# Ackerman(n)
# Biographical Dictionary

# Volume 2

Including the variations of:
Acarman, Acherman, Achuman, Ackerman,
Ackermans, Ackermann, Ackermon, Acreman,
Acremen, Akarman, Akarmans, Akereman,
Akerman, Akermen, Akkerman, Akkermans,
Akorman, Akurman, Akyrman, Auckerman,
Aukerman, Eckerman, Eckermann, Ockerman

# 𝕶𝖆𝖗𝖊𝖓 𝕷. 𝕬𝖈𝖐𝖊𝖗𝖒𝖆𝖓𝖓

HERITAGE BOOKS
2009

# HERITAGE BOOKS

*AN IMPRINT OF HERITAGE BOOKS, INC.*

## Books, CDs, and more—Worldwide

For our listing of thousands of titles see our website
at
www.HeritageBooks.com


Published 2009 by
HERITAGE BOOKS, INC.
Publishing Division
100 Railroad Ave. #104
Westminster, Maryland 21157

International Standard Book Numbers
Paperbound: 978-0-7884-1800-6
Clothbound: 978-0-7884-8274-8

# TABLE OF CONTENTS

# PREFACE

The bulk of this book is arranged as was *Volume 1*. Individuals are listed alphabetically by first name and known biographical information is given in the subjects' entries. This information includes, when available, dates of birth, marriage, and death; the names of parents, spouse(s), and children; occupation and residence; as well as military service, religion, education, and political affiliation.

New to this volume is the family group section at the back of the book. I believe this will provide an easier way to follow a particular family from one generation to the next. Each family of three or more generations begins with an outline of descent from the oldest known ancestor. This is followed by biographical sketches, in alphabetical (not descent) order, which contain information on the individuals' vital statistics, parents, spouse(s), etc.

The vast majority of the information contained herein is new to this volume. Corrections and additions to *Volume 1* have been included, however.

That's enough for the serious news.

Imagine my surprise when, one day, I turned on the television to find actor Charlie Sheen playing a character named David Ackerman in the movie, *The Rookie*.[1] Although it was not a film worth watching through to the end, it did make me wonder just how many other

---

[1] *The Rookie* was produced in 1990 and directed by Clint Eastwood. Film critic Leonard Maltin gave it the overly generous rating of 1.5 stars (out of a possible 4). Maltin, Leonard, *1999 Movie & Video Guide* (New York: Signet, 1998), p. 1161.

fictitious Ackermans were out there. Not too many, apparently. As a matter of idle curiosity, I share the few whom I found. Daniel Ackerman appears as a lieutenant in Roger MacBride Allen's *Allies and Aliens.*[2] Colonel Curie Ackerman ran a traveling circus in *Trouble Shooter* by William Colt MacDonald.[3] Paul Ackermann, lumberjack from Alaska, becomes a resident of the city of Mahagonny in *The Rise and Fall of Mahagonny.*[4] In one of Woody Allen's early plays, *Death Knocks*, a Nat Ackerman appears.[5] And, lastly, an old man is called Ackermann in *Pawns of War.*[6]

## ACKNOWLEDGEMENTS

I would like to thank everyone who shared their family research with me and graciously allowed me to include their work in this collection.

I would also like to thank Kathy (Erlanson) Liston for exposing me to e-bay.com and the other surprising things that can be found on computers with e-mail and Internet connections.

---

[2] Allen, Roger MacBride, *Allies and Aliens* (New York: Baen Publishing Enterprises), 1995. This is a revised and combined publication of two earlier books, *The Torch of Honor* and *Rogue Powers.*

[3] MacDonald, William Colt, *Trouble Shooter* (----: Berkley Medallion), 1965.

[4] Sharp, Harold S. and Marjorie Z. Sharp, *Index to Characters in the Performing Arts, part II - Operas and Muscial Productions: A-L* (Metuchen: The Scarecrow Press, Inc., 1969), p. 5. "*The Rise and Fall of Mahagonny (Aufsteig und Fall der Stadt Mahagonny*), opera (3) (Kurt Weill); Bertolt Brecht, originally a singspiel, first performed at the Chamber Music Festival, Baden Baden, July 17, 1927. Performed as opera, Leipzig, March 9, 1930. Sharp, Harold S. and Marjorie Z. Sharp, *Index to Characters in the Performing Arts, part II - Operas and Muscial Productions: M-Z and Symbols* (Metuchen: The Scarecrow Press, Inc., 1969), p. 1221.

[5] In the late 1970s, by pure coincidence, the part of Nat Ackerman was played by Nicholas John George Ackermann in a college film adaptation. For Nicholas's lineage, see the *Ackerman(n) Biographical Dictionary, Vol. 1.*

[6] Crocker, Bosworth, *Pawns of War* (----: ----, 1918), as listed in Sharp, Harold S. and Marjorie Z. Sharp, *Index to Characters in the Performing Arts, part I - Non-musical Plays: Volume 1* (New York: The Scarecrow press, 1966), p. 6.

# INTRODUCTION

The surname Ackerman(n) had its origins in a person's occupation and referred to a cultivator of the ground, a farmer, husbandman, or ploughman.[7] The word, indicating an occupation, first appeared in print about the year 1000. Today, the term is obsolete but its legacy as a surname lives on.[8] Although most sources agree on the name's origin, another interpretation suggests that Ackerman is "derived from the Saxon word *Acker*, oaken, made of oak, and man. The brave, firm, unyielding man."[9] Yet another source traces Akerman from the Anglo-Saxon 'Aecer-mon,' a "fieldman, farmer, ploughman, clown."[10] While one may readily accept the flattering interpretation of being firm as an oak tree, one wonders how the concept of a clown was tacked on to the noble occupation of farmer. Perhaps those who tilled

---

[7] Reaney, P. H., *A Dictionary of British Surnames* (London: Routledge and Kegan Paul, 1958), p.1. Ackerman, as well as Hickman, Aikman, Winkleman, and Swinklelman, are identified as one "who sweats through toil." ----, *Personal and Family Names* (Glasgow: H. Nisbet and Co., ----. Facsimile reprint Bowie: Heritage Books, Inc. and Rutland: Charles E. Tuttle, Co., Inc., 1988), p. 232. "The German Ackermann is the same as the English Farmer." Anderson, William, *Genealogy and Surnames: with some heraldic and biographical notices* (Edinburgh: William Ritchie, MDCCCLXV), p. 54.

[8] ----, *The Compact Edition of the Oxford English Dictionary.* (Oxford: Oxford University Press, 1985), p. 88.

[9] Holmes, Frank R., *Directory of the Ancestral Heads of New England Families, 1620-1700* (New York: ----, 1923. Reprint Baltimore: Genealogical Publishing Co., Inc., 1989), p. i.

[10] "Sometimes the Akermanni were a peculiar class of feudal tenants, the tenure of whose lands is uncertain, as it is stated that the lord could take them into his hands when he would, yet without injury to the hereditary succession. These holdings were very small, consisting insome instances of five acres only." Lower, Mark Antony, *A Dictionary of the Family Names of the United Kingdom* (----: ----, c1860. Facsimile reprint Bowie: Heritage Books, Inc., 1996).

the soil were considered buffoonish by those of higher rank and better dress in society.

Interestingly, the name spelled as Ackerman is the 1,401st most popular surname in the United States while the name spelled as Ackermann is the 12,282nd most popular.[11]

Ackerman(n)s have left their appelation upon the land, in the business world, and in other unique places.

Many different locations throughout the world carry the name of Ackerman or one of its many variations. Located in Choctaw County, Mississippi, the town of Ackerman was named for a landowner.[12] The town is the county seat.[13] It is 1443 acres in size (2.25 square miles) and had 1573 residents in 1990.[14] Another town of Ackerman is located in Logan County, Colorado.[15] Ackermans Mills is a locale in New Jersey, Ackerman Canyon Ranch is a locale in Nevada, Ackerman's Trailer Park is located in New Hampshire, and Ackermanville and Ackermans are towns in Pennsylvania.[16]

The town of Akkerman, on the Dniester River where it opens into the Dniester Liman and empties into the Black Sea, has had more than one name and has been located in more than one country as political boundaries have changed over time. In the 1930s, it was also known as Cetatea Alba and located in the Basarabia area of Romania.[17] In the 1940s, it was also known as Belgorod Dnestrovski and was located in Moldavia in the Ukraine, which was part of the Soviet Union.[18]

---

[11] Placesnamed.com/a/c/ackerman.asp, accessed 9 December 2000.

[12] Gannett, Henry, *The Origin of Certain Place Names in the United States* (Washington: Government Printing Office, 1902.  Facsimile reprint Bowie: Heritage Books, Inc., 1996), p. 18.

[13] Abate, Frank R., *American Places Dictionary, Volume Two: South* (Detroit: Omnigraphics, Inc., 1994), p. 390. It sits at an elevation of 520 feet. Ibid.

[14] Placesnamed.com/a/c/ackerman.asp, accessed 9 December 2000.

[15] Ibid.

[16] Abate, Frank R., *Omni Gazetteer of the United States of America. Volume 10 - National Index* (Detroit: Omnigraphics, Inc.), p. 3.

[17] Bartholomew, John, *The Oxford Advanced Atlas* (London: Oxford University Press, 1936), p. 50.

[18] Goode, J. Paul, *Goode's School Atlas: physical, political, and economic for American schools and colleges, revised and enlarged* (New York: Rand McNally & Company, 1946), p. 131.

Bodies of water include Ackerman Branch, a stream in Indiana; Ackerman Brook, East Branch of the Shepaug River in Connecticut; Ackerman Creek, appearing as a name for streams in California, Illinois, Kansas, and Texas, while Ackermans Creek, a stream, appears in New Jersey; Ackerman Lake, appearing as a name for lakes in Alaska, Michigan (it actually has two such lakes), and Wisconsin, while an Ackerman Lakes, which is apparently only a single lake, appears in Minnesota; Ackerman Slough, a stream, appears in Texas; and Ackerman Spring, a spring, appears in Nevada.[19]

Miscellaneous land forms, natural and man-made, include the Ackerman Canyon, a valley in Nevada; the Ackerman Cut, a channel in Iowa; the Ackerman Ditch, appearing as a name for canals in Indiana and Missouri; the Ackerman Drain, a canal appearing in Michigan; Ackerman Hill, a summit in South Dakota; the Ackerman Mine, a mine in Nevada; and, islands named Ackerman appear in Pennsylvania and Washington.[20] Ackermans Cave, possibly named after John Ackerman, a speologist who explored the cave, is located on Manggaard Farm in Fillmore County, Minnesota.[21]

An Akerman Road in London partially covered the Loughborough House and grounds that had been standing in 1825. Other roads running over and obliterating the estate were the Evandale, Claribel, and parts of Loughborough and Lilford.[22]

Buildings of various sorts also carry the name of Ackerman. The Abram Ackerman House (historic), David Ackerman House (historic), Garret and Maria Ackerman House, Garret Augustus Ackerman House, Ackerman-Boyd House (historic), Ackerman-Dater House (historic), Ackerman-Demarest House (historic), Ackerman-Dewsnap House (historic), Ackerman-Hopper House (historic), Ackerman House (historic), Ackerman-Smith House (historic), Ackerman-Van Emburgh House (historic), and Ackerman-Zabriskie-

---

[19] Abate, Frank R., *Omni Gazetteer of the United States of America. Volume 10 - National index* (Detroit: Omnigraphics, Inc.), p. 3.
[20] Ibid.
[21] Ackerman, John and David Gerboth, "Historical Review of Ackermans Cave," *Minnesota Speleology Monthly*, Vol. 25 #2, p. 144.
[22] Sheppard, F. H. W., *Survey of London, Volume XXVI: the parish of St. Mary Lambeth, part two, southern area* (London: The Athlone Press, 1956).

Steuben House (historic) are all located in New Jersey. Schools include the Ackerman Attendance Center and the Ackerman Elementary School in Mississippi, the Ackerman Junior High School in Oregon, and the Ackerman School in California and in South Dakota. Churches include the Ackerman Baptist Church, the Ackerman Church of Christ, the Ackerman Church of God, and the Ackerman United Methodist Church, all in Mississippi. The Ackerman Bar, a bar, is located in Washington.[23]

Ackerman family cemeteries can be found in Iowa, New York, and South Carolina.[24]

The Ackerman Choctaw County Airport is in Mississippi, not too far from the town of Ackerman one might suppose.[25]

The types of businesses carrying the Ackerman(n) name are as varied as their locations. Ackerman Bros. were photographers in Boonville, New York, from about 1870 to 1880.[26] Another Ackerman Bros. firm bought the *Record and Farmer* newspaper published in Brattleboro, Vermont, circa 1868.[27] Moss & Ackerman were undertakers in Hamilton County, Ohio, in 1869.[28] Ackerman & Cooke are currently in business as "purveyors of quality food" in Green Bay, Wisconsin.[29] Ackerman's of Colby, Kansas, sold International Harvester items, and perhaps others items as well such as Whirlpool Appliances and Toro Lawn Mowers.[30] Akerman-Hein Werner were manufacturers of heavy

---

[23] Abate, Frank R., *Omni Gazetteer of the United States of America. Volume 10 - National Index* (Detroit: Omnigraphics, Inc.), p. 3. It is likely that all of the houses are connected to the prolific David Ackerman family that arrived in New Amsterdam in 1662. For more information on the family, contact the society for David Ackerman Descendants - 1662 at 806 Phelps Road, Franklin Lakes, New Jersey 07417.

[24] Abate, Frank R., *Omni Gazetteer of the United States of America. Volume 10 - National Index* (Detroit: Omnigraphics, Inc.), p. 3.

[25] Ibid..

[26] memory.loc.org

[27] Hubbard, C. Horace and Justus Dartt, *History of the Town of Springfield, Vermont, with a genealogical record, 1752-1895* (Boston: Geo. H. Walker & Co., 1895. Facsimile reprint Bowie: Heritage Books, Inc., 1998), p. 152.

[28] Hughes, Lois E., *Hamilton County, Ohio, Death Records, 1865-1869, Volume I* (Bowie: Heritage Books, Inc., 1992), p. 1.

[29] Mail order catalog, Holiday 2000.

[30] Business pen with company information printed on it advertised for sale on e-bay.com, accessed summer 2000.

excavation equipment near Thurmont, Maryland.[31] A combination try, mitre, and bevel square was patented 26 June 1855 by J. S. Halsted and C. J. Ackerman.[32]

William S. Ackerman, mechanical engineer, and Albert Randolph Ross were architects working out of New York. They were selected through a competition to design the Washington Public Library located at Mount Vernon Square in Washington D.C. The cornerstone was laid on 23 April 1901. "Although in announcing their selection the *Star* called Ackerman and Ross a 'well-known New York firm,' they never achieved great fame. They were a short-lived partnership lasting from about 1897-1902. Ackerman was the senior partner, while Ross had the design capability."[33] They later went on to design the Union County Courthouse located at the northwest corner of Broad Street and Rahway Avenue in Elizabeth, New Jersey. "It was erected in 1903 on the site of the old borough courthouse burned by the British in 1780."[34] Ackerman formed a new firm [apparently after 1921], called Ackerman and Partridge, and "designed a Carnegie Library for Bucknell University."[35]

The Ackerman(n) name can also be found in other unique places. An unidentified Ackerman, superintendant of the Continental yard, was mentioned in the nineteenth century song, *Our Yankee Monitor*.[36] The Ackerman Law was passed in Ohio in 1933, making legal beer available once again in the state.[37]

---

[31] Ackermann, Nicholas John George, *Journal of...*, Vol. 9, p. 356.

[32] Tool for sale on e-bay.com, accessed summer 2000.

[33] Historic American Buildings Survey/Historic American Engineering Record at memory.loc.gov, accessed 17 February 2000.

[34] Federal Writers' Project, *New Jersey: a guide to its present and past* (New York: The Viking Press, 1939).

[35] Historic American Buildings Survey/Historic American Engineering Record at memory.loc.gov, accessed 17 February 2000.

[36] ----, *Our Yankee Monitor*. New York: H. De Marsan, publisher, no date; posted at memory.loc.gov, accessed 17 February 2000.

[37] Roseboom, Eugene Holloway and Francis Phelps Weisenburger, *A History of Ohio* (New York: Prentice-Hall, Inc., 1934), p. 497.

# ABBREVIATIONS

b = born
bapt = baptized
bc = born circa
bro/o = brother of
bur = buried
c = circa
capt = captain
cem = cemetery
ch = child/children
chr = christened
c/o = child of
co = county/company
d = died/day
dc = died circa
d/o = daughter of
div = divorced
edu = education
lic = license
lt = lieutenant

m = married/month
m1 = married first
m2 = married second
mc = married circa
mil = military service
occ = occupation
qv = indicates that a separate entry is available for this individual
rel = religion
res = residence
s/o = son of
sis/o = sister of
st = saint/street
twp = township
unk = unknown
unm = unmarried
y = year

Plus United States Postal Service state abbreviations and postal abbreviations for foreign countries:

AA = Australia
CN = Canada
EN = England
FR = France
GE = Germany
HO = Holland
RU = Russia
WE = Wales

# HOW TO USE THIS BOOK

This volume is divided into two main sections, both of which can be read in similar ways. The main section of the book is made up of individuals with no known connections to other Ackerman(n)s or of families with only two known generations. The other section is made up of family groups comprising three or more generations; an outline of the descendants appears first for easy reference (beginning with the first known ancestor), followed by the biographical sketches.

Families can be traced in two ways regardless of the section. One, by following the subject's father's listing back from entry to entry until no father is given; this indicates that there is no more information on that line. Two, children who are carried forward are identified with "qv." (Children who are not carried forward generally have little or no data associated with them, in which case their data appear with them in their parents' entry, or they died young.) People with significant information or people who have no known parents are given their own entries.

The entries are arranged alphabetically by the first name regardless of the spelling of the surname. Within similar given names, the subjects are arranged chronologically as well as possible. Ideally, everyone would have birth dates so that the chronological arrangement would readily identify different people who happened to have the same name. Such is not the case, however; marriage and death dates must often suffice, and, sometimes, the date used is that of the birth of a child or the subject's assumed participation in a specific event identified in the entry. Those subjects who have no dates associated with them appear before those subjects who do have dates. For instance, John Ackermann would be listed before John Ackermann b1705.

Effort has been made to combine data from various sources when it is undoubtedly the same person in the records. When it is probable but not certain that two or more entries are actually the same person, it is so noted in the text. The researcher is encouraged to look over all possible entries, however, in case the compiler has missed a clue.

To prevent the cumbersomeness of coded sources, the full source is cited with the entry. In the case of a multi-source entry, the sources are generally given as footnotes to allow for the greatest ease in reading the entry. A complete listing of the sources can be found in the Bibliography.

These sources are predominantly from public domain publications, primary documents, and material contributed by researchers who have given their permission for use. Factual material abstracted from copyrighted publications falls within the Fair Use Act guidelines.

The focus in this dictionary is on men and women who were born with the Ackerman(n) name, in any of its many variations. The custom of men retaining their surname at marriage makes it certain that all the men included here were born Ackerman(n)s; exceptions would cover adoptions, legal name changes, and the like, of course. Women, on the other hand, generally take the surname of their husbands upon marriage. While effort has been made to identify women as either having been born an Ackerman(n) or as having married one, and their entries arranged accordingly, the researcher should keep in mind the possibility that a woman with her own entry might actually be an Ackerman(n) because she married into the family.

AKERMAN, ---- - m Mary Bratton alive 1729, d/o ---- Bratton & Prudence ----. (Prudence (----) (Bratton) Spoore was a resident of Portsmouth when she made her will in 1729 and left Mary her silver tankard.) [Metcalf, Henry Harrison. *Probate Records of the Province of New Hampshire, Volume 2: 1718-1740. State papers series, Volume 32.* Bristol: R. W. Musgrove, Printer, 1914. Facsimile reprint Bowie: Heritage Books, Inc., 1989, p. 364.]

AKERMAN, ---- - m Lydia A ---- bc1763 [based on age at death], d 24 May 1859 Portsmouth, age 96 years. [Chipman, Scott Lee. *New England Vital Records from the "Exeter News-Letter," 1859-1865.* Camden: Picton Press, 1996, p. 18.]

AKERMAN, ---- - m Abigail ---- bc1768 [based on age at death], dc 2 Aug 1858 Portsmouth, "in her 90th year." [Chipman, Scott Lee. *New England Vital Records from the "Exeter News-Letter," 1853-1858.* Camden: Picton Press, 1994, p. 261.]

AKERMAN, ---- - m Sarah Jackson d by 1775. [Evans, Helen F. *Abstracts of the Probate Records of Rockingham County, New Hampshire, 1771-1799.* Bowie: Heritage Books, Inc., 2000, p. 492.]

AKERMAN, ---- - m Susan ---- bc1784 [based on age at death], dc 19 Mar 1860 Portsmouth, age 76. [Chipman, Scott Lee. *New England Vital Records from the "Exeter News-Letter," 1859-1865.* Camden: Picton Press, 1996, p. 59.]

ACKERMAN, ---- - m Louise Cloutman bc1876 [based on age at death] Alexandria, d/o N B Cloutman & Sarah Paige, d 5/4/1936 age 60/6/13; d before 5/4/1936. [Roberts, Richard P. *Alton, New Hampshire, Vital Records, 1890-1998.* Bowie: Heritage Books, Inc., 1999, p. 375.]

ACKERMAN, ---- - m Ranghild V ----. Wife was alive in 1960 with a house at 30 Auburn Ave, Hampton, & she apparently also resided in Hampton Falls. [Husband's name may be Oliver H Akerman.] [----. *Exeter, Brentwood, East Kingston, Greenland, Kensington, Newfield, and Stratham [New Hampshire] Directory, 1960.* New Haven: The Price & Lee Co., 1960, p. 472.]

ACKERMANN, ---- - m ----; ch: Jean m ---- Radtke & d 2 Dec 1998, George m Lorraine ----, John m Marion ----, Norman. [Obituary published in the *Chicago Daily Herald* 5 Dec. 1998 for daughter and posted at ancestry.com, accessed 4 Aug. 2000.]

AKERMAN, ---- - m Elizabeth ----; div or d by 1802 when Elizabeth married Arthur Melcher. [Chipman, Scott Lee. *Genealogical Abstracts from Early New Hampshire Newspapers, Volume 1*. Bowie: Heritage Books, Inc., 2000, p. 118.]

ACKERMAN, ----- - m Eunice Lewis alive 1822, d/o Samuel Lewis of Monroe (Orange Co) NY. [----. "Orange County Wills." *The Orange County [New York] Genealogical Society Quarterly*, Vol. 29 #1 (May 1999), p. 8.]

ACKERMAN, ---- - m Jessie Borenstein b1900 & d 19 Mar 1975. [Cohen, Edward A. & Lewis Goldfarb. *Jewish Cemeteries of Hartford, Connecticut, Volume 1*. Bowie: Heritage Books, Inc., 1995, p. 1.]

ACKERMAN, ---- - m 1680 in Beinheim to ----; ch: Anna Barbara bapt 1697 Beinheim. [Book review for Robichaux, Albert J. Jr. *German Coast Families: European origins and settlement in colonial Louisiana*. Rayne: Hebert Publications, 1997 appearing in *The American Genealogist*, Vol. 74 #3 (July 1999), p. 234.]

AKERMAN, ---- - m Sarah ---- of Portsmouth; ch: Mary alive 1713 qv; d between 1693 & 1719. [Identified as a "West of England surname" in this entry.] [Noyes, Sybil et al. *Genealogical Dictionary of Maine and New Hampshire*. Portland: ----, 1928-1939. Reprint Baltimore: Genealogical Publishing Company, 1996, p. 59.]

AKERMAN, ---- - alive 1798; res: Canton Bern, SW. [Advertisement for Rohrbach, Lewis Bunker. *Men of Bern: the 1798 burgerverzeichnisse of Canton Bern, Switzerland*. Rockport: Picton Press, 1999 appearing in *Everton's Genealogical Helper*, Vol. 53 #4 (July-Aug. 1999), p. 191.]

ACKERMAN, ---- - occ: sail-maker on the privateer *Surprise*; d 15 Apr 1815, cause: drowning. [Marine, William M. *The British*

*Invasion of Maryland, 1812-1815.* ----: ----, c1899. Facsimile reprint Bowie: Heritage Books, Inc., 1998, p. 199.]

AKERMAN, ---- - bc1825 [based on age at death]; d/o Walter Akerman & ----; m Peletiah M Moulton; dc 30 May 1853 Portsmouth, age 28. [Chipman, Scott Lee. *New England Vital Records from the "Exeter News-Letter," 1853-1858.* Camden: Picton Press, 1994, p. 17.]

ACKERMAN, ---- - (female); bc1853 [based on age at death]; res: 210 Betts; race: white; d 14 Jan 1867, age 14, cause: consumption. [Hughes, Lois E. *Hamilton County, Ohio, Death Records, 1865-1869, Volume I.* Bowie: Heritage Books, Inc., 1992, p. 1.]

AKERMAN, ---- - alive 1853; m Martha A ---- of Portsmouth. [Chipman, Scott Lee. *New England Vital Records from the "Exeter News-Letter," 1853-1858.* Camden: Picton Press, 1994, p. 38.]

AKERMAN, ---- - alive 1879; m Josephine ----; ch: son b 9 May 1879. [Nichipor, Ruth L. *Vital Statistics from the Town Records of Hampton Falls, New Hampshire, Through 1899.* ----: ----, 1976, p. 1.]

ACKERMAN, ---- - alive 1918; occ: newspaper correspondent for the New York *Times.* [Radzinsky, Edvard. *The Last Tzar: the life and death of Nicholas II.* Translated from the Russian by Marian Schwartz. New York: Anchor Books, 1992, p. 361.]

ACKERMAN, ---- - sis/o Clinton W Ackerman; m by 1930 H A Taylor; res: [Bucyrus?] OH. [Scholl, Allen W. *Descendants of Moses and Isabell (Clark) Crawford of Bucks County, Pennsylvania.* Bowie: Heritage Books, Inc., p. 511.]

AKERMAN, A - bc1818 [based on age at enlistment]; mil: mustered into Co E, 10th Reg SC (Confederate) at White's Bridge on 19 Jul 1861 as a private, age 43. [Boddie, William Willis. *History of Williamsburg. Something about the people of Williamsburg County, South Carolina, from the first settlement by Europeans about 1705 until 1923.* Columbia: ----, 1923. Facsimile reprint Baltimore: Clearfield Company, Inc., 1995, p. 349.]

ACKERMAN, A - alive 1869; established the Warrenton *Chronicle* in 1869. [Williams, Walter. *A History of Northeast Missouri, Volume 1*. Chicago: The Lewis Publishing Company, 1913, p. 678.]

ACKERMAN, A D - alive 1995. Author of "An Introduction to Violone Playing" posted on the Internet. [Music.indiana.edu/som/emi/ackerman/html, accessed 23 January 2000.]

-----

The following three entries may be the same man.

AKERMAN, AARON - mc 17 May 1842 in Salem to Susan H Hart; res: Portsmouth. [Chipman, Scott Lee. *New England Vital Records from the "Exeter News-Letter," 1841-1846*. Camden: Picton Press, 1993, p. 40.]

AKERMAN, AARON - bc1817 NH [based on age in 1850 census]; m Susan[?] H ---- b NH & age 28 in 1850; ch: Howard H[?] b NH & age 6 in 1850, Alice F[?] b NH & age 2/12 in 1850; occ: grocer; res: Portsmouth, Rockingham Co NH. Aaron Akerman was 33 in 1850. They were family #735 in dwelling #446[?].[1] In the 1860 census, Aaron Akerman's age is given as 43y & he is still a grocer; his real estate is valued at 6000 & his personal estate at 1000. His wife, Susan H, is age 39. Their children are Howard W (age 16), Alice F (age 10), and Grace L (age 4). They are family #1325 in dwelling #1063 & live in Portsmouth, 2<sup>nd</sup> Ward, Rockingham Co NH.[2]

AKERMAN, AARON - alive 1852. Bought the Old Bell Tavern, with J P Morse & Henry M Clark. [Brewster, Charles W., *Rambles About Portsmouth: second series*. ----: Lewis W. Brewster, 1869. Facsimile reprint Somersworth: New Hampshire Publishing Company, 1972, p. 343.]

-----

---

[1] *New Hampshire 1850 Census*, p. 50 at familytreemaker.com, accessed 27 August 2000.
[2] *New Hampshire 1860 Census*, microfilm, p. 777.

AKERMAN, AARON - alive 1861; ch: ---- death announced in newspaper 1 Apr 1861. [Chipman, Scott Lee. *New England Vital Records from the "Exeter News-Letter," 1859-1865*. Camden: Picton Press, 1996, p. 105.]

AKKERMANS, ABIGAEL - alive 1709; rel: joined the church 4 Apr 1709 "with certificate from Hakkinsak." [Versteeg, Dingman and Thomas E. Vermilye, Jr. *Bergen Records. Records of the Reformed Protestant Dutch Church of Bergen in New Jersey, 1666 to 1788*. Originally published in the *Year Book of the Holland Society of New York*, 1915. Reprint Baltimore: Clearfield Publishing Co., Inc., 1990, p. 60.]

AKKERMAN, ABIGAIL - alive 1708; m Andries Hoppe. [Versteeg, Dingman and Thomas E. Vermilye, Jr. *Bergen Records. Records of the Reformed Protestant Dutch Church of Bergen in New Jersey, 1666 to 1788*. Originally published in the *Year Book of the Holland Society of New York, 1913*. Reprint Baltimore: Clearfield Publishing Co., Inc., 1990, p. 56.]

AKERMAN, ABIGAIL - b NH; age 86 in 1850; res: Portsmouth, Rockingham Co NH. Living with Abigail Foster, age 56, & her family. [Is Abigail Foster d/o Abigail Akerman?] [*New Hampshire 1850 Census*, p. 92 at familytreemaker.com, accessed 27 August 2000.]

ACKERMAN, ABNER ATWOOD - bc1835 MA [based on him being 45 in 1880]; occ: stock raiser; res: San Bernardino Co CA. Registered 23 Sep 1882 in the Great Register of San Bernardino Co. [----. "1880 Great Register of San Bernardino County." *Valley Quarterly*, Vol. XXXVI #3 (September 1999), p. 43.]

ACKERMAN, ABRAHAM - m Margt ----; ch: Elizabeth Jane m 8 Nov 1855 qv. [Sherman, Renee Britt. *Brooke County, West Virginia, Licenses and Marriages, 1797-1874*. Bowie: Heritage Books, Inc., 1991, p. 1, 135.]

AKERMAN, ABRAHAM - alive 1808; m Louisa ----; ch: Louisa chr 2 Oct 1808 at London (St Giles Cripplegate). [Correspondence (undated) from Bob G.[?], courtesy of Robert H. Ackerman, 22 Mar. 2000.]

ACKERMAN, ABRAHAM - alive 1812; res: Rockland Co NY; mil: awarded $58.00 claim as a soldier of the War of 1812. [----. *Index of Awards on Claims of the Soldiers of the War of 1812, as audited and allowed by the adjutant and inspector generals, pursuant to chapter 176, of the laws of 1859.* Albany: Weed, Parsons and Company, Printers, 1860, p. 4.]

ACKERMAN, ABRAHAM - alive 1819; m Maregrietye Ackerman; ch: William b 18 Jul 1819 & bapt 22 Aug 1819. [Durie, Howard I. "Pascack Reformed Dutch Church Baptisms 1814-1850." *The American Genealogist*, Vol. 47 #3 (July 1971), p. 176.]

ACKERMAN, ABRAHAM - alive 1860; mil: 170 Infantry. [Wilt, Richard A., *New York Soldiers in the Civil War: a roster of military officers and soldiers who served in New York regiments in the Civil War as listed in the annual reports of the Adjutant General of the State of New York.* Bowie: Heritage Books, Inc., 1999, p. 2.]

ACKERMON, ABRAM - alive 1763; one of the grantees of Duxbury 7 Jun 1763. [Batchellor, Albert Stillman. *The New Hampshire Grants being transcripts of the charters of townships and minor grants of lands made by the provincial government of New Hampshire, within the present boundaries of the State of Vermont, from 1749 to 1764. With an appendix containing petitions to King George the Third, in 1766, by the proprietors and settlers under the New Hampshire Grants, and lists of the subscribers; also historical and bibliographical notes relative to the towns in Vermont, by Hiram A. Huse, State Historian. Volume XXVI. Town charters, Volume III.* Concord: Edward N. Pearson, Public Printer, 1895, p. 141.]

ACKERMAN, ABRAM - alive 1815; m Margaret Haldrom; ch: Williampe b23 Jan 1815 & bapt 12 Feb 1815. [Durie, Howard I. "Pascack Reformed Dutch Church Baptisms 1814-1850." *The American Genealogist*, Vol. 47 #3 (July 1971), p. 176.]

ACKERMAN, ABRAM - alive 1816; m Jane Debaan; ch: John b 5 May 1816 & bapt 2 Jun 1816. [Durie, Howard I. "Pascack Reformed Dutch Church Baptisms 1814-1850." *The American Genealogist*, Vol. 47 #3 (July 1971), p. 177.]

ACKERMAN, ABRAM - bc1843; res: KY; d 5 Mar 1845. Death reported in the *Covington Licking Valley Register*. [Eddlemon, Sherida K. *A Genealogical Collection of Kentucky Birth & Death Records, Volume 1.* Bowie: Heritage Books, Inc., p. 1.]

ACKERMAN, ABRAM - alive 1860; mil: 83 Infantry. [Wilt, Richard A. *New York Soldiers in the Civil War: a roster of military officers and soldiers who served in New York regiments in the Civil War as listed in the annual reports of the Adjutant General of the State of New York.* Bowie: Heritage Books, Inc., 1999, p. 2.]

ACKERMAN, ADAM - alive 1860; mil: 15 Artillery. [Wilt, Richard A. *New York Soldiers in the Civil War: a roster of military officers and soldiers who served in New York regiments in the Civil War as listed in the annual reports of the Adjutant General of the State of New York.* Bowie: Heritage Books, Inc., 1999, p. 2.]

ACKERMAN, ADOLPH - m Christine Yeaton b 7 Feb 1880, d/o Benjamin B Yeaton & Mary Elizabeth James/Jones, d 28 Dec 1935. [Jones, William Haslet. *The Yeaton Family of New England, 1650-1900.* Bowie: Heritage Books, Inc., 1997, p. 90.]

ACKERMANN, ADOLPHUS - m Elizabeth Barnes; ch: Phobbe [Phoebe?] Charlotte chr 24 Feb 1847 at Kennington St Mark, Kate chr 28 Apr 1847 at Kennington St Mark, Henry chr 28 Apr 1847 at Kennington St Mark, Ernest Charles chr 24 Feb 1847 at Kennington St Mark. [Correspondence (undated) from Bob G.[?], courtesy of Robert H. Ackerman, 22 Mar. 2000.][3]

ACKERMAN, AGNES - m license obtained c 6 Sep 1911 by Ray Duncan; res: Covello. [Mendocino Coast Genealogical Society. *Births, Deaths and Marriages on California's Mendocino Coast: Volume Two, 1910-1919.* Bowie: Heritage Books, Inc., 1997, p. 194.]

---

[3] In Ackermann, *Ackerman(n) Biographical Dictionary, Volume 1*, similar information was contributed by Brian I. L. Ackerman and appears as follows (on pages 11 and 12): Ackermann, Adolphus - s/o Rudolph Ackermann & ----; m Elizabeth Baimer? Freeman; ch: Elizabeth Mary Ann b1840 & d1924, Adolphus William b 24 Oct 1841, Phoebe Charlotte b1845 & d1925, Henry d1897, Ernest Charles b1847, Theodore b1848, Jesse Felicia b1849 & d1932, Edgar Rudolph b 2-5-1851, David Freeman b1853, Septimus Parry b1856, Ferdinand John b 11-8-1858; d1858. Lines for Adolphus William, Henry, and Ernest Charles are continued in *Volume 1*.

ACKERMAN, AL - bc1881 [based on age at death]; occ: performer; d1971, age 90. [Waring, J. P. *American and British Theatrical Biography: a directory.* Metuchen: The Scarecrow Press, Inc., 1979, P. 14.]

ACKERMAN, ALAN - alive 1980; m Donna Armstrong; ch: Ian Cullen b 12 Dec 1980. [Hunt, James K. Jr. *Hampton Vital Records and Genealogy, 1889-1986.* Portsmouth: Peter E. Randall, Publisher, 1988, p. 343.]

ACHERMAN, ALBERT - m ---- d1920 [apparently in Seneca (Nemaha Co) KS]. [----. "WPA Obituary Index." *Nemaha County Genealogical Society Newsletter,* Vol. 6 #1 (Nov. 1998), p. 7.]

ACKERMAN, ALBERT - alive 1860; mil: 13 Infantry. [Wilt, Richard A. *New York Soldiers in the Civil War: a roster of military officers and soldiers who served in New York regiments in the Civil War as listed in the annual reports of the Adjutant General of the State of New York.* Bowie: Heritage Books, Inc., 1999, p. 2.]

ACKERMANN, ALBERT - alive 1890; occ: druggist; res: 5053 S Halsted, Chicago IL. [Correspondence dated 18 Dec. 1979 from Larry C. Winterburn, courtesy of Robert H. Ackerman, 22 Mar. 2000. Mr. Winterburn cites his source as an 1890-1893 Chicago city directory.]

ACKERMAN, ALBERT - alive 1898; mil: served in the Philippine Campaign of the Spanish-American War in Co F 1$^{st}$ Battalion MT & discharged 6 Oct 1898 at Cavite, Philippine Islands; occ: saloon-keeper; res: MT. [Dougherty, Marilyn. "The Spanish-American War, The Phillipine Campaign, Montana Edition." *Treasure State Lines,* Vol. 24 #1 (1999), p. 12.]

ACKERMAN, ALBERT A - b 9 Mar 1931; mil: permanent grade of Major received 22 Aug 1958; edu: Master's degree. [----. *U. S. Army Register, Volume I: regular army active list, 1 January 1974.* Washington: U. S. Government Printing Office, 1974, p. 1.]

ACKERMAN, ALBERT G - alive 1889; occ: clerk at 120 Lasalle, Chicago IL; res: 44 Beethoven Pl, Chicago IL. [Is he related to John

W Ackermann who resided at the same place?] [Correspondence dated 18 Dec. 1979 from Larry C. Winterburn, courtesy of Robert H. Ackerman, 22 Mar. 2000. Mr. Winterburn cites his source as an 1889 Chicago city directory.] Albert G Ackermann may have actually clerked at 122 Lasalle. [Correspondence dated 18 Dec. 1979 from Larry C. Winterburn, courtesy of Robert H. Ackerman, 22 Mar. 2000. Mr. Winterburn cites his source as an 1890-1893 Chicago city directory.]

AKERMAN, ALBERT S - b NH; occ: painter; res: Exeter, Rockingham Co NH. The index lists him as Albert S but the census record looks like Albert E. No wife is listed but he apparently had a daughter, Helen A, b NH & age 1 in 1850. They are family #137 in dwelling #121 and live with Nathan T Bachelder (age 30) and Clarissa E Bachelder (age 30). Albert S Akerman is age 28 in 1850. [*New Hampshire 1850 Census*, p. 207 at familytreemaker.com, accessed 27 August 2000.

ACHERMAN, ALEX - alive 1860. Listed as a juror for the 1860 September term of the Forsyth Co NC court of pleas & quarter session.[4] This may be the same Alex Acherman who is listed as a juror for the 1861 March term of the Forsyth Co NC court of pleas & quarter session.[5]

ACKERMAN, ALEXANDER - alive 1450?; occ: musician. "This was the most productive period for the musicians in the Netherlands [mid-1400s?]: apart from the ten or so 'great names' such as...Alexander Ackerman (Agricola) [residence?],...there were any number of others...." [Prevenier, Walter and Wim Blockmans. *The Burgundian Netherlands*. Cambridge: Cambridge University Press, 1986, p. 301.]

---

[4] Alson, Rebecca R., "Forsyth County Court of Pleas and Quarter Sessions, June Term 1860," *The Forsyth County [North Carolina] Genealogical Society Journal*, Vol. XVII #1 (Fall 1998), p. 8. Listed as a grand juror for this court in the September 1860 session. Alson, Rebecca R., "Forsyth County Court of Pleas and Quarter Session, September Term 1860," *The Forsyth County [North Carolina] Genealogical Society Journal*, Vol. XVII #3 (Spring 1999), p. 34.
[5] Alson, Rebecca R., "Forsyth County Court of Pleas and Quarter Sessions, March Term 1861," *The Forsyth County [North Carolina] Genealogical Society Journal*, Vol. XVIII #1 (Fall 1999), p. 2.

ACKERMAN, ALEXANDER S - b 23 Oct 1879 MA; mil: appointed from RI, capt in corps of engineers 1 Jul 1920.[6] Mil: Lt Col 26 Jul 1940, retired 30 Jun 1942.[7]

ACKERMAN, ALICE - m 28 Nov 1878 Frank A Daboll; res: Prattsburgh NY. [Jackson, Mary S. and Edward F. Jackson. *Marriage Notices from Steuben County, New York, Newspapers, 1797-1884.* Bowie: Heritage Books, Inc., 1998, p. 213.]

ACKERMAN, ALLAN DOUGLAS - b 13 Jun 1947 London; s/o John B Ackerman & Anne Faith Donaldson; m 14 Mar 1970 Mary Abigail King; ch: Molly, Samuel; occ: energy conservation consultant, architect; edu: BA Dartmouth College 1968, M Arch Harvard 1974; res: Arlington MA. [----. *Who's Who in Frontier Science and Technology.* Chicago: Marquis Who's Who, Inc., 1984, p. 3.]

ACKERMAN, ALLEN - dc1861. "Ordered by the Court that the Indentures binding John Brindle to Allen Ackerman be rescinded the said Allen Ackerman now being dead in all respects except that his administrator furnish said Apprentice with 2 suits of clothing."[8] This is probably the same Allen Ackerman - dc1861. An inventory of the estate "was returned by the adms & ordered to be recorded" in the September Term 1861, Court of Pleas and Quarter Session.[9]

AKERMAN, ALMIRA - bc1802 [based on age at death]; d/o Jos Akerman & ----; m Simon Pender; d 17 Sep 1845 Salem, age 43.[10]

---

[6] ----, *Official Army Register January 1, 1922* (Washington: U. S. Government Printing Office, 1922), p. 310.
[7] ----, *Official Army Register January 1, 1945* (Washington: U. S. Government Printing Office, 1945), p. 1055.
[8] Alson, Rebecca R., "Forsyth County Court of Pleas and Quarter Sessions, June Term 1861," *The Forsyth County [North Carolina] Genealogical Society Journal,* Vol. XVIII #1, Fall 1999, p. 14.
[9] Alson, Rebecca R., "Forsyth County Court of Pleas and Quarter Session, September Term 1861," *The Forsyth County [north Carolina] Genealogical Society Journal,* Vol. XVIII #3, Spring 2000, p. 54.
[10] Chipman, Scott Lee, *New England Vital Records from the "Exeter News-Letter," 1841-1846* (Camden: Picton Press, 1993), p. 147.

This may be the same Almira Akerman m Simon ---- b 1 Aug 1800; d 17 Sep 1845.[11]

AKERMAN, ALPHEUS - mc 28 Sep 1841 Harriet Sanborn; res: Danvers. [Chipman, Scott Lee. *New England Vital Records from the "Exeter News-Letter," 1841-1846.* Camden: Picton Press, 1993, p. 21.]

ACKERMAN, ALVIS - alive 1849; res: Frankfort Twp, IL. Purchased 40 acres of federal land, at $1.25/acre, on 21 Apr 1849 in Frankfort Twp.[12] This may be the same Alvis Ackerman - alive 1852; res: Frankfort Twp, IL. Purchased 27 acres of federal land, at $1.25/acre, on 16 Sep 1852 in Frankfort Twp.[13]

ACKERMAN, AMANDA - m 1 Mar 1854 Noah B Hoyt b 5 Mar 1829 Yonkers, s/o Belding Hoyt & Rebecca ----; res: Yonkers NY. [Is Amanda sis/o Harriet Ackerman m 14 Sep 1853?] [Hoyt, David W. *A Genealogical History of the Hoyt, Haight, and Hight Families: with some account of the earlier Hyatt families, a list of the first settlers of Salisbury and Amesbury, Mass., etc.* ----: ----, 1871. Facsimile reprint Bowie: Heritage Books, Inc., 1992, p. 459.]

ACKERMAN, AMEN - mil: private in 2nd Reg of Dragoons, Co K; d 19 Nov 1839, drowned en route to Black Creek. [----. "Indian War Casualities from the Florida War, 1835-1842." *The Southern Genealogists Exchange Quarterly*, Vol. 39 #166 (June 1998), p. 50]

AKERMAN, AMOS TAPPAN - b 20 Aug 1900 GA; mil: 12 Jun 1942. [----. *Official Army Register January 1, 1945.* Washington: U. S. Government Printing Office, 1945, p. 12.]

ACKERMAN, ANDREW - b1813 PA; m Sarah Schades b1818; ch: Jane b1839 VA, Elizabeth b1843 VA, Druzilla b1848 VA, Malissa b 15 Jul 1850 VA qv; occ: laborer. [Pedigree chart prepared 1984 and contributed by Teresa Durbin.]

---

[11] Stickney, Matthew Adams, *The Fowler Family: a genealogical memoir, ten generations: 1590-1882* (----: ----, 1883. Reprint Charleston: Garnier & Company, 1969), p. 90.
[12] ----, "Original Land Owners - Frankfort Township," *Where the Trails Cross*, Vol. 29 #2 (Winter 1998/1999), p. 41.
[13] ----, "Original Land Owners - Frankfort Township," *Where the Trails Cross*, Vol. 29 #2 (Winter 1998/1999), p. 37.

ACKERMAN, ANDREW - alive 1860; mil: 2 Mounted Rifles. [Wilt, Richard A. *New York Soldiers in the Civil War: a roster of military officers and soldiers who served in New York regiments in the Civil War as listed in the annual reports of the Adjutant General of the State of New York*. Bowie: Heritage Books, Inc., 1999, p. 2.]

AKERMAN, ANN - alive 1791; unm; res: Portsmouth. Determined to be mentally incapacitated as an adult & put under the guardianship of Nathaniel Adams of Portsmouth. [Evans, Helen F. *Abstracts of the Probate Records of Rockingham County, New Hampshire, 1771-1799, Volume 1.* Bowie: Heritage Books, Inc., 2000, p. 6.]

ACKERMANN, ANN - alive 1966; edu: MS Ohio State University 1966; occ: assistant professor & assistant dean at the College of Biological Sciences, Ohio State University 1997. [Biosci.ohio-state.edu/%7Emicrobio/aab.html, accessed 23 January 2000.]

AKERMAN, ANN C - bc1817 [based on age at death]; d/o ---- Akerman & Ann B Akerman; res: Portsmouth NH, Boston; dc 5 Dec 1837 age 20. [Chipman, Scott Lee. *New England Vital Records from the "Exeter News-Letter," 1831-1840.* Camden: Picton Press, 1993, p. 147.]

AKERMAN, ANN M - mc 6 Dec 1831 in Portsmouth to Albert J Badger. [Chipman, Scott Lee. *New England Vital Records from the "Exeter News-Letter," 1831-1840.* Camden: Picton Press, 1993, p. 26.]

AKKERMANS, ANNA - alive 1708. [Pearson, Jonathan. "Extracts from the Doop-Boek, or Baptismal Register of the Reformed Protestant Dutch Church of Schenectady, N. Y." *The New England Historical & Genealogical Register*, Volume XIX (January 1865), p. 70.]

ACKERMANN, ANNA - b 3 Jul 1899; res: Dublin, Cheshire Co NH; d Oct 1982. [Social Security Death Index at ancestry.com]

ACKERMANN, ANNA J - d 14 Nov 1886. [----. "R. L. Polk & Co.'s Toledo [OH] Directory: mortuary list 1 Apr. 1886 to 1 Apr.

1887." *Fort Industry Reflections,* Vol. XX #1 (January-February-March 2000), p. 2.]

ACKERMANS, ANNETJE - alive 1680; witnessed bapt of Jannetje on 18 Apr 1680, who was the d/o Laurus Ackerman & Geertje Egberts. [Versteeg, Dingman and Thomas E. Vermilye, Jr. *Bergen Records. Records of the Reformed Protestant Dutch Church of Bergen in New Jersey, 1666 to 1788.* Originally published in the *Year Book of the Holland Society of New York,* 1913. Reprint Baltimore: Clearfield Publishing Co., Inc., 1990, p. 27.]

ACKERMAN, ANNETTE MARY - b 14 Apr 1863 Alexandria; d/o Jacob Hanson Ackerman & Sarah Hall; unm; occ: keeping a boarding house in Winchester MA. [Musgrove, R. W. *History of the Town of Bristol, New Hampshire.* ----: Richard W. Musgrove, 1904. Reprint with a new foreword by Charles E. Greenwood, Somersworth: New Hampshire Publishing Company, 1976, p. 2 (Volume II).]

-----

The following are probably the same woman.

AKERMAN, ANNIE E - alive 1915; umn; occ: bookkeeper for J A Lane & Co's; res: boarded with Mrs E F Akerman in Hampton NH. [Crowley & Lunt. *Exeter & N. H. Coast Directory.* Beverly: Crowley & Lunt, Publishers, 1915, p. 181.]

AKERMAN, ANNIE E - alive 1924; occ: bookkeeper for J A Lane & Co; res: boarded at Mrs Elizabeth F Akerman's house on Lafayette Rd in Hampton NH. [See Charles P Akerman for data on his widow, Elizabeth F Akerman.] [Crowley & Lunt. *Exeter, Newmarket, & N. H. Coast Directory.* Beverly: Crowley & Lunt, Publishers, 1924, p. 266.]

AKERMAN, ANNIE E - alive 1935; unm; occ: bookkeeper; res: boarded with J P Blake on RFD 1 in Hampton NH. [Crowley & Lunt. *Exeter, Hampton, & N. H. Coast Directory.* Beverly: Crowley & Lunt, Publishers, 1935, p. 315.]

AKERMAN, ANNIE E - alive 1936; occ: secretary for the Lane Fund Trustees; d by 1948. [Randall, Peter Evans. *Hampton, a century of town and beach, 1888-1988.* Portsmouth: Peter E. Randall, Publisher, 1989, p. 807.]

AKERMAN, ANNIE E - alive 1941; unm; res: boarded at J P Blake's on RFD 1, Hampton NH. [Crowley & Lunt. *Exeter, Hampton, & N. H. Coast Directory.* Beverly: Crowley & Lunt, Publishers, 1941, p. 324.]

-----

ACKERMANN, ANTJE JURGENS - b 28 Oct 1828 Strackholt GE; d/o Jurgen Eden Ackermann & Trientje Eilers; m 20 Jul 1849 in Strackholt GE to Reiner Heyen Ackermann (a first cousin); d 25 Dec 1875 Sudhorn GE. [Correspondence dated 1 Oct. 2000 from Eddie Dirks.]

ACKERMAN, ANTHONY - d 22 Jul 1885. [----. "Deaths Extracted from R. L. Polk & Co.'s Toledo Directory 1885-1886. Mortuary List. Extending from April 1, 1885 to April 1, 1886. Compiled from official records." *Fort Industry Reflections,* Vol. 18 #4, p. 30]

ACKERMAN, ANTOINE - alive 1860; mil: 176 Infantry. [Wilt, Richard A. *New York Soldiers in the Civil War: a roster of military officers and soldiers who served in New York regiments in the Civil War as listed in the annual reports of the Adjutant General of the State of New York.* Bowie: Heritage Books, Inc., 1999, p. 2.]

ACKERMANN, ANTOINETTE - alive 1993; edu: "Dip Tch (Auck), B Ed, M Ed (CCAE);" occ: lecturer in health education at the University of Canberra. [education.canberra.edu.au/staff/pace/ ackermann/ackermann.html, accessed 23 January 2000.]

ACKERMANN, ANTON - alive 1860; mil: 7 Veteran Infantry. [Wilt, Richard A. *New York Soldiers in the Civil War: a roster of military officers and soldiers who served in New York regiments in the Civil War as listed in the annual reports of the Adjutant General of the State of New York.* Bowie: Heritage Books, Inc., 1999, p. 2.]

ACKERMAN, ARLENE A - b 24 Mar 1936; edu: Master's degree; mil: permanent grade of Captain. [----. *U. S. Army Register, Volume*

*II: army, NGUS, USAR, and other active lists, 1 January 1970.* Washington: U. S. Government Printing Office, 1970, p. 3.]

ACKERMAN, ARTHUR H - b 25 Jun 1928; edu: college graduate; mil: permanent grade of Major received 2 Jun 1967. [----. *U. S. Army Register, Volume 1: regular army active list, 1 January 1970.* Washington: U. S. Government Printing Office, 1970, p. 1]

ACKERMAN, ARTHUR W - b 15 Oct 1944; mil: permanent rank of 1st Lt received 5 Jun 1971; edu: college graduate. [----. *U. S. Army Register, Volume 1: regular army active list, 1 January 1974.* Washington: U. S. Government Printing Office, 1974, p. 1.]

ACKERMAN, ASA C - alive 1812; res: Brownville, Jefferson Co NY; mil: awarded $31.00 claim as a soldier of the War of 1812. [----. *Index of Awards on Claims of the Soldiers of the War of 1812, as audited and allowed by the adjutant and inspector generals, pursuant to chapter 176, of the laws of 1859.* Albany: Weed, Parsons and Company, Printers, 1860, p. 4.]

ACKERMAN, AUGUST - alive 1911; m Augusta Anderson; ch: Edward Augustus b 5 Dec 1911 qv. [Debus, Allen G. *World Who's Who in Science: a biographical dictionary of notable scientists from antiquity to the present.* Chicago: Marquis-Who's Who, Inc., 1968, p. 8.]

ACHERMAN, AUGUSTUS C - m Eve Acherman d 20 Jan 1845; ch: Augusta B bc1840 [based on age at death] & d 3 Sep 1844 aged 4y 13d. [Augusta is listed as a son in the article. Wife and daughter are buried in the Old Catholic Cem, Henry Twp, Marshall Co IL.] [Bogner, Tom. "The Old Catholic Cemetery." *The Prospector*, Vol. 19 #2 (February 1999), p. 13.]

ACKERMAN, BALTZER - alive 1790; res: Lancaster Borough in Lancaster Co. Free white males 16+ years old = 1; free white women = 3. [----. *Heads of Families at the First Census of the United States Taken in the Year 1790: Pennsylvania.* Baltimore: Genealogical Publishing Company, 1966, p. 136.]

AKKERMAN, BARBARA - alive 1790; res: Salisbury District in Stokes Co. Free white males less than 16 = 1, free white females = 3.

[North, S. N. D. *Heads of Families at the First Census of the United states Taken in the Year 1790: North Carolina.* Washington: Government Printing Office, 1908. Reprint Spartanburg: The Reprint Company, 1961, p. 181.]

AKERMAN, BARNARD - alive 1790; res: Portsmouth Town NH. Free white males of 16y & upwards, including heads of families = 1. Free white males under 16y = 3. Free white females, including heads of families = 1. [----. *Heads of Families at the First Census of the United States Taken in the Year 1790: New Hampshire.* Washington: Government Printing Office, 1907. Reprint Baltimore: Genealogical Publishing Company, 1966, p. 78.]

AKERMAN, BARNARD - b NH; m Margaret ---- b NH & age 55 in 1850 census; ch: Margaret b NH & age 20 in 1850 census, Lucy b NH & age 18 in 1850 census; occ: laborer; res: Portsmouth, Rockingham Co NH. Barnard Akerman was 63 in the 1850 census. They were family #808 & lived in dwelling #598; they lived with Whidden & Rice/Bice families. [*New Hampshire 1850 Census*, p. 54 at familytreemaker.com, accessed 27 August 2000.]

AKERMAN, BARNET - owned a house on Congress Street. [Brewster, Charles W. *Rambles About Portsmouth: first series.* ----: Charles W. Brewster, 1859. Facsimile reprint of second edition published 1873 Somersworth: New Hampshire Publishing Company, 1971, p. 355.]

AKERMAN, BARNET - ch: Catharine J bc1799 [based on age at death] & d 12 Mar 1856 Portsmouth age 57. [Chipman, Scott Lee. *New England Vital Records from the "Exeter News-Letter," 1853-1858.* Camden: Picton Press, 1994, p. 151.]

AKERMAN, BARNET - alive 1776; signed Association Test of 1776 in which he agreed to "oppose the Hostile Proceedings of the British Fleets, and Armies, against the United American Colonies." [Brewster, Charles W. *Rambles About Portsmouth: first series.* ----: Charles W. Brewster, 1859. Facsimile reprint of second edition published 1873 Somersworth: New Hampshire Publishing Company, 1971, p. 215.]

AKERMAN, BARNET - alive 1776; res: Portsmouth. [Batchellor, Albert Stillman. *Miscellaneous Revolutionary Documents of New Hampshire including the association test, the pension rolls, and other important papers. Vol. 30.* Manchester: The John B. Clarke Co., 1910, p. 113.]

AKERMAN, BARNET - alive 1784; m Sarah ----; ch: Mark bapt 25 May 1784 at North Church in Portsmouth NH, Barnet bapt 17 Dec 1786 at North Church in Portsmouth NH, Walter bapt 14 Dec 1788 at North Church in Portsmouth NH, Sarah bapt 12 Jun 1791 at North Church in Portsmouth NH, Hannah bapt 30 Jun 1793 at North Church in Portsmouth NH.[14]

AKERMAN, BARNET - bc1787 [based on age at death]; d 30 Mar 1856 Portsmouth, age 69. [Chipman, Scott Lee. *New England Vital Records from the "Exeter News-Letter," 1853-1858.* Camden: Picton Press, 1994, p. 153.] [Is this the Barnet Akerman bapt 1786; s/o Barnet Akerman alive 1784?]

AKERMAN, BARNET - alive 1800; res: Portsmouth. Free white males under 10y = 0, 10-16y = 2, 16-26y (including heads of households) = 0, 26-45y (including heads of households) = 0, 45y & upwards (including heads of households) = 0. Free white females under 10y = 0, 10-16y = 0, 16-26y (including heads of households) = 0, 26-45y (including heads of households) = 0, 45y & upwards (including heads of households) = 1. [----. *Heads of Families at the Second Census of the United States Taken in the Year 1800: New Hampshire.* Madison: John Brooks Threlfall, 1973, p. 144.]

AKERMAN, BARNET - alive 1817; ch: (eldest son) Barnet W bc1817 qv. [Chipman, Scott Lee. *New England Vital Records from the "Exeter News-Letter," 1847-1852.* Camden: Picton Press, 1994, p. 230.]

---

[14] Tibbetts, Charles W., *The New Hampshire Genealogical Record. An illustrated quarterly magazine devoted to genealogy, history and biography. Vol. VII, January 1910 - April 1910* (Dover:Charles W. Tibbetts, 1910. Facsimile reprint Bowie: Heritage Books, Inc., 1988), p. 15, 74, 75, 77, 78. Is this the same Barnet Akerman who married Sarah March? Brewster, Charles W., *Rambles About Portsmouth: first series* (----: Charles W. Brewster, 1859. Facsimile reprint of second edition published 1873 Somersworth: New Hampshire Publishing Company, 1971), p. 129.

AKERMAN, BARNET W - bc1815 [based on age at death]; s/o Barnet Akerman & ----; res: Portsmouth, Boston; dc 18 Oct 1852 Portsmouth, age 35. [Chipman, Scott Lee. *New England Vital Records from the "Exeter News-Letter," 1847-1852.* Camden: Picton Press, 1994, p. 230.]

AKERMAN, BARNETT - bapt 8 Apr 1722 North Church, Portsmouth NH. [Tibbetts, Charles W. *The New Hampshire Genealogical Record. An illustrated quarterly magazine devoted to genealogy, history and biography. Vol. V, January 1908 - October 1908.* Dover: Charles W. Tibbetts, 1908. Facsimile reprint Bowie: Heritage Books, Inc., 1988, p. 38.]

ACKERMAN, BARTLEY C - b 27 Jul 1948; mil: permanent grade of 2nd Lt received 9 Jun 1971; edu: high school graduate. [----. *U. S. Army Register, Volume 1: regular army active list, 1 January 1974.* Washington: U. S. Government Printing Office, 1974, p. 1.]

ACKERMAN, BEATRICE M - b1902 Lebanon, Lebanon Co PA; d/o Frank R Ackerman & Ella Black; m 15 Apr 1922 in Annville PA to Winfield Charles Gerber b 21 Jul 1900 Lebanon (Lebanon Co) PA, s/o William J Gerber & Sarah Ann Heilman; d 19 May 1968. [Heilman, Robert A. *The Heilman Family Genealogy comprising three Heilman lines in one volume: John Peter, John Adam, and William B. Heilman.* Bowie: Heritage Books, Inc., p. 196, 197 (part 1).]

ACKERMAN, BEN - b Oct 1850 GE; m ----; naturalized in 1872; res: PA?, WA; occ: farmer, owned 190 acres; d 1 Sep 1907 age 56y 11m, cause: cancer; bur: 4 Sep 1907 in NE 87-4 Line 7. [Gilman, Gerry. "Old City Cemetery." *Trail Breakers*, Vol. 25 #1, p. 21.]

AKERMAN, BENJ JR - alive 1749; ch: Barnet bapt 14 Jan 1749/50 at North Church in Portsmouth NH. [Tibbetts, Charles W. *The New Hampshire Genealogical Record. An illustrated quarterly magazine devoted to genealogy, history and biography. Vol. V, January 1908 - October 1908.* Dover: Charles W. Tibbetts, 1908. Facsimile reprint Bowie: Heritage Books, Inc., 1988, p. 88.]

AKERMAN, BENJA - alive 1722? Listed as one of the original proprietors of Barrington NH, which was incorporated in 1722. He had 120 acres, 60 rods wide, rate of 1 pound. [Bouton, Nathaniel. *Town Papers. Documents and Records Relating to Towns in New Hampshire; with an appendix embracing the constitutional conventions of 1778-1779; and of 1781-1783; and the State Constitution of 1784. Volume IX.* Concord: Charles C. Pearson, State Printer, 1875, p. 41.]

ACREMAN, BENJA - alive 1722; with John Cutt, he received one proprietor's share of the town of Chester chartered 1722. [Batchellor, Albert Stillman. *State of New Hampshire. Town Charters including grants of territory within the present limits of New Hampshire, made by the government of Massachusetts, and a portion of the grants and charters issued by the government of New Hampshire, with an appendix, consisting of papers relating to the granting of the various lines and bodies of towns, with acts in regard to town bounds in general, and many documents produced by disputes between towns concerning their boundary lines, with illustrative maps and plans and complete indexes. Volume XXIV. Town charters, Volume I.* Concord: Edward N. Pearson, Public Printer, 1894, p. 569.]

AKARMAN, BENJA - alive 1748. Signed a petition requesting the grant of a "Tract of Land for a Township on Merrimack River or as Near the River as you think Proper...." [Batchellor, Albert Stillman. *State of New Hampshire. Township Grants of Lands in New Hampshire included in the Masonian Patent issued subsequent to 1746 by the Masonian Proprietary. Volume XXVII. Town Charters, Volume IV. Masonian Papers, Volume 1.* Concord: Edward N. Pearson, Public Printer, 1896, p. 63.]

AKARMAN, BENJA - alive 1755; settled the estate of William Adams of Portsmouth, 22 Oct 1755. [Hammond, Otis G. *Probate Records of the Province of New Hampshire, Vol. 4, 1750-1753. State Papers Series Vol. 34.* ----: The State of New Hampshire, 1933. Facsimile reprint Bowie: Heritage Books, Inc., 1989, p. 281.]

AKERMAN, BENJA - alive 1759. "Richard Wibird Esqr Chairman of the Committee for the Expedition Against Canada, 1759...Discharges himself from the Aforesaid Sums by the following payments...." Benja Akerman was paid 31 pounds, 8 shillings, & 10 pence in 1759. [Hammond, Isaac W. *The State of New Hampshire.*

*Miscellaneous Provincial and State Papers 1725-1800. Vol. XVIII.* Manchester: John B. Clarke, Public Printer, 1890, p. 501.]

AKERMAN, BENJA - alive 1773; a grantee of Success Twp 12 Feb 1773. [Batchellor, Albert Stillman. *State of New Hampshire. Town Charters granted within the present limits of New Hampshire, being the continuation and conclusion of the grants of townships issued by the provincial government of New Hampshire, presented in alphabetcical arrangement, and including all subsequent to the letter E, will illustrative maps, plans, bibliographical citations and complete indexes, and an appendix containg documents relating to the most ancient towns of this State, and historical notes and monographs. Volume XXV. Town charters, Volume II.* Concord: Edward N. Pearson, Public Printer, 1895, p. 555.]

AKERMAN, BENJA - alive 1775; res: Portsmouth. Signed a petition (dated 4 May 1775) regarding certain election returns. [Bouton, Nathaniel. *Town Papers. Documents and Records Relating to Towns in New Hampshire; with an appendix embracing the constitutional conventions of 1778-1779; and of 1781-1783; and the State Constitution of 1784. Volume IX.* Concord: Charles C. Pearson, State Printer, 1875, p. 714.]

AKERMAN, BENJA - alive 1776; res: Portsmouth. [Batchellor, Albert Stillman. *Miscellaneous Revolutionary Documents of New Hampshire including the association test, the pension rolls, and other important papers. Vol. 30.* Manchester: The John B. Clarke Co., 1910, p. 113.]

AKERMAN, BENJA JR - witness to land transaction between John Mason Jr & Ichabod Rawlins; res: Somersworth. [Rollins, Alden M. *The Rollins Family in the New Hampshire Provincial Deeds, 1655-1771.* Bowie: Heritage Books, Inc., 1997, p. 148, 149.]

AKERMAN, BENJA JR - alive 1745. On 25 Jun 1745, the "Journal of the Assembly" records that "a vote of the House for an allowance to Benja Akerman jun. of 35 [shillings] as an Express carrying Proclamations thro' the Province which were read at the board & concurred & assented to by the Governour." [Bouton, Nathaniel. *Provincial Papers. Documents and Records Relating to the Province of New-Hampshire, from 1738 to 1749: containing very valuable and interesting records and papers relating to the expedition against Louisbourg, 1745. Volume V.* Nashua: Orren C. Moore, State Printer, 1871, p. 761.]

AKARMAN, BENJA JR - alive 1748. Signed a petition requesting the grant of a "Tract of Land for a Township on Merrimack River or as Near the River as you think Proper...." [Batchellor, Albert Stillman. *State of New Hampshire. Township Grants of Lands in New Hampshire included in the Masonian Patent issued subsequent to 1746 by the Masonian Proprietary. Volume XXVII. Town Charters, Volume IV. Masonian Papers, Volume 1.* Concord: Edward N. Pearson, Public Printer, 1896, p. 63.]

ACKERMAN, BENJA SR - res: Portsmouth or New Castle; petitioned against having a bridge at New Castle [undated]. [Bouton, Nathaniel. *Town Papers. Documents and Records Relating to Towns in New Hampshire; with an appendix embracing the constitutional conventions of 1778-1779; and of 1781-1783; and the State Constitution of 1784. Volume IX.* Concord: Charles C. Pearson, State Printer, 1875, p. 561.]

ACKERMAN, BENJAMEN - land abutted that of Peter Wells. [Hammond, Otis G. *Probate Records of the Province of New Hampshire, Vol. 9, 1767-1771. State Papers Series Vol. 39.* ----: The State of New Hampshire, 1941. Facsimile reprint Bowie: Heritage Books, Inc., 1990, p. 205.]

AKERMAN, BENJAMIN - mil: rank of corporal; res: Portsmouth. [See Mass Rolls vol. 1 p. 96.] [Batchellor, Albert Stillman. *Miscellaneous Revolutionary Documents of New Hampshire including the association test, the pension rolls, and other important papers. Vol. 30.* Manchester: The John B. Clarke Co., 1910, p. 174.]

AKERMAN, BENJAMIN - res: a "house on Islington near Cass Street." [Brewster, Charles W. *Rambles About Portsmouth: first series.* ----: Charles W. Brewster, 1859. Facsimile reprint of second edition published 1873 Somersworth: New Hampshire Publishing Company, 1971, p. 326.]

AKERMAN, BENJAMIN - owned a pew in North Church. [Brewster, Charles W. *Rambles About Portsmouth: first series.* ----:

Charles W. Brewster, 1859. Facsimile reprint of second edition published 1873 Somersworth: New Hampshire Publishing Company, 1971, p. 329.]

AKERMAN, BENJAMIN - m Olive ---- dc 4 Mar 1834 Portsmouth, [age 47?]. [Chipman, Scott Lee. *New England Vital Records from the "Exeter News-Letter," 1831-1840*. Camden: Picton Press, 1993, p. 86.]

ACREMAN, BENJ[AMI]N - m Mary ----; ch: Simeon b 29 Nov 1832. [----. "Births, Marriages, and Deaths in Portsmouth, N.H." *The New England Historical and Genealogical Register*, Vol. XXV (April 1871), p. 120.]

AKERMAN, BENJAMIN - alive 1711. Was to receive 5 pounds for "one year's service in attending the General Assembly" as recorded in the journal of Council & Assembly, 19 Apr 1711.[15] This is probably the same Benjamin Akerman who received 5 pounds "for his Attendance on the Council and Assembly" as recorded in the journal of the Council & Assembly on 5 May 1712.[16] This is probably the same Benja Akerman who is noted as receiving 5 pounds in the journal of the Council & Assembly on 8 May 1714.[17] This is probably the same Benj Akerman who was to receive 7 pounds per annum "for the future for his service in waiting on the Governmt" as recorded in the journal of the Council & Assembly recorded 7 Apr 1716.[18] This is probably the same Benj Akerman who was to receive 8 shillings "for going post to Newbury" as recorded on 14 May 1716 in the journal of the Council & Assembly.[19]

AKERMAN, BENJAMIN - alive 1714. Reported on the division of the estate of Joseph Dennett, deceased, of Portsmouth. [Metcalf, Henry Harrison. *Probate Records of the Province of New Hampshire, Volume 1: 1635-1717. State papers series, Volume 31.* Concord:

---

[15] Bouton, Nathaniel, *Provincial Papers. Documents and Records Relating to the Province of New-Hampshire, from 1692 to 1722: being part II. of papers relating to that period. Containing the "Journal of the Coucil and General Assembly." Volume III* (Manchester: John B. Clarke, State Printer, 1869), p. 470.
[16] Ibid., p. 528.
[17] Ibid., p. 567.
[18] Ibid., p. 636.
[19] Ibid., p. 641.

Rumford Printing Co., 1907. Facsimile reprint Bowie: Heritage Books, Inc., 1989, p. 749.]

ACERMAN, BENJAMIN - alive 1716. The House of Representatives, meeting on 7 Apr 1716, "Voted That Benjamin Acerman be Allowed Seven Pounds [per] annum for the future out of the Treasury for his Attending the Councel And Assembly[.]" [Batchellor, Albert Stillman. *Provincial Papers of New Hampshire including the records of the president and council.... Vol. XIX.* Manchester: John B. Clarke, Public Printer, 1891, p. 84.]

AKARMAN, BENJ[AMIN] - alive 1722. According to the journal of the House dated 4 May 1722, he was paid 40 shillings [no reason given].[20]

AKERMAN, BENJA[MIN] - alive 1722. Recorded in the journal of the General Assembly for 5 May 1722 as being paid 4 shillings. [Bouton, Nathaniel. *Provincial Papers. Documents and Records Relating to the Province of New-Hampshire, from 1722 to 1737: containing important records and papers, pertaining to the settlement of the boundary lines between New-Hampshire and Massachusetts. Volume IV.* Manchester: John B. Clarke, State Printer, 1870, p. 32.]

AKERMAN, BENJA[MIN] - alive 1723. Recorded in the journal of the General Assembly for 30 May 1723 that he was to receive, "for attena & express to Boston: ye Ballce allowed," 10 pounds. [Bouton, Nathaniel. *Provincial Papers. Documents and Records Relating to the Province of New-Hampshire, from 1722 to 1737: containing important records and papers, pertaining to the settlement of the boundary lines between New-Hampshire and Massachusetts. Volume IV.* Manchester: John B. Clarke, State Printer, 1870, p. 97.]

AKARMANS, BENJ[AMIN] - alive 1723. The journal of the House dated 30 May 1723 shows him paid 13 pounds 15 shillings. [Bouton, Nathaniel. *Provincial Papers. Documents and Records Relating to the Province of New-Hampshire, from 1722 to 1737: containing*

---

[20] Bouton, Nathaniel, *Provincial Papers. Documents and Records Relating to the Province of New-Hampshire, from 1722 to 1737: containing important records and papers, pertaining to the settlement of the boundary lines between New-Hampshire and Massachusetts. Volume IV* (Manchester: John B. Clarke, State Printer, 1870), p. 313. There may be two Benjamins serving the state and receiving payment for it.

*important records and papers, pertaining to the settlement of the boundary lines between New-Hampshire and Massachusetts. Volume IV.* Manchester: John B. Clarke, State Printer, 1870, p. 357.]

-----

The following two Benja[min]s may be the same person being paid twice, or two different people.

AKERMAN, BENJA[MIN] - alive 1726. Paid 5 pounds; the journal of the General Assembly, dated 1 Dec 1726, does not give a reason for the payment. [Bouton, Nathaniel. *Provincial Papers. Documents and Records Relating to the Province of New-Hampshire, from 1722 to 1737: containing important records and papers, pertaining to the settlement of the boundary lines between New-Hampshire and Massachusetts. Volume IV.* Manchester: John B. Clarke, State Printer, 1870, p. 230.]

AKERMAN, BENJA[MIN] - alive 1726. Paid 1 pound 5 shillings; the journal of the General Assembly, dated 1 Dec 1726, does not give a reason for the payment. [Bouton, Nathaniel. *Provincial Papers. Documents and Records Relating to the Province of New-Hampshire, from 1722 to 1737: containing important records and papers, pertaining to the settlement of the boundary lines between New-Hampshire and Massachusetts. Volume IV.* Manchester: John B. Clarke, State Printer, 1870, p. 230.]

-----

AKERMAN, BENJA[MIN] - alive 1726. The House of Representatives voted on 30 Sep 1726 that he "be allowed and paid out of ye Publick Treasury 25 [shillings] in full Satisfaction for his horse when he went to Penny Cook. [Bouton, Nathaniel. *Provincial Papers. Documents and Records Relating to the Province of New-Hampshire, from 1722 to 1737: containing important records and papers, pertaining to the settlement of the boundary lines between New-Hampshire and Massachusetts. Volume IV.* Manchester: John B. Clarke, State Printer, 1870, p. 436.]

AKERMAN, BENJA[MIN] - alive 1727. According to the journal of the General Assembly dated 26 Jan 1727, he was to receive 6 shillings for "a day service & Canoe."[21] This may be the same Benja Akerman who the House of Representatives allowed "himself & Cannoe Carrying the Comittee to let the wheels and Carryages out Jun 1727" for 6 shillings, as recorded 20 Dec 1727.[22]

AKERMAN, BENJA[MIN] - alive 1727. According to the journal of the General Assembly dated 18 May 1727, he was to be paid 10 pounds.[23] This may be the same Benja[min] Akerman for which was recorded in the journal of the House: "Eodm Die. allowed Benja akerman ten pounds for his Service attending Govr and Councill & assembly for the ye yeare 1726."[24]

AKERMAN, BENJAMIN - alive 1727; taxpayer in Portsmouth in 1727. [Brewster, Charles W. *Rambles About Portsmouth: first series.* ----: Charles W. Brewster, 1859. Facsimile reprint of second edition published 1873 Somersworth: New Hampshire Publishing Company, 1971, p. 160.]

AKERMAN, BENJA[MIN] - alive 1728. According to the journal of the General Assembly dated 31 May 1728, he was to receive 13 pounds 6 shillings for one year's service (10 pounds), extra service (3 pounds) and a day's service (6 shillings).[25] This is probably the same Mr Akerman recorded in the journal of the House, dated 24 May 1728, who was voted to receive 3 pounds for his "exterordinary attendance for the yeare 1727 Ending as above [Apr 1728]."[26] This is probably the same Benja Akerman recorded in the journal of the House on 31 May 1728, who was to receive 10 pounds for his service in 1727.[27]

---

[21] Bouton, Nathaniel, *Provincial Papers. Documents and Records Relating to the Province of New-Hampshire, from 1722 to 1737: containing important records and papers, pertaining to the settlement of the boundary lines between New-Hampshire and Massachusetts. Volume IV* (Manchester: John B. Clarke, State Printer, 1870), p. 280.
[22] Ibid., p. 466.
[23] Ibid., p. 248.
[24] Ibid., p. 451.
[25] Bouton, Nathaniel, *Provincial Papers. Documents and Records Relating to the Province of New-Hampshire, from 1722 to 1737: containing important records and papers, pertaining to the settlement of the boundary lines between New-Hampshire and Massachusetts. Volume IV.* Manchester: John B. Clarke, State Printer, 1870, p. 304.
[26] Ibid., p. 497.
[27] Ibid., p. 500.

AKERMAN, BENJ[AMIN] - alive 1730. The journal of the House dated 1 Sep 1730 records him as receiving 10 pounds for 1729 but gives no reason. [Bouton, Nathaniel. *Provincial Papers. Documents and Records Relating to the Province of New-Hampshire, from 1722 to 1737: containing important records and papers, pertaining to the settlement of the boundary lines between New-Hampshire and Massachusetts. Volume IV.* Manchester: John B. Clarke, State Printer, 1870, p. 571.]

AKERMAN, BENJAMIN - alive 1731. Signed on the inventory accounting of Robert Pike, deceased, of Portsmouth. [Metcalf, Henry Harrison. *Probate Records of the Province of New Hampshire, Volume 2: 1718-1740. State papers series, Volume 32.* Bristol: R. W. Musgrove, Printer, 1914. Facsimile reprint Bowie: Heritage Books, Inc., 1989, p. 426.]

AKERMAN, BENJAMIN - alive 1736; m Mary ----; ch: Nahum b 21 Jan 1736-7. [----. "Births, Marriages, and Deaths in Portsmouth, N.H." *The New England Historical and Genealogical Register*, Vol. XXVI (Oct. 1872), p. 378.]

ACREMEN, BENJA[MIN] - alive 1737. Was to be paid 6 pounds 10 shillings for "fetching ye Commiso from Boston" so that the Commissioners could settle the boundary lines between NH & MA. [Batchellor, Albert Stillman. *Provincial Papers of New Hampshire including the records of the president and council, January 1, 1679, to December 22, 1680.... Vol. XIX.* Manchester: John B. Clarke, Public Printer, 1891, p. 421.]

AKERMAN, BENJAMIN - alive 1737. His land abutted that of Edward Wells, deceased, of Portsmouth. [Metcalf, Henry Harrison, *Probate Records of the Province of New Hampshire, Volume 2: 1718-1740. State papers series, Volume 32.* Bristol: R. W. Musgrove, Printer, 1914. Facsimile reprint Bowie: Heritage Books, Inc., 1989, p. 680. Map (on next page) is from page 682.]

AKERMAN, BENJ[AMI]N - alive 1737; m Mary ----; ch: Josiah b 1 May 1737. [----. "Births, Marriages, and Deaths in Portsmouth, N.H." *The New England Historical and Genealogical Register*, Vol. XXVI (Oct. 1872), p. 380.]

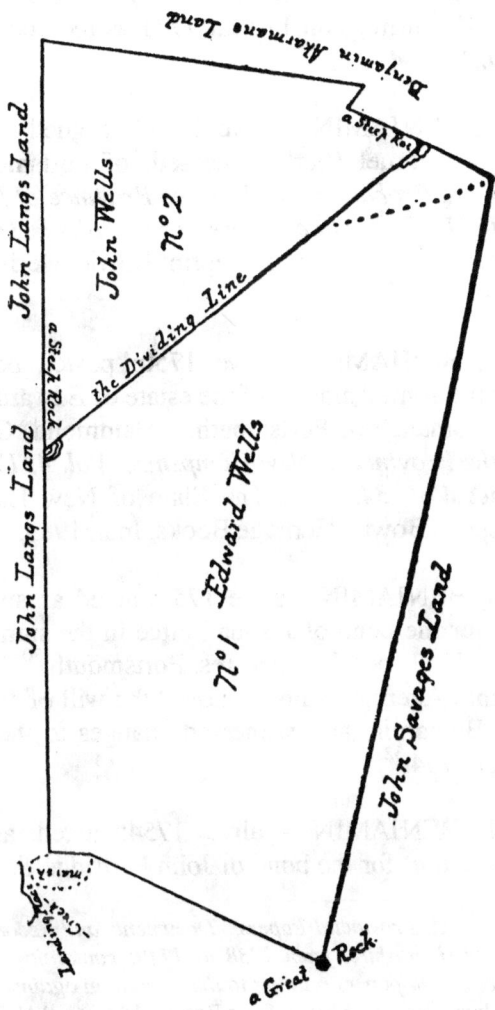

One end of Benjamin Akerman's property (his name appears as Benjamin Akarman on the map) is shown abutting the land of Edward Wells and John Wells. [See citation on page 26.]

AKERMAN, BENJA[MIN] - alive 1741; the House voted to give him 20 pounds (to "be allowed & paid out of the Publick Treasury") for "Extre. Attenda." on 29 Jan 1841 [*sic*; this entry in the "Journal of the House" is preceeded & followed by records dated 1741].[28] This is probably the same Benja Akerman who was "allow'd Express money" of 4 pounds 10 shillings on 17 Mar 1741 as recorded in the "Journal of the House."[29]

AKERMAN, BENJAMIN - alive 1742. Signed on the inventory accounting of Samuel Clark, deceased, of Portsmouth. [Metcalf, Henry Harrison, *Probate Records of the Province of New Hampshire, Volume 3: 1741-1749. State papers series, Volume 33.* Concord: The Rumford Press, 1915. Facsimile reprint Bowie: Heritage Books, Inc., 1989, p. 105.]

AKERMAN, BENJAMIN - alive 1750; posted bond (with John Phillips) for the administration of the estate of Edward Phillips, 25 Jul 1750; occ: yeoman; res: Portsmouth. [Hammond, Otis G., *Probate Records of the Province of New Hampshire, Vol. 4, 1750-1753. State Papers Series Vol. 34.* ----: The State of New Hampshire, 1933. Facsimile reprint Bowie: Heritage Books, Inc., 1989, p. 52.]

AKERMAN, BENJAMIN - alive 1751; acted as surety (with John Wentworth) for the bond of Joshua Peirce in the sum of 500 pounds, dated 26 Nov 1751; occ: butcher; res: Portsmouth.[30] This may be the same Benjamin Akerman who witnessed the will of Joshua Peirce, 18 Jul 1754.[31] Benjamin later witnessed changes to the will of Joshua Peirce, 27 Jul 1754.[32]

AKERMAN, BENJAMIN - alive 1754; acted as surety (with Benjamin Dockum) for the bond of John Partridge & wife Priscilla in

---

[28] Bouton, Nathaniel, *Provincial Papers. Documents and Records Relating to the Province of New-Hampshire, from 1738 to 1749: containing very valuable and interesting records and papers relating to the expedition against Louisbourg, 1745. Volume V* (Nashua: Orren C. Moore, State Printer, 1871), p. 141.]
[29] Ibid., p. 153.
[30] Hammond, Otis G., *Probate Records of the Province of New Hampshire, Vol. 4, 1750-1753. State Papers Series Vol. 34* (----: The State of New Hampshire, 1933. Facsimile reprint Bowie: Heritage Books, Inc., 1989), p. 182.
[31] Otis G. Hammond, *Probate Records of the Province of New Hampshire, Vol. 5, 1754-1756. State Papers Series Vol. 35* (----: The State of New Hampshire, 1936. Facsimile reprint Bowie: Heritage Books, Inc., 1989), p. 137.
[32] Ibid., p. 138.

the sum of 500 pounds, dated 28 Aug 1754; res: Portsmouth. [Hammond, Otis G., *Probate Records of the Province of New Hampshire, Vol. 5, 1754-1756. State Papers Series Vol. 35.* ----: The State of New Hampshire, 1936. Facsimile reprint Bowie: Heritage Books, Inc., 1989, p. 153.]

AKERMAN, BENJAMIN - alive 1756; posted bond for the administration of the estate of Joseph Mead, 21 Jun 1756; occ: tanner; res: Portsmouth. [Hammond, Otis G., *Probate Records of the Province of New Hampshire, Vol. 5, 1754-1756. State Papers Series Vol. 35.* ----: The State of New Hampshire, 1936. Facsimile reprint Bowie: Heritage Books, Inc., 1989, p. 472, 473. ]

AKERMAN, BENJ[AMIN] - alive 1757; "The Council concurred in votes of allowance, to...Benj. Akerman, in behalf of Benj. Pitman, deed, for support of two Indians in prison-- 15 [pounds]." [Bouton, Nathaniel. *Provincial Papers. Documents and Records Relating to the Province of New-Hampshire, from 1749 to 1763: containing very valuable and interesting records and papers relating to the Crown Point expedition, and the "Seven Years French and Indian Wars," 1755-1762. Volume VI.* Manchester: James M. Campbell, State Printer, 1872, p. 594.]

AKERMAN, BENJAMIN - alive 1759; witnessed bond of Dorothy Reed, 1759. [Hammond, Otis G., *Probate Records of the Province of New Hampshire, Vol. 6, 1757-1760. State Papers Series Vol. 36.* ----: The State of New Hampshire, 1938. Facsimile reprint Bowie: Heritage Books, Inc., 1989, p. 444.]

AKERMAN, BENJAMIN - alive 1759; res: Portsmouth; appointed sole executor by Thomas Mead. [Hammond, Otis G., *Probate Records of the Province of New Hampshire, Vol. 6, 1757-1760. State Papers Series Vol. 36.* ----: The State of New Hampshire, 1938. Facsimile reprint Bowie: Heritage Books, Inc., 1989, p. 428, 429.]

AKERMAN, BENJAMIN - alive 1761; acted as surety (with John Folsom) for the bond of Gideon Walker in the sum of 500 pounds, dated 25 Feb 1761; res: Portsmouth; occ: tanner. [Hammond, Otis G., *Probate Records of the Province of New Hampshire, Vol. 7, 1760-1763. State Papers Series Vol. 37.* ----: The State of New Hampshire, 1939. Facsimile reprint Bowie: Heritage Books, Inc., 1990, p. 110.]

AKERMAN, BENJAMIN - alive 1768; acted as surety (with John Penhallow) for bond of George Sherburne in the sum of 500 pounds, dated 9 Feb 1768; res: Portsmouth; occ: tanner. [Hammond, Otis G., *Probate Records of the Province of New Hampshire, Vol. 9, 1767-1771. State Papers Series Vol. 39.* ----: The State of New Hampshire, 1941. Facsimile reprint Bowie: Heritage Books, Inc., 1990, p. 69.]

AKERMAN, BENJAMIN - alive 1771. Voted to serve as selectman for Portsmouth 1771, 1772, 1773, 1774, 1775. [Tibbetts, Charles W., *The New Hampshire Genealogical Record. An illustrated quarterly magazine devoted to genealogy, history and biography. Vol. II, July 1904 - April 1905.* Dover: Charles W. Tibbetts, 1905. Facsimile reprint Bowie: Heritage Books, Inc., 1988, p. 159.]

AKARMAN, BENJAMIN - alive 1772; signed a "petition relative to market, fire-wards, taverns, small-pox, etc." which was read before the assembly on 26 May 1772; res: selectman of Portsmouth.[33] In the census of 1773, Benjamin is listed as a selectman for Portsmouth, Rockingham Co NH.[34]

AKERMAN, BENJAMIN - alive 1772; res: Franconia NH. One of several men petitioning John Wenworth on 22 Jan 1772. [Bouton, Nathaniel, *Town Papers. Documents and Records Relating to Towns in New Hampshire; with an appendix embracing the constitutional conventions of 1778-1779; and of 1781-1783; and the State Constitution of 1784. Volume IX.* Concord: Charles C. Pearson, State Printer, 1875, p. 301.]

AKERMAN, BENJAMIN - alive 1773; res: Portsmouth; occ: tanner. [Evans, Helen F., *Abstracts of the Probate Records of Rockingham*

---

[33] Hammond, Isaac W., *Town Papers. Documents Relating to Towns in New Hampshire, New London to Wolfeborough, with an appendix, embracing some docuemnts, interesting and valuable, not heretofore published, including the census of New Hampshire of 1790 in detail. Volume XIII* (Concord: Parsons B. Cogswell, State Printer, 1884), p. 275.

[34] Bouton, Nathaniel, *Provincial and State Papers. Miscellaneous Documents and Records Relating to New Hampshire at Different Periods.... Volume X* (Concord: Edward A. Jenks, State Printer, 1877), p. 627.

*County, New Hampshire, 1771-1799.* Bowie: Heritage Books, Inc., 2000, p. 880.]

AKERMAN, BENJAMIN - alive 1775; mil: enlisted 15 May 1775 as corporal in Capt Ebenezer Sullivan's co "(Berwick Me.)" of Col Scammon's regiment; res: Portsmouth. [Hammond, Isaac W., *The State of New Hampshire. Rolls of the Soldiers in the Revolutionary War, May, 1777 to 1780: with an appendix, embracing names of New Hampshire men in Massachusetts regiments. Volume II of the War Rolls. Volume XV of the Series.* Concord: Parsons B. Cogswell, State Printer, 1886, p. 749.]

AKARMAN/AKERMAN, BENJAMIN - alive 1776; mil: "privat" in the field artillery co commanded by Ebenezer Dearing, Esq, for one month's pay from 7 Dec 1776 to 7 Jan 1777. He was to be paid 2 pounds 1 shilling & acknowledged receipt of said amount on 14 Jan 1777. [His name is also abbreviated as Benja.][35] Listed as a private in Capt Ebenezer Dearing's co of artillery in the NH regiment commanded by Col Pierse Long & fit to march to Ticonderoga. He was to receive one month's pay from 7 Jan 1777 to 7 Feb 1777 in the amount of 2 pounds 1 shilling.[36] Benjamin refused to march [presumeably to Ticonderoga] under command of Capt. Dearing & was put on board the *Raleigh.*[37]

AKERMAN, BENJAMIN - b 3 Feb 1776; d 20 Feb 1867, age 91.[38] This is probably the same Benjamin Akerman - bapt 18 Feb 1776 North Church, Portsmouth NH; s/o Joseph Akerman & ——.[39]

AKERMAN, BENJAMIN - bc1776 NH [based on age of 74y in 1850]; res: Portsmouth, Rockingham Co NH. Living with Martha H

---

[35] Hammond, Isaac W., *The State of New Hampshire. Rolls of the Soldiers in the Revolutionary War, 1775, to May, 1777: with an appendix, embracing diaries of Lieut. Jonathan Burton. Volume I of the War Rolls. Volume XIV of the Series* (Concord: Parsons B. Cogswell, State Printer, 1885), pp. 484, 499.
[36] Ibid., pp. 511, 512.
[37] Ibid., p. 518.
[38] Brewster, Charles W., *Rambles About Portsmouth: second series* (——: Lewis W. Brewster, 1869. Facsimile reprint Somersworth: New Hampshire Publishing Company, 1972), p. 15.
[39] Tibbetts, Charles W., *The New Hampshire Genealogical Record. An illustrated quarterly magazine devoted to genealogy, history and biography. Vol. VI, January 1909 - October 1909* (Dover: Charles W. Tibbetts, 1909. Facsimile reprint Bowie: Heritage Books, Inc., 1988), p. 77.

Akerman, b NH & age 26 in 1850, & Benjamin [I? or T?], b NH & age 24 in 1850 (occ: tailor). [*New Hampshire 1850 Census*, p. 64 at familytreemaker.com, accessed 27 August 2000.]

AKERMAN, BENJAMIN - alive 1776; signed Association Test of 1776 in which he agreed to "oppose the Hostile Proceedings of the British Fleets, and Armies, against the United American Colonies." [Brewster, Charles W., *Rambles About Portsmouth: first series.* ----: Charles W. Brewster, 1859. Facsimile reprint of second edition published 1873 Somersworth: New Hampshire Publishing Company, 1971, p. 215.]

AKERMAN, BENJAMIN - alive 1780; res: Portsmouth NH. [Evans, Helen F., *Abstracts of the Probate Records of Rockingham County, New Hampshire, 1771-1799, Volume 1.* Bowie: Heritage Books, Inc., 2000, p. 436.]

AKARMAN, BENJAMIN - alive 1782; signed a petition, as one of several wardens of the "North and South Parishes in Portsmouth in the county of Rockingham and State aforesaid [NH]," regarding parish bounds on 18 Dec 1782; res: Portsmouth, Rockingham Co NH. [Hammond, Isaac W., *Town Papers. Documents Relating to Towns in New Hampshire, New London to Wolfeborough, with an appendix, embracing some docuemnts, interesting and valuable, not heretofore published, including the census of New Hampshire of 1790 in detail. Volume XIII.* Concord: Parsons B. Cogswell, State Printer, 1884, p. 293.]

AKERMAN, BENJAMIN - res: Portsmouth; occ: tanner; dc1783. "Divisees: Walter Akerman (oldest son, two shares); Joseph Akerman; Barnet Akerman; Richard Jenkins and Elizabeth his wife in her right; Salome Akerman, only child and rep. of Mark Akerman a son decd." [Evans, Helen F., *Abstracts of the Probate Records of Rockingham County, New Hampshire, 1771-1799, Volume 1.* Bowie: Heritage Books, Inc., 2000, p. 6.]

AKERMAN, BENJAMIN - bc1789 [based on age at death]; res: Portsmouth, Boston; dc 22 Sep 1840 Boston, age 51. [Chipman, Scott Lee, *New England Vital Records from the "Exeter News-Letter," 1831-1840.* Camden: Picton Press, 1993, p. 204.]

AKERMAN, BENJAMIN - alive 1814; attested to inventory amounting to $1353.00 on 14 Jun 1814. [Hammond, Otis G., *Probate Records of the Province of New Hampshire, Vol. 9, 1767-1771. State Papers Series Vol. 39.* ----: The State of New Hampshire, 1941. Facsimile reprint Bowie: Heritage Books, Inc., 1990, p. 259.]

AKERMAN, BENJAMIN - alive 1820; res: Portsmouth. [Evans, Helen F., *Abstracts of the Probate Records of Rockingham County, New Hampshire, 1771-1799.* Bowie: Heritage Books, Inc., 2000, p. 743.]

AKERMAN, BENJAMIN JR - alive 1752; ch: Benjamin bapt 18 Sep 1752 at North Church in Portsmouth NH. [Tibbetts, Charles W., *The New Hampshire Genealogical Record. An illustrated quarterly magazine devoted to genealogy, history and biography. Vol. V, January 1908 - October 1908.* Dover: Charles W. Tibbetts, 1908. Facsimile reprint Bowie: Heritage Books, Inc., 1988, p. 91.]

ACKERMAN, BENJAMIN F - alive 1860; mil: 6 Battery. [Wilt, Richard A., *New York Soldiers in the Civil War: a roster of military officers and soldiers who served in New York regiments in the Civil War as listed in the annual reports of the Adjutant General of the State of New York.* Bowie: Heritage Books, Inc., 1999, p. 2.]

ACKERMAN, BENJAMIN G - alive 1897; joined the Society of Sons of the Revolution in 1897; great-great-grandson of Private Johannes Ackerman b1725 qv. [----, *Year Book of the Society of Sons of the Revolution in the State of New York.* New York: Francis E. Fitch, 1899, p. 49.]

ACKERMAN, BENSON F - m 6 Jun 1850 in Eddyville to Mary Elizabeth Carmichael; res: High Falls. [Klinkenberg, Audrey M., *Marriages from "The Saugerties Telegraph," 1846-1870, and Obituaries, Death Notices and Genealogical Gleanings from "The Ulster Telegraph," 1846-1848.* Bowie: Heritage Books, Inc., 1998, p. 166.]

ACKERMAN, BERNARD - m1842 ----. [Hughes, Lois E., *Hamilton County, Ohio, Marriage index, 1817-1845, Volume I.* Bowie: Heritage Books, Inc., 1994, p. 1.]

ACKERMANN, BERNARD - bc1856 [based on age of 24y in 1880; although he may have actually been 24y in 1883]; res: GE, OH. Immigrated through Rotterdam & arrived at NY City on 4 Sep 1880. Made his declaration of intention on 18 Oct 1883 but no naturalization record is listed. [Hughes, Lois E., *Hamilton County, Ohio, Citizenship Record Abstracts, 1837-1916*. Bowie: Heritage Books, Inc., 1991, p. 1.]

ACKERMAN, BERNICE - b1924; occ: meterologist; edu: BS University of Chicago 1948 & MS 1955 & PhD in geophysical science 1965; mil: member of the US Navy's Women Accepted for Voluntary Emergency Services (WAVES). "She was the first woman weather forecaster in the United States, the only woman research meteorologist in the Cloud Physics Laboratory at the University of Chicago, and the first woman meteorologist at Argonne National Laboratory." [Bailey, Martha J., *American Women in Science: a biographical dictionary*. Denver: ABC-CLIO, 1994, p. 4.]

AKERMAN, BETSY - alive 1800; res: Portsmouth. Free white males under 10y = 1, 10-16y = 0, 16-26y (including heads of households) = 0, 26-45y (including heads of households) = 0, 45y & upwards (including heads of households) = 0. Free white females under 10y = 1, 10-16y = 0, 16-26y (including heads of households) = 1, 26-45y (including heads of households) = 0, 45y & upwards (including heads of households) = 0. [----, *Heads of Families at the Second Census of the United States Taken in the Year 1800: New Hampshire*. Madison: John Brooks Threlfall, 1973, p. 145.]

AKARMAN, BETTY - alive 1799. [Evans, Helen F., *Abstracts of the Probate Records of Rockingham County, New Hampshire, 1771-1799*. Bowie: Heritage Books, Inc., 2000, p. 716.]

ACKERMAN, BETTYE - b1928; occ: acted in film *Face of Fire* (1959) and in television 1955-1980. [Lentz, Harris M. III, *Science Fiction, Horror & Fantasy Film and Television Credits: Volume 1*. Jefferson: McFand & Company, Inc., Publishers, 1983, p. 2.]

ACKERMAN, BETTYE - alive 1970; occ: dramatic artist with Creative Management Associates. [----, *Who's Who in Show Business*. New York: Who's Who in Show Business, Inc., 1971, p. 122.]

AKERMAN, BRINA - b 1 Dec 1949; d 28 Jun 1984; bur: United Synagogues, Wethersfield, Hartford Co CT. [Cohen, Edward A. & Lewis Goldfarb, *Jewish Cemeteries of Five Counties of Connecticut, Volume 2.* Bowie: Heritage Books, Inc., 1998, p. 3.]

ACKERMAN, BRUCE - alive 1998; occ: Sterling Professor of Law and Political Science at Yale University, author of *We The People, Volume 1: Foundations, We The People, Volume 2: Transformations,* and other books (1974- ). [Ackerman, Bruce, *We The People, Volume 2: Transformations.* Cambridge: The Belknap Press, 1998.]

ACKERMAN, BRUCE A - b1943; res: US; occ: author of nonfiction. [Havlice, Patricia Pate, *Index to Literary Biography:first supplement. Volume I: A-K.* Metuchen: The Scarecrow Press, Inc., 1983, p. 5.]

ACKERMAN, C M - alive 1872; age 26; res: GE, OH. Immigrated through Bremen & arrived at NY City in Mar 1872. Made his declaration of intention on 7 Nov 1882 but no naturalization date is listed. [Hughes, Lois E., *Hamilton County, Ohio, Citizenship Record Abstracts, 1837-1916.* Bowie: Heritage Books, Inc., 1991, p. 1.]

ACKERMAN, C W - alive 1878; occ: wrote music including "Charms of Life Waltz" (1879), "Hill side Waltz," "La Galante" (polka gracieuse) (1878), "Hill-side Echo Waltz" (1879), and "Happy Return" (1880). [memory.loc.org; see next page for sample song sheet cover.]

ACKERMANN, CARL - alive 1858; res: Columbus OH; edu: Wooster OH 12 Sep 1858, AB Capital 1879 & AM 1882 & PhD 1901; occ: pastor 1884-1907, emer[itus?] prof 1936-    . [Cattell, Jaques, *Directory of American Scholars.* Lancaster: The Science Press, 1942, p. 3.]

ACKERMAN, CARL J - bc1909 [based on age at death]; d 17 Jul 1993, age 84. ["*San Diego-Tribune* Obituaries, 1993-94" database posted at ancestry.com, accessed 15 July 2000.]

Sample song sheet cover for music written by C. W. Ackerman.
[memory.loc.org]

ACKERMAN, CARL W - s/o Daniel Ackerman & ----; mil: private in 18 Co 164 Dep Brig, Co H 353 Inf & entered the service on 26 Apr 1918; res: Merriam KS; d 1 Nov 1918, killed in action. [Sanderson, Ruth Bennett, "Kansas Casualties in the World War - 1917-1919," *Kansas Review*, Vol. 25 #2 (1999), p. 53]

ACKERMAN, CARL WILLIAM - b 16 Jan 1890 Richmond IN;[40] s/o John F Ackerman & Mary Allice Eggemeyer; m 24 May 1914 Mabel Vander Hoof; ch: ---- d Oct 1970 NY City;[41] edu: Richmond IN 16 Jan 1890, Chicago 1910, AB Earlham College 1911 & honorary AM 1917 & LLD 1935, B Litt Columbia 1913, LLD Richmond 1935 & Northwestern 1935, honorary doctorate University San Marcos (Peru) 1937;[42] occ: wrote for United Press International & *New York Tribune*, war correspondent for the *Saturday Evening Post* 1917-1918 & the *New York Times* 1918-1919 reporting from Mexico, western Europe, & Siberia, directed the foreign news service of the *Philadelphia Ledger* for 2y, opened a public relations business called Carl W. Ackerman Inc. 1921-1930, assistant to the president of General Motors Corporation 1930,[43] dean of Columbia University Graduate School of Journalism (1931- ),[44] author of several books on current events in Germany, Mexico, & Russia, & biographies of Charles Dawes & George Eastman[45] such as *Mexico's Dilemma* (1918), *Trailing the Bolsheviki* (1919), *Biography of George Eastman* (1930) etc;[46] res: NY City NY.[47]

---

[40] Burke, W. J. and Will D. Howe, *American Authors and Books, 1640-1940* (New York: Gramercy Publishing Co., 1943)
[41] Ohles, Frederik, et al, *Biographical Dictionary of Modern American Educators* (Westport: Greenwood press, 1997), p. 1.
[42] Cattell, Jaques, *Directory of American Scholars* (Lancaster: The Science Press, 1942), p. 2. Education also appears as IN University, Earlham College BA 1911 & MA 1917, Columbia University School of Journalism B Litt 1913 (first in his class of twelve). Ohles, Frederik, et al, *Biographical Dictionary of Modern American Educators* (Westport: Greenwood Press, 1997), p. 1.
[43] Ibid.
[44] Burke, W. J. and Will D. Howe, *American Authors and Books, 1640-1940* (New York: Gramercy Publishing Co., 1943).
[45] Ohles, Frederik, et al, *Biographical Dictionary of Modern American Educators* (Westport: Greenwood Press, 1997), p. 1.
[46] Burke, W. J. and Will D. Howe, *American Authors and Books, 1640-1940* (New York: Gramercy Publishing Co., 1943). Was dean until 1956 when he became emer[itus?] dean 1956- . Cattell, Jaques, *Directory of American Scholars: a biographical directory, 3rd edition* (New York: R. R. Bowker Company, 1957), p. 2.
[47] Ibid.

ACKERMAN, CAROLINE E - d/o Jonathan C Ackerman & Maria S Ackerman; m1842 Abraham Coles b 26 Dec 1813, d 3 May 1891; d1845. [Ricord, F. W., *History of Union County, New Jersey*. Newark: East Jersey History Company, 1897, p. 63.]

ACKERMANN, CAROLINE AUGUSTA - b 1 Nov 1801 Saxony?; m 24 May 1818 in Limbach, Saxony to Samuel Frederick Voight d1847 on board ship & buried at sea; left from Bremen in 1847 on board the *Charles N Cooper* & arrived in Galveston TX on 23 Oct 1847; d 15 Nov 1880; bur: Pettytown, Bartrop & Caldwell Cos TX. [Correspondence dated 2/3/[19]94 & various materials dated 17 Dec 1999 from Christy Baize Cave. On the Galveston Immigration Database report, "Caroline Augusta" is listed as "Auguste," her age is given as 47, & the family's country of origin is listed as "Meinnger." A deed from Augusta Voight to Christian Wilke appears to be Caroline Augusta (Ackermann) Voight since the next available Augusta in the Voight family was only 3 yrs old in 1852. On 10 Nov 1852, Augusta sold 3 parcels of land for $625.00: 80 acres, 1.5 acres, & 5 acres. Photograph of tombstone (see next page) received with letter dated 21 July 2000.]

AKERMAN, CAROLINE F - mc 2 Oct 1843 in Greeland to Paul Hoyt; res: Portsmouth.[48] Caroline F Ackerman m Paul G Hoyt b 14 Dec 1815; res: Portsmouth NH.[49]

ACKERMAN, CARRIE - m Theodore Reed b 1 Aug 1872. [Lee, Francis Bazley, *Genealogical and Personal Record of Mercer County, New Jersey*. New York: The Lewis Publishing Company, 1907. Facsimile reprint Bowie: Heritage Books, Inc., 1989, p. 568, 664.]

---

[48] Chipman, Scott Lee, *New England Vital Records from the "Exeter News-Letter," 1841-1846* (Camden: Picton Press, 1993), p. 84.
[49] Hoyt, David W., *A Genealogical History of the Hoyt, Haight, and Hight Families: with some account of the earlier Hyatt families, a list of the first settlers of Salisbury and Amesbury, Mass., etc* (----: ----, 1871. Facsimile reprint Bowie: Heritage Books, Inc., 1992), p. 180.

Tombstone of Caroline Augusta Ackerman, born 1 Nov. 1801 and died 15 Nov. 1880. Courtesy of Christy Baize Cave.

ACKERMAN, CATH - m 22 Dec 1833 George Krotz. [Kieffer, Henry Martyn, *Some of the First Settlers of "The Forks of the Delaware" and Their Descendants. Being a translation from the German of the record books of the First Reformed Church of Easton, Penna. From 1760 to 1852.* Easton: ----, 1902. Facsimile reprint Bowie: Heritage Books, Inc., 1995, p. 383.]

ACKERMAN, CATHARINA - b1871; res: Ward 23; race: white; d 3 Sep 1871, age 2m, cause: anemia; bur: Walnut Hills. [Hughes, Lois E., *Hamilton County, Ohio, Death Records, 1870-1873, Volume II, Book A, A-K.* Bowie: Heritage Books, Inc., 1992, p. 2.]

ACKERMAN, CATHARINE - m 8 Feb 1821 Henry Schuck. [Kieffer, Henry Martyn, *Some of the First Settlers of "The Forks of the Delaware" and Their Descendants. Being a translation from the German of the record books of the First Reformed Church of Easton, Penna. From 1760 to 1852.* Easton: ----, 1902. Facsimile reprint Bowie: Heritage Books, Inc., 1995, p. 370.]

AKERMAN, CHARITY - b NH; age 41 or 61 in 1850; res: Alexandria, Grafton Co NH. The following children are presumabley hers: David b NH & age 12 in 1850, P D (male) b NH & age 7 in 1850, J P (male) b NH & age 5 in 1850, R H (female) b NH & age 4 in 1850. No husband listed. They were family #10 in dwelling #9. [*New Hampshire 1850 Census*, p. 155 at familytreemaker.com, accessed 27 August 2000.]

ACKERMAN, CHARLES - m 8 Nov 1774 in "Montgomery Ref Ch" (Orange Co NY) to Maria Sensebaugh/Sensebach, d/o Jacob Sensebaugh/Sensebach; rel: "forereader and foresinger of Cong." [Weller, Ralph H., "Orange County, New York, Early Marriages," *The Orange County Genealogical Society Quarterly*, Vol. 30 #3 (August 2000), p. 22.]

AKERMAN, CHARLES - b 27 Feb 1812 Portsmouth NH; s/o Joseph Akerman & Esther ----; m Lucy E Metcalf; ch: Caroline E, Louise M; d 14 Apr 1879 Providence RI. [Correspondence dated August 2000 from Marjorie Jackson.]

ACKERMAN, CHARLES - alive 1860; mil: 5 Infantry, 26 Infantry, 38 Infantry, 55 Infantry, 165 Infantry. [Wilt, Richard A., *New York*

*Soldiers in the Civil War: a roster of military officers and soldiers who served in New York regiments in the Civil War as listed in the annual reports of the Adjutant General of the State of New York.* Bowie: Heritage Books, Inc., 1999, p. 2.]

ACKERMANN, CHARLES - alive 1860; mil: 7 Infantry. [Wilt, Richard A., *New York Soldiers in the Civil War: a roster of military officers and soldiers who served in New York regiments in the Civil War as listed in the annual reports of the Adjutant General of the State of New York.* Bowie: Heritage Books, Inc., 1999, p. 2.]

ACKERMANN, CHARLES - alive 1880; age 32; res: GE, OH. Immigrated through Havre & arrived at NY City on 2 Nov 1880. Made his declaration of intention on 13 Dec 1887 but no naturalization record is listed. [Hughes, Lois E., *Hamilton County, Ohio, Citizenship Record Abstracts, 1837-1916.* Bowie: Heritage Books, Inc., 1991, p. 1.]

ACKERMAN, CHARLES - alive 1897; m Rebecca ----; ch [the following children are all presumed to be by this couple, due to their appearance in the same church baptismal records and the short span of time over which the births occurred]: Julia E b 8 Dec 1897 & bapt 2 Jan 1898 [see p. 74 of the church baptismal records], Ernest b 16 Jan 1899 & bapt 26 Feb 1899 [see p. 76], Adalaid F b [6? or 7?] Dec 1906 & bapt 14 Jan 1906 [see p. 89, should this be 1907?]. [Ruppert, Gary B., "Martin Luther Lutheran Church Records," *Maryland Genealogical Society Bulletin,* Vol. 40 #3 (Summer 1999), p. 314, 315.]

ACKERMAN, CHARLES A - m 30 Dec 1900 in Ukiah to Elizabeth Drever. [Mendocino Coast Genealogical Society, *Births, Deaths and Marriages on California's Mendocino Coast: Volume One, 1889-1909.* Bowie: Heritage Books, Inc., 1995, p. 223.]

ACKERMAN, CHARLES A JR - m Phyllis ---- d 12 Feb 1994 San Diego CA; ch: Charles, Dean, Tamar M. ["*San Diego-Tribune* Obituaries, 1993-94" database posted at ancestry.com, accessed 15 July 2000.]

ACKERMAN, CHARLES D - alive 1860; mil: 174 Infantry. [Wilt, Richard A., *New York Soldiers in the Civil War: a roster of military officers and soldiers who served in New York regiments in the Civil War as listed in the annual reports of the Adjutant General of the State of New York.* Bowie: Heritage Books, Inc., 1999, p. 2.]

ACKERMAN, CHARLES G - alive 1890; res: Clark Co WA. According to the article, he is supposed to have seen Civil War service but no record of it appears in the article. [Germann, Jane, "Clark County and the Civil War," *Trail Breakers*, Vol. 26 #1 (Fall 1999), p. 25]

ACKERMAN, CHARLES G - d before 1922; res: Florence, Lane Co OR; mil: served in WWI. [----, "Oregon's Roll of Honor," *Trees From the Grove*, Vol. XI #2, (April-May-June 1998), p. 12]

ACKERMAN, CHARLES H - bc1832 MA [based on age at death]; mil: served in the Civil War, member of the Grand Army of the Republic; d 5 May 1892 Ukiah, age 60. [Mendocino Coast Genealogical Society, *Births, Deaths and Marriages on California's Mendocino Coast: Volume One, 1889-1909.* Bowie: Heritage Books, Inc., 1995, p. 71.]

AKERMAN, CHARLES I - b 9 May 1879 Hampton Falls NH; grandson of John C Akerman [probably through his son John E Akerman b1864/5 because John C Akerman's daughter would not have continued the Akerman surname, unless she had an illegitimate child?]; m 10 Nov 1903 in Hampton Falls to Mary M McConnell b1881/2 Sandwich MA; ch: Priscilla A b 26 Nov 1906 qv, Oliver H b 29 Jul 1908 & d 9 Jan 1988, Charlotte Rosa b 10 Jan 1911, Josephine Ruth b 25 Oct 1914, Lincoln H b 20 Mar 1916 qv, Charles I Jr b 12 May 1922; occ: first rural mail carrier in Hampton Falls;[50] res: house in Hampton Falls NH 1915,[51] Main [St?] in Hampton Falls NH

---

[50] Hunt, James K. Jr., *Hampton Vital Records and Genealogy, 1889-1986* (Portsmouth: Peter E. Randall, Publisher, 1988), p. 2. Charles I. Akerman was one of four men who took the examination to become rural carrier. "The contract was awarded to Charles I. Akerman who scored 99.70 of 100 points, which was perfection. On February 15, 1904, he entered upon his duties and has continued until the present time, 1916." Brown, Warren, *History of Hampton Falls, N. H., Volume II: containing the church history and many other things not previously recorded* (Concord: The Rumford Press, 1918), p. 161.
[51] Crowley & Lunt, *Exeter & N. H. Coast Directory* (Beverly: Crowley & Lunt, Publishers, 1915), p. 227.

1924,[52] owned house on Lafayette Rd in Hampton Falls NH 1935;[53] d 16 Jul 1935.[54] In 1900, Charles I Akerman was 21 years old, single, a farmer, and living with his grandmother Charlotte A Akerman.[55]

AKERMAN, CHARLES I - alive 1941; edu: student at "N'port High;" res: boarded with Mrs M M Akerman in Hampton Falls NH. [M M Akerman may be the Mary M Akerman who was the widow of Charles I Akerman]. [Crowley & Lunt, *Exeter, Hampton, & N. H. Coast Directory*. Beverly: Crowley & Lunt, Publishers, 1941, p. 420. If this is the Charles I. Akerman, Jr. listed above, then he would have been 19 years old in 1941, and probably in his last year of high school.]

ACKERMAN, CHARLES LOUIS - alive 1871; edu: graduated Harvard Law School 1871; occ: admitted to the Suffolk bar 9 Oct 1871. [Davis, William T., *Professional and Industrial History of Suffolk County, Massachusetts, Volume 1: history of the bench and bar*. ----: The Boston History Company, 1894, p. 457.]

ACKERMAN, CHARLES NELSON - b 7 Dec 1871 Union City MI; s/o Harvey Ackerman & Mary Elizabeth Manvel; m 26 Jan 1946 in Chicago IL to Lillian Gayda, d/o Frank Gayda; ch: none; occ: inventor, manufacturer; edu: "public grade and high schools of his native place;" rel: Roman Catholic; pol: Republican; d 22 Oct 1955 Waukegan IL. "He was variously employed until 1893, when he went to Chicago, Ill., to work for a fountain pen company at its exhibit at the Columbian Exposition. ... In the late 1890s he and an associate organized the Ackerman-Boland Telephone Co., Chicago, Ill., to make and install inter-communicating telephones within offices and residences. ... In 1912, in association with John L. Johnson, he organized the Ackerman-Johnson Co., Chicago, manufacturers of toggle bolts and other specialties such as expansion bolts, clamps, and screw anchors. ... In 1915, he invented the Ackerman-Johnson toggle screw anchor for attaching fixtures to concrete and the

---

[52] Crowley & Lunt, *Exeter, Newmarket, & N. H. Coast Directory* (Beverly: Crowley & Lunt, Publishers, 1924), p. 330.
[53] Crowley & Lunt, *Exeter, Hampton, & N. H. Coast Directory* (Beverly: Crowley & Lunt, Publishers, 1935), p. 398.
[54] Hunt, James K. Jr., *Hampton Vital Records and Genealogy, 1889-1986* (Portsmouth: Peter E. Randall, Publisher, 1988), p. 2.
[55] See dwelling 3, family 4 in Hampton Falls, *Rockingham County, New Hampshire, 1900 Census*.

companion tool for setting same (U. S. Pat. No. 1,664,903), 1915. He also devised screw holding inserts and a pressure tool for setting them (Pat. Nos. 1,137,443 and 1,177,843), 1915 and 1916." [----, *The National Cyclopaedia of American Biography... Vol. XLIV.* New York: James T. White & Company, 1962., p. 326. A photograph appears on page 326a.]

ACKERMAN, CHARLES O - alive 1886; res: road 19 in Alexandria (Grafton Co) NH; occ: farmer with his father. [Child, Hamilton, *Business Directory of Grafton County, N. H., 1885-1886.* Syracuse: The Syracuse Journal Company, Printers and Binders, c1886, p. 3.]

ACKERMAN, CHAS P - m Elizabeth F Blake b 19 Dec 1842. [Pierce, Frederick Clifton, *Batchelder, Batcheller Genealogy. Descendants of Rev. Stephen Bachiler, of England, a leading nonconformist who settled the town of New Hampton, N. H. and Joseph, Henry, Joshua, and John Batcheller of Essex Co., Massachusetts.* Chicago: author, 1898. Facsimile reprint Bowie: Heritage Books, Inc., 1992, p. 196.]

AKERMAN, CHARLIE - alive 1941; edu: member of the high school basketball team 1941-1942. [Randall, Peter Evans, *Hampton, a century of town and beach, 1888-1988.* Portsmouth: Peter E. Randall, Publisher, 1989, p. 731.]

ACKERMANN, CHARLOTTE - b1757; occ: actress; d1774. [Waring, J. P., *American and British Theatrical Biography: a directory.* Metuchen: The Scarecrow Press, Inc., 1979, p. 14.]

AKERMAN, CHARLOTTE A - bc1839 Hampton Falls [based on age at death]; d/o M F Akerman & Mary M ----; unm; occ: housework; res: Hampton; d 31 Dec 1858 age 19y 9m, cause: typhoid fever.[56]

AKERMAN, CHARLOTTE S - m 5 May 1842 in Hampton Falls to Nicholas Dodge Jr of Wenham MA; res: Hampton Falls. [Chipman,

---

[56] Sanborn, George Freeman Jr. & Melinde Lutz Sanborn, *Vital Records of Hampton, New Hampshire, to the end of the year 1900* (Boston: New England Genealogical Society, 1992), p. 301, 329. This is probably the Charlotte Ann Akerman - d 31 Dec 1858 Hampton, age 19. Chipman, Scott Lee, *New England Vital Records from the "Exeter News-Letter," 1859-1865* (Camden: Picton Press, 1996), p. 2.

Scott Lee, *New England Vital Records from the "Exeter News-Letter," 1841-1846*. Camden: Picton Press, 1993, p. 41.]

AKERMAN, CHASE - alive 1840; bro/o Charles/Charles E Akerman; occ: shoemaker; res: he "built his house and buildings a little east of the Baptist meeting house, late in the decade" (1840-1850). [Brown, Warren, *History of Hampton Falls, N. H., Volume II: containing the church history and many other things not previously recorded.* Concord: The Rumford Press, 1918, p. 282.]

ACKERMAN, CHAYNE BENJAMIN - alive 1999. Descendant of Joseph Locklear, pioneer of Alachua FL. [----, "The Florida Pioneer Descendants Committee 1999 Certificate Awards Presentation," *The Florida Genealogist*, Volume XXII #4 (Winter 1999), p. 126.]

ACKERMAN/AUKERMAN/OCKERMAN, CHRISTOPER - b1758 NJ; m Susana ----; mil: enlisted 1775; res: Westmoreland Co PA in 1833; d 7 Jul 1845. Christoper's military service was witnessed by William Ackerman in 1847. [Correspondence dated 3 Sep. 2000 from Dorothy Pray Wilson.]

ACKERMAN, CHRISTOPHER - owned a lot in the western part of Oregon Twp. [----, *An Illustrated Historical Atlas of Lucas and Part of Wood Counties, Ohio.* Chicago: Andreas & Baskin, 1875. Facsimile reprint Bowie: Heritage Books, Inc., 1999, p. 87. See map on next page.]

ACKERMAN, CLARA ESTELLE - b 14 Feb 1870 Brooklyn NY; m 21 Jun 1899 Arthur Powers Dunkly b 12 Oct 1870, s/o George Randolph Dunkly & Mary Elizabeth Rogers, d 11 Sep 1902; res: Brooklyn NY. [Jewett, Frederic Clarke, *History and Genealogy of the Jewetts of America... Vol. II.* Rowley: The Jewett Family of America. Facsimile reprint Bowie: Heritage Books, Inc., 1992, p. 925.]

ACKERMAN, CLARK - alive 1886; res: road 9 in Alexandria (Grafton Co) NH; occ: farmer with his father. [Child, Hamilton, *Business Directory of Grafton County, N. H., 1885-1886.* Syracuse: The Syracuse Journal Company, Printers and Binders, c1886, p. 3.]

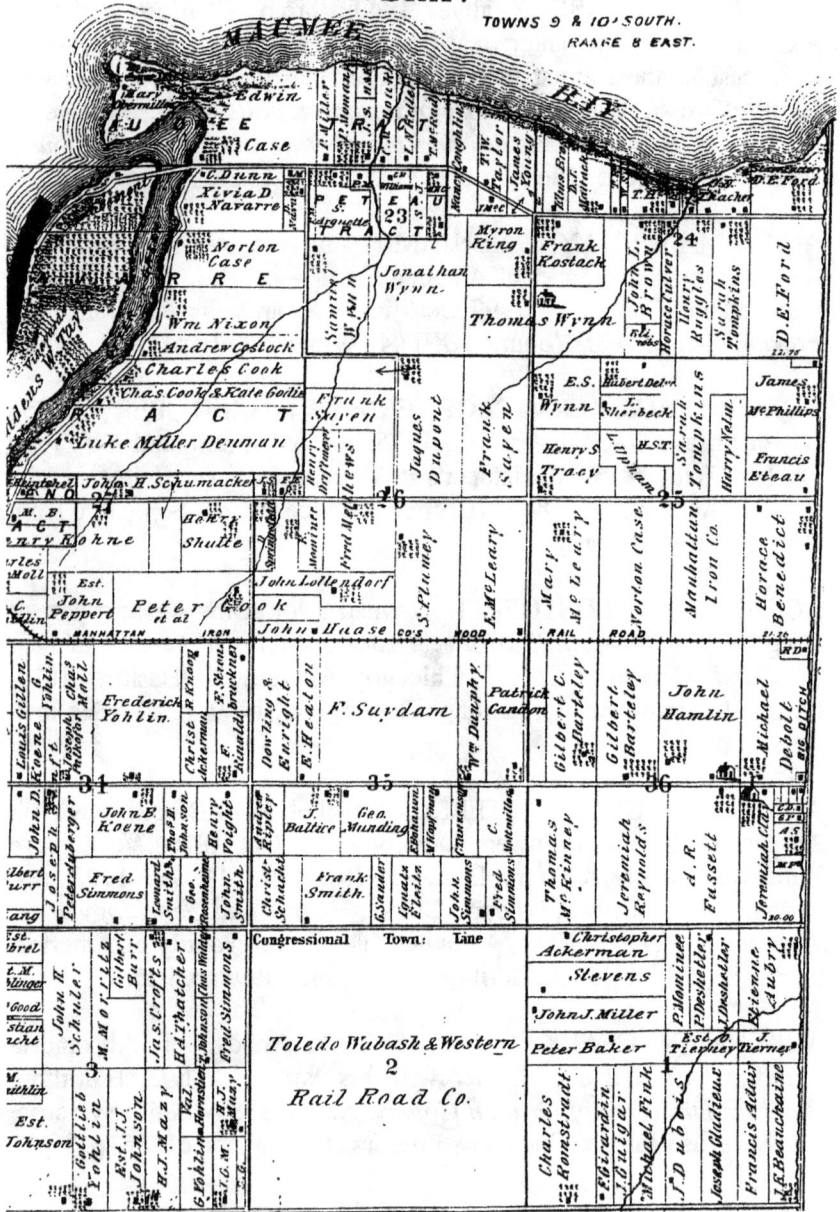

Lot owned by Christopher Ackerman. [See citation on page 45.]

46

ACKERMAN, CLINTON J - alive 1888; res: Scott City, Scott Co KS. Listed on the Farmers Loan & Trust tax register 1 Jan 1888. [Sanders, Ruth Bennett, "Farmers Loan & Trust, tax register, 1886-1889," *Kansas Review*, Vol. 24 #2, p. 57]

ACKERMAN, CLINTON W - b 26 Dec 1903; m 21 Jun 1930 Ethel C Leonard b 14 Jun 1904, d1972, bur: Bucyrus Cem in Bucyrus OH; ch: John Norman b 7 Feb 1932 qv, Joan Elizabeth 6 Sep 1937 qv; res: Bucyrus OH; occ: "owned and operated a Shell Oil bulk station with his brother-in-law H A Taylor." [Scholl, Allen W., *Descendants of Moses and Isabell (Clark) Crawford of Bucks County, Pennsylvania.* Bowie: Heritage Books, Inc., p. 511.]

ACKERMAN, CONRAD - alive 1901; edu: attended Union School & a notice for his perfect attendance in Oct 1901 was posted in the Nunda *Herald*, 7 Nov 1902. [Wells, Ann, "Perfect Attendance, Union School - Crystal Lake," *McHenry County, Illinois, Connection Quarterly*, Vol. XVI #1 (Jan-Mar 1998), p. 23]

ACKERMANN, CONRAD ERNEST/ERNST - b1710; res: GE; occ: comedian; d1771. [Hyamson, Albert M., *A Dictionary of Universal Biography of All Ages and All Peoples.* London: ----, 1916. Reprint Baltimore: Clearfield Company, Inc., 1995, p. 4.]

ACKERMANN, CONRAD THEODOR - b 17 Sep 1825 Wismar GE; occ: physician; edu: MD University of Rostock (GE) 1852; d1896. "Described angle at skull base characteristic of kyphosis, 1882 (known as Ackermann's angle)." [Debus, Allen G., *World Who's Who in Science: a biographical dictionary of notable scientists from antiquity to the present.* Chicago: Marquis-Who's Who, Inc., 1968, p. 8.]

ACKERMANN, CONSTANCE - m 29 Jan 1853 in Richmond VA to Charles Eckert. [Reddy, Anne Waller and Andrew Lewis Riffle, *Richmond City, Virginia, Marriage Bonds, 1797-1853.* Baltimore: Genealogical Publishing Co., Inc., 1976, p. 119.]

ACKERMAN, CORNELIUS - alive 1816; m Caty Banta; ch: Henry b 19 Feb 1816 & bapt 17 Mar 1816. [Durie, Howard I., "Pascack Reformed Dutch Church Baptisms 1814-1850," *The American Genealogist*, Vol. 47 #3 (July 1971), p. 177.]

AKERMAN, COUNT - res: Bessarabia. [Burke, Bernard, *A Genealogical and Heraldic History of the Colonial Gentry.* Baltimore: Genealogical Publishing Company, 1970, p. 779.]

AKERMAN, CYRUS - member of the Independent City Guard (1st Brigade, 4th Division) in Sacramento CA. The militia unit was organized 28 Jun 1858 and disbanded 19 Mar 1880. No specific year is given for Cyrus Akerman's participation. [----, "City Guard - A California Militia Unit,", *Root Cellar Preserves*, Vol. 21 #3 (Jun-Jul-Aug-Sep 1999), p. 103.]

ACKERMAN, D - m Eliza Spurgeon; ch: G W [George?] b OR & res: Waverly KS & m Gertie Ramey. [Correspondence dated 13 Sep. 2000 from Gail R. Thomas. Mr. Thomas suggests that the "D" is an error; see the Descendants of John Ackerman in the Family Groups section.]

ACKERMAN, D E - alive 1904; res: OK. Publisher (with J L Morgan) of *The Waurika News*, Waurika, Jefferson Co OK.[57] This may be the same D E Ackerman who was US Court Commissioner in 1904.[58]

ACKERMAN, D E - alive 1984; mil: staff sergeant; res: 152-W 12 Patch at Fort Monroe, moved in Mar 1984 & moved out Jul 1986. [McClellan, Phyllis I., *The Artillerymen of Historic Fort Monroe, Virginia.* Bowie: Heritage Books, Inc., 1991, p. 101.]

ACKERMAN, D S H - alive 1854. Granted to Lawrence B Ackerman 550 acres on south side of Edisto River. Date of instrument: 1854; date of record: 24 Sep 1870; kind of instrument: title. [For the full record, see Book D p. 338 of the Direct Index to Deeds, 1865-1974, for Colleton County SC.] [McElligott, Carroll Ainsworth and Ronald J. McElligott II, *A Guide to the Pre-Civil War Land Records of Colleton County, South Carolina.* Bowie: Heritage Books, Inc., 2000, p. 3.]

---

[57] Garrison, Linda Norman, "*The Waurika News,*" *The Tree Tracers*, Vol. XXIII #2 (Dec. 1998-Feb. 1999), p. 91.
[58] Ibid., p. 93.

ACKERMAN, D VERPLANK - alive 1839; mil: rank of lieutenant. Served as special judge advocate at a court martial held 14 Aug 1839. [Ladd, Kevin, *Gone to Texas: genealogical abstracts from "The Telegraph & Texas Register," 1835-1841.* Bowie: Heritage Books, Inc., 1994, p. 146.]

ACKERMAN, DANIEL - ch: Carl W d 1 Nov 1918 qv; res: Merriam KS. [Sanderson, Ruth Bennett, "Kansas Casualties in the World War - 1917-1919," *Kansas Review*, vol. 25 #2, (1999), p. 53]

ACKERMAN, DANIEL - alive 1812; res: Springville, Adams Co WI; mil: awarded $36.00 claim as a soldier of the War of 1812. [---, *Index of Awards on Claims of the Soldiers of the War of 1812, as audited and allowed by the adjutant and inspector generals, pursuant to chapter 176, of the laws of 1859.* Albany: Weed, Parsons and Company, Printers, 1860, p. 4.]

OCKERMAN, DANIEL - alive 1820; res: Bath Co KY. Accounted for in the census are 4 males 10y & under, 1 male age 26-45 plus 1 female 10y & under, 1 female age 26-45. [Lawson, Rowena, *Bath County, Kentucky, 1820-1840 Censuses.* Bowie: Heritage Books, Inc., 1985, p. 1.]

ACKERMAN, DANIEL - m1843 ----. [Hughes, Lois E., *Hamilton County, Ohio, Marriage index, 1817-1845, Volume I.* Bowie: Heritage Books, Inc., 1994, p. 1.]

AKERMAN, DANIEL - b NH; age 42 in 1850; res: Portsmouth, Rockingham Co NH. A pauper, he lived with many other individuals, probably in the alms house. [*New Hampshire 1850 Census*, p. 105 at familytreemaker, accessed 27 August 2000.]

AKERMAN, DANIEL F - bc1826 NH [based on age of 54y in 1880]; s/o ---- b NH & ---- b NH; m Maria L ---- b NH & age 49 in 1880 census; ch: Charles E b NH & age 24 in 1880 census (occ: grocer), Edward A b NH & age 20 in 1880 census (occ: clerk in store); occ: painter; res: Ward 3, Portsmouth NH. They were family #82 living in dwelling #70.[59] This probably the same Daniel F Akerman mc 7 Aug 1848 in Portsmouth to Maria L Hayes.[60]

ACKERMANN, DANKWART - b 11 Nov 1878 Halle-S GE; s/o Theodor Ackermann & Mathilde Fritzsche; m Marianne von Frey; ch: 3; res: West GE; occ: chemist. [Debus, Allen G., *World Who's Who in Science: a biographical dictionary of notable scientists from antiquity to the present*. Chicago: Marquis-Who's Who, Inc., 1968, p. 8.]

AKERMAN, DARELL ROY - b 12 Sep 1945; s/o George Mongon & Patricia Butler. [Was Darell Roy Akerman adopted?] [Hunt, James K. Jr., *Hampton Vital Records and Genealogy, 1889-1986.* Portsmouth: Peter E. Randall, Publisher, 1988, p. 343.]

ACKERMAN, DAVID - m Ann Gale; ch: Maria m 10 Jan 1875 qv. David Ackerman has the title of captain in the book. [Labaw, George Warne, *A Genealogy of the Warne Family in America: principally the descendants of Thomas Warne, born 1652, died 1722, one of the twenty-four proprietors of east New Jersey.* New York: Frank Allaben Genealogical Company, 1911, p. 574]

ACKERMAN, DAVID - alive 1812; res: NY City; mil: awarded $11.00 claim as a soldier of the War of 1812. [----, *Index of Awards on Claims of the Soldiers of the War of 1812, as audited and allowed by the adjutant and inspector generals, pursuant to chapter 176, of the laws of 1859.* Albany: Weed, Parsons and Company, Printers, 1860, p. 4.]

AUCKERMAN, DAVID - b 19 Apr 1825; s/o John Auckerman & Annie Dorrathea Shaver; m 12-9-1850 in Lawrence Co OH to Minerva Brooks. [Correspondence dated 3 Sep. 2000 from Dorothy Pray Wilson.]

ACKERMAN, DAVID - m 3 Jul 1838 Cath Flick. [Kieffer, Henry Martyn, *Some of the First Settlers of "The Forks of the Delaware" and Their Descendants. Being a translation from the German of the record books of the First Reformed Church of Easton, Penna. From*

---

[59] *Rockingham County, New Hampshire, 1880 Census*, p. 82.
[60] Chipman, Scott Lee, *New England Vital Records from the "Exeter News-Letter," 1847-1852* (Camden: Picton Press, 1994), p. 55.

*1760 to 1852*. Easton: ----, 1902. Facsimile reprint Bowie: Heritage Books, Inc., 1995, p. 389.]

ACKERMAN, DAVID - alive 1908; m Bertha Greenberg; ch: Nathan Ward b 22 Nov 1908 qv. [----, *Who's Who in American History - Science and Technology*. Chicago: Marquis Who's Who, Inc., 1976, p. 3.]

ACKERMAN, DAVID ALAN - b 18 Jul 1949; unm; race: Caucasian; res: Derry NH; rel: Congregational Christian; mil: "PFC - E3 - Army - Regular" - 25th Inf Division, tour of duty in Vietnam began 9 May 1968; d 6 Jun 1968 Binh Duong, South Vietnam, cause: multiple fragmentation wounds. [See panel 60W, line 24 on the Vietnam War Memorial.] [thewall-usa.com, accessed 16 August 2000.]

ACKERMAN, DAVID G - b 29 Dec 1928; edu: college graduate; mil: permanent rank of major received 8 Jul 1966. [----, *U. S. Army Register, Volume 1: regular army active list, 1 January 1970*. Washington: U. S. Government Printing Office, 1970, p. 1]

ACKERMAN, DAVID J - alive 1812; res: Rockland Co; mil: awarded $60.50 claim as a soldier of the War of 1812. [----, *Index of Awards on Claims of the Soldiers of the War of 1812, as audited and allowed by the adjutant and inspector generals, pursuant to chapter 176, of the laws of 1859*. Albany: Weed, Parsons and Company, Printers, 1860, p. 4.]

ACKERMAN, DELORES M - alive 1984; res: Bellingham WA. [Martin, David Kendall, "Uncovering the Elphick Ancestry of Harriet J. Allen of Susquehanna Co., Penn." *The American Genealogist*, Vol. 64 #1 (January 1989), p. 16.]

ACKERMAN, DONALD C - b 24 Sep 1934; mil: permanent grade of Major received 4 Jan 1972; edu: college graduate. [----, *U. S. Army Register, Volume 1: regular army active list, 1 January 1974*. Washington: U. S. Government Printing Office, 1974, p. 1.]

ACKERMAN, DONALD R - res: Minnehaha Co SD; mil: corp; dc1946 in a non-battle area. [----, "Honor List of State's WWII Casualties," *Pioneer Pathfinder*, Vol. 25 #2 (April 1999), p. 45.]

ACKERMAN, DORIE - res: 118 Bank; race: white; d 18 Jun 1872, age 18m, cause: inflamation of brain; bur: St John. [Hughes, Lois E., *Hamilton County, Ohio, Death Records, 1870-1873, Volume II, Book A, A-K*. Bowie: Heritage Books, Inc., 1992, p. 2.]

ACKERMANN, DOROTHEA - b1752; occ: actress; d1821. [Waring, J. P., *American and British Theatrical Biography: a directory*. Metuchen: The Scarecrow Press, Inc., 1979, p. 14.]

ACKERMAN, DOROTHY - alive 1929; m Frank W Cole. [Hooff, Ronald L. and Barbara M. Hooff, *Descendants of Lorenz and Anna M. Hoff/Hooff*. Bowie: Heritage Books, Inc., 2000, p. 74.]

ACKERMAN, DORRA - b1842; d 5 Jun 1916; bur: Agudater Achim Cem Assoc on Zion St in Hartford CT. [Cohen, Edward A. & Lewis Goldfarb, *Jewish Cemeteries of Hartford, Connecticut, Volume 1*. Bowie: Heritage Books, Inc., 1995, p. 1.]

ACKERMAN, DUANE V - b 1 May 1940; edu: college graduate; mil: permanent rank of Captain received 16 Jun 1969. [----, *U. S. Army Register, Volume 1: regular army active list, 1 January 1970*. Washington: U. S. Government Printing Office, 1970, p. 1]

ACHERMAN, E - alive 1861; res: Forsyth Co NC. Listed as a petit juror for the 1861 March term of the Forsyth Co court of pleas & quarter session. [Alson, Rebecca R., "Forsyth County Court of Pleas and Quarter Sessions, March Term 1861," *The Forsyth County Genealogical Society Journal*, Vol. XVIII #1 (Fall 1999), p. 3, 4]

ACKERMAN, E - d 17 Sep [1867?]. [Kelsey, Michael et al, *Miscellaneous Texas Newspaper Abstracts - Deaths, Volume 2*. Bowie: Heritage Books, Inc., 1997, p. 340.]

ACKERMAN, E C - member of the Navasota Lodge #299, Novasota, Grimes Co. [Kelsey, Michael et al, *Texas Masonic Deaths with Selected Biographical Sketches*. Bowie: Heritage Books, Inc., 1998, p. 57.]

ACHERMAN, E T - alive 1861; res: Forsyth Co NC. "Inspectors bond - E T Acherman enters into bond in the sum of One Thousand dollars with Chas Brietz & R L Patterson securities which is accepted." [Alson, Rebecca R., "Forsyth County Court of Pleas and Quarter Sessions, March Term 1861," *The Forsyth County Genealogical Society Journal*, vol. XVIII #1 (Fall 1999), p. 12]

ACKERMAN, EARL - bur: 1897, Greenwood Cem, Boonton, NJ. [Morris Area Genealogy Society Indexing Group, "Index to Records of Greenwood Cemetery, Boonton, 1872-1899," *Morris Area Genealogy Society Newsletter*, Vol. 12 #2 (June 1999), p. 13.]

ACKERMAN, EDNA B - bc1902 [based on age at death]; d 1 Jun 1909 Hudson NH, age 7y. [Nash, Gerald Q. et al, *The Vital Records of Hudson, New Hampshire, 1734-1985.* Bowie: Heritage Books, Inc., 1997, p. 492.]

AKERMAN, EDNA K - dc1920s-1960. [For full record, see administration record, file #13526.] [----, "General Index to Estates - Palm Beach County," *Ancestry: quarterly bulletin of the Palm Beach County Genealogical Society*, Vol. XXXV #1 (January 2000), p. 3.]

ACKERMANN, EDO JURGENS - b 5 May 1823 Strackholt GE; s/o Jurgen Eden Ackermann & Trientje Eilers; m 30 Apr 1849 in Neustadt-Godens GE to Tahlke M Rickels; d 29 Nov 1872 Neustadt-Godens GE. [Correspondence dated 1 Oct. 2000 from Eddie Dirks.]

ACHERMAN, EDWARD - alive 1860; appointed inspector of flour for Salem, Forsyth Co NC. [Alson, Rebecca R., "Forsyth County Court of Pleas and Quarter Sessions, March Term 1860," *The Forsyth County Genealogical Society Journal*, Vol. XVI #3 (Spring 1998), p. 40.]

ACKERMAN, EDWARD - alive 1861; served as juror for March term 1861 in court of pleas & quarter sessions, Forsyth Co NC. [Alson, Rebecca R., "Forsyth County Court of Pleas and Quarter Sessions, June Term 1860," *The Forsyth County Genealogical Society Journal*, Vol. XVII #4 (Summer 1999), p. 17.]

ACKERMAN, EDWARD A - b1911; res: US; occ: author of nonfiction; d1973. [Havlice, Patricia Pate, *Index to Literary Biography: first supplement. Volume 1: A-K.* Metuchen: The Scarecrow Press, Inc., 1983, p. 5.]

ACKERMAN, EDWARD AUGUSTUS - b 5 Dec 1911 Post Falls ID; s/o August Ackerman & Augusta Anderson; m 24 Sep 1949 Adrienne Aymard Desjardins; ch: Helen Augusta, Frances Edward, Julia Hardy, Justin Kemp, Elizabeth Chantal; edu: PhD Harvard 1939; occ: geographer. [Debus, Allen G., *World Who's Who in Science: a biographical dictionary of notable scientists from antiquity to the present.* Chicago: Marquis-Who's Who, Inc., 1968, p. 8.]

ACKERMAN, EDWARD EDWIN - b 4 Jan 1830 Salem, Stokes Co NC; s/o Johannes Ackerman & Anna Johanna Spaugh; m1 1857 Mary Elizabeth "Bettie" Davis; m2 Sarah Jane "Sallie" Veach; d 11 Feb 1911. [Tesh, Peggy J., "Heinrich Peter Tesch and His Descendants," *The Forsyth County Genealogical Society Journal*, vol. XVII #1 (Fall 1998), p. 51]

ACKERMAN, EDWIN D - b1855; m after 1872 Anna Lord b Apr 1854; ch: Harry b 28 Sep 1875 & d 26 Jan 1876, James Arthur b 18 Feb 1878 qv; occ: expressman; d 3 Apr 1882. [Locke, Arthur H., *A History and Genealogy of Captain John Locke (1627-1696) of Portsmouth and Rye, N. H., and His Descendants. Also of Nathaniel Locke of Portsmouth and a short account of the history of the Lockes in England.* ----: ----, ----. Facsimile reprint Bowie: Heritage Books, Inc., 1993, p. 400, 522.]

ACKERMAN, EDWIN M - alive 1848. Granted Stephen O Ackerman, et al, property near Maple Cane. Date of instrument: 1848; date of record: 24 Sep 1870; kind of instrument: title. [For the full record, see Book D p. 337 of the Direct Index to Deeds, 1865-1974, for Colleton County SC.] [McElligott, Carroll Ainsworth and Ronald J. McElligott II, *A Guide to the Pre-Civil War Land Records of Colleton County, South Carolina.* Bowie: Heritage Books, Inc., 2000, p. 3.]

ACKERMANN, EILERT - b 14 May 1820 Strackholt GE; s/o Jurgen Eden Ackermann & Trientje Eilers; m 23 Oct 1842 in Strackholt GE to Ette Janssen Eilers; d US. [Correspondence dated 1 Oct. 2000 from Eddie Dirks.]

ACKERMAN, ELIESABET - alive 1739; m Abraham Brouwer. [Versteeg, Dingman and Thomas E. Vermilye, Jr., *Bergen Records. Records of the Reformed Protestant Dutch Church of Bergen in New*

*Jersey, 1666 to 1788.* Originally published in the *Year Book of the Holland Society of New York,* 1913. Reprint Baltimore: Clearfield Publishing Co., Inc., 1990, p. 71.]

ACKERMANS, ELISABET - alive 1719. [Pearson, Jonathan, "Extracts from the Doop-Boek, or Baptismal Register of the Reformed Protestant Dutch Church of Schenectady, N. Y.," *The New England Historical & Genealogical Register,* Volume XXI (April 1867), p. 130.]

ACKERMAN, ELISABETH - m 14 Jun 1804 in "Shawangunk Dutch Ref Ch" (Orange Co NY) to Frederick Ackerman. [Weller, Ralph H., "Orange County, New York, Early Marriages," *The Orange County Genealogical Society Quarterly,* Vol. 30 #3 (August 2000), p. 22.]

ACKERMAN, ELIZ - m 12 Oct 1834 Tobias Schmidt. [Kieffer, Henry Martyn, *Some of the First Settlers of "The Forks of the Delaware" and Their Descendants. Being a translation from the German of the record books of the First Reformed Church of Easton, Penna. From 1760 to 1852.* Easton: ----, 1902. Facsimile reprint Bowie: Heritage Books, Inc., 1995, p. 384.]

ACKERMAN, ELIZA - alive 1849; m Peter Demarest. [Durie, Howard I., "Pascack Reformed Dutch Church Baptisms 1814-1850," *The American Genealogist,* Vol. 48 #2, p. 115.]

ACKERMAN, ELIZA - b Cincinnati; res: 569 Main; d 11 Jun 1876, 8m, cause: "variola;" bur: Carthage Rd. [Hughes, Lois E., *Hamilton County, Ohio, Death Records, 1874-1877, Volume III, Book A, A-K.* Bowie: Heritage Books, Inc., 1992, p. 1.]

ACKERMAN, ELIZABETH - m Frederick Westfall. Their son, having lost his German marriage certificate, was remarried in 1863 at age 43. It is unclear whether she was alive or not at the time of his remarriage. [----, "New Jersey Tidbits," *The German Connection,* Vol. 22 #4, p. 81]

AKYRMAN, ELIZABETH - alive 1530. "Elizabeth Bedell, alias Akyrman, of London. Pardon for having, on 24 Aug. 19 Hen. VIII., stolen certain monies belonging to John Granger, draper, at the priory of St. Bartholomew the Greater in Westsmythfield, London. Del.

Westm., 29 June 22 Hen. VIII. - S. B. Pat. p. 1, m. 4." [Brewer, J. S., *Letters and Papers, Foreign and Domestic, of the Reign of Henry VIII. ... Vol. IV. - Part III. 1529-1530. With a general index.* London: Her Majesty's Stationary Office, 1876. Reprint Vaduz: Kraus Reprint Ltd., 1965, p. 2921.]

AKERMAN, ELIZABETH - bapt Jul 1715 North Church, Portsmouth NH. [Baptized as an adult?] [Tibbetts, Charles W., *The New Hampshire Genealogical Record. An illustrated quarterly magazine devoted to genealogy, history and biography. Vol. IV, January 1907 - October 1907.* Dover: Charles W. Tibbetts, 1907. Facsimile reprint Bowie: Heritage Books, Inc., 1988, p. 51.]

ACREMAN, ELIZ[ABE]TH - m 23 Feb 1728-9 Eben[eze]r Jackson; res: Portsmouth NH. [----, "Births, Marriages, and Deaths in Portsmouth, N.H.," *The New England Historical and Genealogical Register*, Vol. XXV (April 1871), p. 117.]

AKERMAN, ELIZABETH - alive 1800; res: Portsmouth. Free white males under 10y = 1, 10-16y = 0, 16-26y (including heads of households) = 0, 26-45y (including heads of households) = 0, 45y & upwards (including heads of households) = 0. Free white females under 10y = 1, 10-16y = 0, 16-26y (including heads of households) = 1, 26-45y (including heads of households) = 0, 45y & upwards (including heads of households) = 0. [----, *Heads of Families at the Second Census of the United States Taken in the Year 1800: New Hampshire.* Madison: John Brooks Threlfall, 1973, p. 145.]

ACKERMAN, ELIZABETH - bc1790 [based on age at death]; dc 4 Mar 1802, age 12y 2m 11d. She resided in or was buried in Plainfield. [Kieffer, Henry Martyn, *Some of the First Settlers of "The Forks of the Delaware" and Their Descendants. Being a translation from the German of the record books of the First Reformed Church of Easton, Penna. From 1760 to 1852.* Easton: ----, 1902. Facsimile reprint Bowie: Heritage Books, Inc., 1995, p. 296.]

AKERMAN, ELIZABETH - mc 31 Aug 1846 in Portsmouth to Charles G Foster of Boston; res: Portsmouth. [Chipman, Scott Lee, *New England Vital Records from the "Exeter News-Letter," 1841-1846.* Camden: Picton Press, 1993, p. 186.]

AKERMAN, ELIZABETH - d/o Joseph Akerman Jr & ----; mc 31 Jan 1832 in Portsmouth to Andrew H Jones. [Chipman, Scott Lee, *New England Vital Records from the "Exeter News-Letter," 1831-1840*. Camden: Picton Press, 1993, p. 34.]

EKERMAN, ELISABETH - alive 1850; res: Northfield, Merr[imack] Co NH. [See page 90 of the original census for full record.] [Jackson, Ronald Vern and Gary Ronald Teeples, *New Hampshire 1850 Index Census*. Bountiful: Accelerated Indexing Systems, Inc., 1978, p. 77.]

AKERMEN, ELIZABETH - m1850 David ---- b 7 Dec 1816; res: Alexandria. [Locke, Arthur H., *A History and Genealogy of Captain John Locke (1627-1696) of Portsmouth and Rye, N. H., and His Descendants. Also of nathaniel Locke of Portsmouth and a short account of the history of the Lockes in England*. ----: ----, ----. Facsimile reprint Bowie: Heritage Books, Inc., 1993, p. 100.]

ACKERMAN, ELIZABETH - bc1903 [based on age at death]; d 15 Sep 1968 Nashua NH, age 65. [Nash, Gerald Q. et al, *The Vital Records of Hudson, New Hampshire, 1734-1985*. Bowie: Heritage Books, Inc., 1997, p. 492.]

AKERMAN, ELIZABETH CHARLOTTE - b 16 Oct 1855; d/o John William Akerman & Jane Stantial; m Dec 1878 Thomas Daniel Barry of Linsmore (Swellendam, Cape Colony), d Oct 1890. [Burke, Bernard, *A Genealogical and Heraldic History of the Colonial Gentry*. Baltimore: Genealogical Publishing Company, 1970, p. 778.]

ACKERMAN, ELIZABETH JANE - b Washington Co PA; d/o Abraham Ackerman & Margt ----; m 8 Nov 1855 Peter Close b Washington Co PA, s/o John Close & Nancy ----; res: Brooke Co VA. Elizabeth Jane Ackerman was 33 yrs old when she married; Peter Close, a widower, was 45 yrs old. [Sherman, Renee Britt, *Brooke County, Virginia/West Virginia, Licenses and Marriages, 1797-1874*. Bowie: Heritage Books, Inc., 1991, p. 1, 135.]

AKERMAN, ELIZABETH T - mc 2 Jun 1840 Alexander Rand. [Chipman, Scott Lee, *New England Vital Records from the "Exeter News-Letter," 1831-1840*. Camden: Picton Press, 1993, p. 192.]

ACKERMAN, ELLEN - bc1833 IR [based on age at death]; d Aug 1860, age 27, Newark (Essex Co) NJ. [----, "1860 U. S. Census Mortality Schedules," *The Genealogical Magazine of New Jersey*, Vol. 74 #1 (January 1999), p. 28.]

AKERMAN, ELLEN E - bc1833 [based on age at death]; dc 23 May 1864 Portsmouth, age 23. [Chipman, Scott Lee, *New England Vital Records from the "Exeter News-Letter," 1859-1865*. Camden: Picton Press, 1996, p. 234.]

ACKERMAN, EMILY - bc1862 [based on age at death]; res: 12 Providence; race: white; d 15 Dec 1867, age 5, cause: typhoid fever. [Hughes, Lois E., *Hamilton County, Ohio, Death Records, 1865-1869, Volume I*. Bowie: Heritage Books, Inc., 1992, p. 1.]

AKERMAN, EMMA - alive 1850; res: Hampton, Rockingham Co NH. [See page 259 of the original census for full record.] [Jackson, Ronald Vern and Gary Ronald Teeples, *New Hampshire 1850 Index Census*. Bountiful: Accelerated Indexing Systems, Inc., 1978, p. 3.]

ACKERMAN, EMMA J - m 25 Dec 1889 James Smith of Willington; div [request? 22 Apr 1898] due to cruelty. [Knox, Grace Louise and Barbara B. Ferris, *Connecticut Divorces: superior court records for the counties of New London, Tolland, & Windham, 1719-1910*. Bowie: Heritage Books, Inc., 1987, p. 236.]

ACKERMAN, ENOCH - ch: Leona qv. [Musgrove, R. W., *History of the Town of Bristol, New Hampshire.* ----: Richard W. Musgrove, 1904. Reprint with a new foreword by Charles E. Greenwood, Somersworth: New Hampshire Publishing Company, 1976, p. 3 (Volume II).]

ACKERMAN, ENOCH - alive 1886; res: road 9 in Alexandria (Grafton Co) NH; occ: farmer with his father. [Child, Hamilton, *Business Directory of Grafton County, N. H., 1885-1886*. Syracuse: The Syracuse Journal Company, Printers and Binders, c1886, p. 3. See map on the next page.]

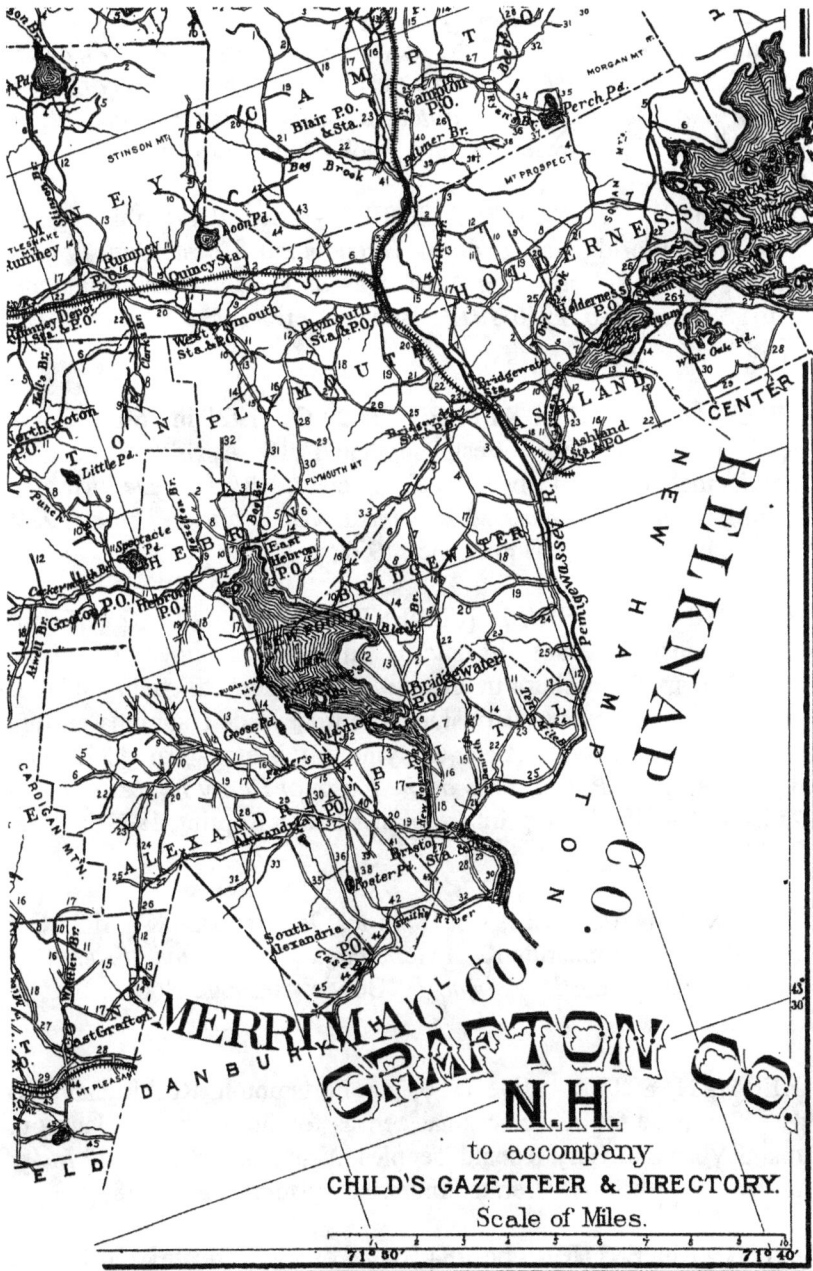

Alexandria, Grafton County, New Hampshire, where Enoch Ackerman, and others, lived. [See citation on page 58.]

ACKERMAN, ERNEST - m 23 Aug 1934 in Tenino WA to Mrs Sigrid Samuelson; res: Fort Bragg. Marriage reported in the *Advocate* dated 5 Sep 1934. [Mendocino Coast Genealogical Society, *Births, Deaths and Marriages on California's Mendocino Coast, Volume Four, 1930-1939*. Bowie: Heritage Books, Inc., 1998. p. 242.]

ACKERMAN, "[ERNEST?] ALFRED" - alive 1917; mil: register #2355 for World War I draft. [Mendocino Coast Genealogical Society, *Births, Deaths and Marriages on California's Mendocino Coast: Volume Two, 1910-1919*. Bowie: Heritage Books, Inc., 1997, p. 243.]

ACKERMAN, ERNEST ALFRED - m 29 Oct 1921 in Fort Bragg to Wendala/Wendla Irene West; separated 18 Apr 1928; ch: 2. [Mendocino Coast Genealogical Society, *Births, Deaths and Marriages on California's Mendocino Coast: Volume Three, 1920-1929*. Bowie: Heritage Books, Inc., 1997, p. 181.]

AKERMAN, ERNISIUM [ERNEST] - alive 1229. "Lucas Russel...constituti sunt justiciarii ad assisam nove dissaisine capiendam apud Shireburn in crastino Sancti Laurentii quam Jordanus Oliveri aramiavit versus...Ernisium Akerman..., de communa pasture in Eteministre, que pertinet etc. in Ryme: salvis etc." Dated 1229 (m. 6d.) Dorset. [----, *Patent Rolls of the Reign of Henry III...A.D. 1225-1232*. ---: ---, 1903. Reprint Germany: Kraus Reprint, 1971, p. 295, 296.]

ACKERMANN, ESTELLA - bc1883; res: Jefferson Co KY; d 22 Oct 1948. [Eddlemon, Sherida K., *A Genealogical Collection of Kentucky Birth & Death Records, Volume 1*. Bowie: Heritage Books, Inc., p. 1.]

AKERMAN, ESTER - alive 1850; res: Portsmouth, Rockingham Co NH. [See page 50 of the original census for full record.] [Jackson, Ronald Vern and Gary Ronald Teeples, *New Hampshire 1850 Index Census*. Bountiful: Accelerated Indexing Systems, Inc., 1978, p. 3.]

ACKERMAN, ESTHER - bc1784 [based on age at death]; ch: J H; dc 19 May 1869 Waterloo NY, age 85y 6m 9d. [Jackson, Mary S. and Edward F. Jackson, *Marriage and Death Notices from Seneca*

*County, New York, Newspapers, 1817-1885*. Bowie: Heritage Books, Inc. 1997, p. 131.]

AKERMAN, ESTHER - b NH; res: Portsmouth NH; age 75 in 1850. Living with Emily Fonart[?] (age 57) as family #736 in dwelling 446[?]; this is the same dwelling where Aaron Akerman & Susan[?] H ---- live. [*New Hampshire 1850 Census*, p. 50 at familytreemaker.com, accessed 27 August 2000.]

AKERMAN, ESTHER ANNIE - d/o Leonard Akerman & ----; mc 26 Nov 1855 in Portsmouth to Geo W Carlisle of Boston. [Chipman, Scott Lee, *New England Vital Records from the "Exeter News-Letter," 1853-1858*. Camden: Picton Press, 1994, p. 138.]

ACKERMAN, ETHEL A - alive 1908; res: Exeter NH. [Mitchell, Harry Edward, *Exeter & Hampton, New Hampshire, Census & Business Directory, 1908*. Augusta: Mitchell-Cony Company, 1908. Facsimile reprint Bowie: Heritage Books, Inc., 1979.]

ACKERMAN, EUGENE - b 8 Jul 1920 Brooklyn NY; s/o Saul Benton Ackerman & Dorothy Salwen; m 5 Jun 1943 Dorothy Hopkirk; ch: Francis H, Emmanuel T, Amy R; res: Rochester MN; edu: PhD University of Wisconsin 1949; occ: biophysicist. [Debus, Allen G., *World Who's Who in Science: a biographical dictionary of notable scientists from antiquity to the present*. Chicago: Marquis-Who's Who, Inc., 1968, p. 8.]

ACKERMAN, EUGENE FRANCIS - b1888; res: US; occ: author of writings for juveniles; d1974. [Havlice, Patricia Pate, *Index to Literary Biography: first supplement. Volume I: A-K*. Metuchen: The Scarecrow Press, Inc., 1983, p. 5.]

ACKERMAN, F - alive 1814. [Kieffer, Henry Martyn, *Some of the First Settlers of "The Forks of the Delaware" and Their Descendants. Being a translation from the German of the record books of the First Reformed Church of Easton, Penna. From 1760 to 1852*. Easton: ----, 1902. Facsimile reprint Bowie: Heritage Books, Inc., 1995, p. 307.]

ACKERMAN, F - m L J Ackerman; ch: Rosa G d 1 Jul 1893 age 10y & bur near the driveway in the St Vrain Ch of the Brethren Cem (Hygiene, Boulder Co CO). [Weissgerber, J. G., "St. Vrain Church of the Brethren Cemetery Records," *Orange County, California, Genealogical Society Journal*, Vol. 36 #1 (April 1999), p. 48.]

ACKERMAN, F DUANE - alive 1999; occ: chairman & CEO of BellSouth Corporation, vice chairman of the Kennedy Center (Washington D.C.) Corporate Fund. [The Kennedy Center, *Stagebill*, December 1999, p. 38]

ACKERMAN, FLORRIE B - b1901; d1987; bur: lot #77, plot #A2 of the Garden of the Resurrection section of Grandview Memorial Gardens, Champaign, Hensley Twp, Champaign Co IL. [Volk, Adam, "Markers in Grandview Memorial Gardens," *Champaign County Genealogical Society Quarterly*, Vol. 20 #2 (Fall 1998), p. 40.]

ACKERMAN, FLOYD FREELAND - b 1 May 1927 Paterson NJ; s/o John L Ackerman & Marian Freeland; m 24 mar 1951 Bertina M Bayless; ch: 2 sons, 1 daughter; occ: producer, personal manager, theatre representative; edu: Ramsay (NJ) High School graduating in 1945; mil: served in WWII, US Navy, Korea - rank PO-2. [Rigdon, Walter, *The Biographical Encyclopaedia & Who's Who of the American Theatre*. New York: James H. Heineman, Inc., 1966, p. 231.]

ACKERMAN, FOREST J - b1916;[61] occ: writer, editor, filmaker, actor; res: Hollywood Hills. Author of "dozens of stories" including "The Shortest SF Story Ever Told" (1973) & editor of six complete anthologies including *Ackermanthology* (1997).[62] Acted in films 1944-1982, appearing as an alien astronaut in TV's *Starstruck* (1978). He "is the world authority on science fiction and fantasy films, having authored over two thousand articles on the genre, published numerous books in the field..., polished scripts..., been Technical Advisor... and Creative Consultant..., and acted in many films...."[63]

---

[61] Havlice, Patricia Pate, *Index to Literary Biography: first supplement. Volume I: A-K* (Metuchen: The Scarecrow Press, Inc.), 1983, p. 5.

[62] Ackerman, Forest J., *Ackermanthology* (Los Angeles: General Publishing Group, Inc., 1997), p. 303.

[63] Lentz, Harris M. III, *Science Fiction, Horror & Fantasy Film and Television Credits: Volume 1* (Jefferson: McFand & Company, Inc., Publishers, 1983), p. x, 2. According to Lentz's supplement, Forrest J Ackerman's acting career went through 1987. Lentz, Harris M. III, *Science Fiction, Horror & Fantasy Film and Television*

AKERMAN, FRANCES ANN - bc1828 [based on age at death]; d 25 Nov 1851 Portsmouth, age 23. [Chipman, Scott Lee, *New England Vital Records from the "Exeter News-Letter," 1847-1852.* Camden: Picton Press, 1994, p. 189.]

ACKERMAN, FRANCIS - b1337; occ: soldier, diplomatist; res: Flanders; d1387. [Hyamson, Albert M., *A Dictionary of Universal Biography of All Ages and All Peoples.* London: ----, 1916. Reprint Clearfield Company, Inc., 1995, p. 4.]

ACKERMAN, FRANCIS - alive 1383. "Grant, for life, to Francis Ackerman of Ghent, late admiral of the fleet of Flanders, of 200 francs in gold (francos auri) or their value in English money yearly at the Exchequer." [---, *Calendar of the Patent Rolls... Richard II. A.D. 1381-1385.* ----: ----, 1897. Reprint Germany: Kraus Reprint, 1971, p. 225.]

ACKERMAN, FRANK - b FR; mil: private, mustered in Jul 1863 & served in Co M, 17th IN Cav, mustered out May 1865; res: FR, San Diego c1925; d 6 Mar 1929. [Palmer, Barbara, *The Civil War Veterans of San Diego.* Unpublished ms, c1998, p. 231.]

ACKERMAN, FRANK - dc 9 Aug 1867; "killed James Reynolds at Haverstraw about a year ago. He committed suicide in jail on Monday." [Klinkenberg, Audrey M., *Obituaries, Death Notices and Genealogical Gleanings from "The Saugerties Telegraph," Volume 3: 1861-18*70. Bowie: Heritage Books, Inc., 1989, p. 218.]

ACKERMAN, FRANK - m Lizzie J Ackerman. Divorce case #3846 recorded in book 8C dated 01/07/1905. [Anderson, Marti, "Boulder County Divorces, 1867-1919, Part I A's - G's," *Boulder [Colorado] Genealogical Society Quarterly,* Vol. 31 #3 (August 2000), p. 100.]

ACKERMAN, FRANK - alive c1872; edu: age 12 in White's Common School Register, undated, Beaver Twp, Mahoning Co OH.[64] This is probably the same Frank Ackerman aged 12 years in register

---

*Credits Supplement: through 1987* (Jefferson: McFand & Company, Inc., Publishers, 1983), p. 2.
[64] Fry, Georgene, "White's Common School Register, [Beaver Township, Mahoning County, Ohio]" *Mahoning Meanderings,* Vol. 22 (January 1998), p. 7

dated 9 Dec 1872 to 15 Mar 1873.[65] This is probably the same Frank Akerman aged 13 years in register dated 3 Nov 1873 to 19 Feb 1874.[66]

ACKERMAN, FRANK - res: 474 Vine; race: white; d 20 Feb 1873, age 9m, cause: bronchitis; bur: St Bernard. [Hughes, Lois E., *Hamilton County, Ohio, Death Records, 1870-1873, Volume II, Book A, A-K*. Bowie: Heritage Books, Inc., 1992, p. 2.]

ACKERMAN, FRANK A - b 3 Aug 1952 [taken from a stone in lot 357 of Empire Cem, Empire CO]. [----, "Empire, Colorado, Empire Cemetery," *The Foothills Inquirer*, Vol. 19 #3 (Fall 1999), p. 85]

ACKERMAN, FRANK L - bc1866 [based on age at death]; d 19 Apr 1938, age 72; bur: Mt View Cem, SD. [Barnes, Donald S., "Behrens' Funeral Home: index to H. J. Behrens' mortuary records, book 4, 1930-1939," *Black Hills Nuggets*, Vol. XXXII #4 (November 1999), p. 9. Frank L. Ackerman is listed as #5867 in the records.]

ACKERMAN, FRANK LESLIE - b 14 May 1865 Alexandria; s/o Jacob Hanson Ackerman & Sarah Hall; unm; res: Burlington VT; occ: manager of the Hygienic Milk Company. [Musgrove, R. W., *History of the Town of Bristol, New Hampshire*. ----: Richard W. Musgrove, 1904. Reprint with a new foreword by Charles E. Greenwood, Somersworth: New Hampshire Publishing Company, 1976, p. 2 (Volume II).]

AKERMAN, FRANK P - alive 1865; m Eunice V ---- bc1841 [based on age at death], dc 6 Nov 1865, age 24. [Chipman, Scott Lee, *New England Vital Records from the "Exeter News-Letter," 1859-1865*. Camden: Picton Press, 1996, p. 295.]

ACKERMAN, FRANK R - alive 1902; m Ella Black; ch: Beatrice M b1902 qv. [Heilman, Robert A., *The Heilman Family genealogy comprising three Heilman lines in one volume: John Peter, John Adam, and William B. Heilman*. Bowie: Heritage Books, Inc., p. 196, 197 (part 1).]

---

[65] Fry, Georgene, "White's Common School Register, [Beaver Township, Mahoning County, Ohio]" *Mahoning Meanderings*, Vol. 21 (October 1997), p. 79.
[66] Fry, Georgene, "White's Common School Register, [Beaver Township, Mahoning County, Ohio]" *Mahoning Meanderings*, Vol. 21 (November 1997), p. 89.

ACKERMAN, FRA[N]KLIN - aged 11 years in register dated 1870-1871.[67] This is probably the same Franklin Acherman aged 11 years in register dated Feb 1872.[68] This is probably the same Franklin Ackerman age 11 in register, probably dated before 1872.[69] This is probably the same Franklin Akerman aged 13 years c1873 in undated register.[70] Is this the same Franklin Akerman aged 15 years in register dated 8 Apr 1873 to 25 Jul 1873 or are there two Franklins?[71]

ACKERMAN, FRED A - bc1899 [based on age at marriage]; m 9 Nov 1936 in Madison Co NC to Helda Josephson; res: IL. At the time of their marriage, Fred A Ackerman was 37 and Helda Josephson was 36. [----, "Marriages of Madison County, NC," *A Lot of Bunkum*, Vol. 21 #3 (August 2000), p. 72.]

ACKERMAN, FREDERICK L - b1875; m Sarah Henrietta (----) Barnes; d1909; bur: Greenwood Cem, Decatur IL. [Birth, death, and burial data from correspondence dated 31 Jan. 2000 with Marian A. Coberly of the Decatur Genealogical Society. Marriage data from affidavit #161559 dated 26 May 1924.]

AKERMAN, FREDRICK [sic?] - alive 1850; res: Portsmouth, Rockingham Co NH. [See page 49 of the original census for full record.] [Jackson, Ronald Vern and Gary Ronald Teeples, *New Hampshire 1850 Index Census*. Bountiful: Accelerated Indexing Systems, Inc., 1978, p. 3.]

ACKERMAN, GENE JR - alive 1969; edu: Master's degree; mil: temporary grade 1st Lt given 18 Aug 1969. [----, *U. S. Army Register, Volume II: army, NGUS, USAR, and other active lists, 1 January 1970*. Washington: U. S. Government Printing Office, 1970, p. 3.]

ACKERMANN, GENOVEFA - b1838; d/o Jakob Ackermann & Elizabeth Oberuck; m Franz Balthasa Kaufmann b1836, d1898; d 1

---

[67] Fry, Georgene, "White's Common School Register, [Beaver Township, Mahoning County, Ohio]" *Mahoning Meanderings*, Vol. 21 (October 1997), p. 79.
[68] Ibid.
[69] Fry, Georgene, "White's Common School Register, [Beaver Township, Mahoning County, Ohio]" *Mahoning Meanderings*, Vol. 22 (January 1998), p. 7.
[70] Fry, Georgene, "White's Common School Register, [Beaver Township, Mahoning County, Ohio]" *Mahoning Meanderings*, Vol. 21 (November 1997), p. 89.
[71] Ibid.

Jul 1917, age 79y 25d. [Correspondence dated 30 July 2000 from Carl W. Weil.]

ACKERMANN, GEORG - alive 1892. Confirmed 15 "Mai" [May?] 1892 at St John's Evangelical Lutheran Church, Brooklyn NY. [----, "Brooklyn Church Records," *The German Connection*, Vol. 23 #3 (Third Quarter 1999), p. 54.]

ACKERMAN, GEORGE - m Lizzie Glenn; ch: Lizzie m Charles Scudder b 2 Aug 1860, George, John. [Lee, Francis Bazley, *Genealogical and Personal Record of Mercer County, New Jersey.* New York: The Lewis Publishing Company, 1907. Facsimile reprint Bowie: Heritage Books, Inc., 1989, p. 167.]

ECKERMAN/AKERMAN, GEORGE - alive 1780; mil: served in Capt Wikert/Wickart's Company from Lower Milford Twp. [Egle, William Henry, *Pennsylvania Archives: 3rd Series, Vol. VI.* Harrisburg: Clarence M. Busch, Printer, 1896, p. 27, 30, 136.]

AKERMAN, GEORGE - alive 1785; res: Portsmouth; occ: mariner. [Evans, Helen F., *Abstracts of the Probate Records of Rockingham County, New Hampshire, 1771-1799.* Bowie: Heritage Books, Inc., 2000, p. 914.]

AKERMAN, GEORGE - alive 1790; res: Portsmouth Town NH. Free white males of 16y & upwards, including heads of families = 1. Free white males under 16y = 0. Free white females, including heads of families = 1. [----, *Heads of Families at the First Census of the United States Taken in the Year 1790: New Hampshire.* Washington: Government Printing Office, 1907. Reprint Baltimore: Genealogical Publishing Company, 1966, p. 78.]

ACKERMAN, GEORGE - alive 1790; res: Lancaster Borough in Lancaster Co. Free white males 16+ years old = 2, free white males less than 16 = 2, free white females = 3. [----, *Heads of Families at the First Census of the United States Taken in the Year 1790: Pennsylvania.* Baltimore: Genealogical Publishing Company, 1966, p. 136.]

AKERMAN, GEORGE - alive 1790; res: Bucks Co. Free white males 16+ years old = 1, free white males less than 16 = 2, free white females = 3. [----, *Heads of Families at the First Census of the United States Taken in the Year 1790: Pennsylvania.* Baltimore: Genealogical Publishing Company, 1966, p. 56.]

ACKERMAN, GEORGE - bc1823 [based on age of 54y in 1877]; b GE; occ laborer. Naturalized 3 Sep 1877 in Los Angeles Co CA, at age 54, & registered 3 May 1884. [Calaway, Louise Meredith, "The 1884 Great Register," *The Searcher*, Vol. 37 #4 (July/August 2000), p. 179.]

ACKERMAN, GEORGE - bc1824 [based on age of 50y in 1874]; occ: pipeman in fire company #19, "Corryville," at the corner of Washington & Charlotte streets, Cincinnati, Hamilton Co OH. At the fire department, "Mr. Ackerman is a veteran from the start." [----, "Our Fire Department: a historical look at the Cincinnati fire department," *The Tracer*, Vol. 20 #4 (December 1999), p. 116.]

ACKERMAN, GEORGE - res: 123 Buckeye; race: white; d 22 Jul 1870, age 10 weeks, cause: convulsions; bur: Lick Run. [Hughes, Lois E., *Hamilton County, Ohio, Death Records, 1870-1873, Volume II, Book A, A-K.* Bowie: Heritage Books, Inc., 1992, p. 2.]

ACKERMAN, GEORGE - m 13 Dec 1870 in Delaware Co OH to Aresa Columber. [Carr, Mary, "Marriages - 1870, Volume 4, Delaware County, Ohio," *The Delaware Genealogist*, Vol. 15 #4 (Winter 1999/2000), p. 67.]

ACKERMAN, GEORGE - alive 1886; res: road 2 in Alexandria (Grafton Co) NH; occ: farmer with 50 acres. [Child, Hamilton, *Business Directory of Grafton County, N. H., 1885-1886.* Syracuse: The Syracuse Journal Company, Printers and Binders, c1886, p. 3.]

ACKERMAN, GEORGE - d1889; bur: Santa Ana Cem. [Although no explanation of the codes is given, the following appears to be the specifics of where he is buried: Service #SU0000508, Gardn Sect SK, Lot 07, Sb 24 Sp 1.] [----, "Orange County Cemetery Records," *Orange County, California, Genealogical Society Journal*, Vol. 34 #2 (October 1997), p. 18.]

ACKERMAN, GEORGE - alive 1889; occ: upholsterer; res: 843 W 21 St, Chicago IL. [Correspondence dated 18 Dec. 1979 from Larry

C. Winterburn, courtesy of Robert H. Ackerman, 22 Mar. 2000. Mr. Winterburn cites his sources as Chicago city directories that cover the years 1889-1893.]

ACKERMAN, GEORGE - alive 1889; occ: horse buyer; res: 500 Hermitage, Chicago IL. [Correspondence dated 18 Dec. 1979 from Larry C. Winterburn, courtesy of Robert H. Ackerman, 22 Mar. 2000. Mr. Winterburn cites his source as an 1889 Chicago city directory.]

ACKERMAN, GEORGE - alive 1889; occ: laborer; res: 62 N Wells [St?], Chicago IL. [Correspondence dated 18 Dec. 1979 from Larry C. Winterburn, courtesy of Robert H. Ackerman, 22 Mar. 2000. Mr. Winterburn cites his source as an 1889 Chicago city directory.]

ACKERMAN, GEORGE - alive 1889; occ: artist; res: 482 N Franklin [St?], Chicago IL. [Correspondence dated 18 Dec. 1979 from Larry C. Winterburn, courtesy of Robert H. Ackerman, 22 Mar. 2000. Mr. Winterburn cites his source as an 1889 Chicago city directory.]

ACKERMAN, GEORGE - alive 1889; occ: clerk at 78 Mich[igan?] Ave, Chicago IL; res: 3716 Johnson Pl, Chicago IL. [Correspondence dated 18 Dec. 1979 from Larry C. Winterburn, courtesy of Robert H. Ackerman, 22 Mar. 2000. Mr. Winterburn cites his source as an 1889 Chicago city directory.]

ACKERMANN, GEORGE - alive 1890; occ: teacher; res: 482 N Franklin, Chicago IL. [Is this the same George who was listed as an artist in 1889?] [Correspondence dated 18 Dec. 1979 from Larry C. Winterburn, courtesy of Robert H. Ackerman, 22 Mar. 2000. Mr. Winterburn cites his source as an 1890-1893 Chicago city directory.]

ACKERMAN, GEORGE A - b Haverstraw NY; m Phoebe Bull Golden b Trenton NJ; ch: Martha Elizabeth b 7 Jun 1865 in NY City & m George Dill Bower; occ: carriage & truck builder. [Lee, Francis Bazley, *Genealogical and Personal Record of Mercer County, New Jersey.* New York: The Lewis Publishing Company, 1907. Facsimile reprint Bowie: Heritage Books, Inc., 1989, p. 501.]

ACKERMAN, GEORGE DEWEY - occ: county engineer 1942-1944 & 1965-1970. [Kilner, Arthur R., *Green County, Ohio - Past and Present.* Bowie: Heritage Books, Inc., 1997, p. 260.]

ACKERMAN, GEORGE E - m 26 Aug 1879 in Cohocton NY to Eugena Van Wormer; res: Kendall NY. [Jackson, Mary S. and Edward F. Jackson, *Marriage Notices from Steuben County, New York, Newspapers, 1797-1884.* Bowie: Heritage Books, Inc., 1998, p. 220.]

AKERMAN, GEORGE H - alive 1856; baggage master of the Eastern Railroad train that derailed c 4 Feb 1856 near Wenham. [Chipman, Scott Lee, *New England Vital Records from the "Exeter News-Letter," 1853-1858.* Camden: Picton Press, 1994, p. 148.]

ACKERMAN, GEORGE H - alive 1889; occ: druggist & partner with George H Vanpeil in George H Ackerman & Co located at 853 W Harrison & 409 S Western, Chicago IL; res: boarder at 292 Marshfield [St?], Chicago IL. [Correspondence dated 18 Dec. 1979 from Larry C. Winterburn, courtesy of Robert H. Ackerman, 22 Mar. 2000. Mr. Winterburn cites his sources as Chicago city directories covering 1889-1893.]

ACKERMAN, GEORGE H - m Julie E ----, alive 1915 & residing in a house at 70 Main [St?] in Exeter NH; d by 1915.[72] Julia E Akerman was alive in 1924 & residing in Exeter NH.[73]

ACKERMAN, GEORGE M - alive 1890; occ: meat market at 680 W Madison, Chicago IL; res: 168 Park, Chicago IL. [Correspondence dated 18 Dec. 1979 from Larry C. Winterburn, courtesy of Robert H. Ackerman, 22 Mar. 2000. Mr. Winterburn cites his source as an 1890-1893 Chicago city directory.]

ACKERMAN, GEORGE W - alive 1890; res: 3716 Elmwood Pl, Chicago IL. [Correspondence dated 18 Dec. 1979 from Larry C. Winterburn, courtesy of Robert H. Ackerman, 22 Mar. 2000. Mr. Winterburn cites his source as an 1890-1893 Chicago city directory.]

ACKERMAN, GEORGE W - alive 1890; occ: horses; res: 502 Hermitage, Chicago IL. [Correspondence dated 18 Dec. 1979 from

---

[72] Crowley & Lunt, *Exeter & N. H. Coast Directory* (Beverly: Crowley & Lunt, Publishers, 1915), p. 79.
[73] Crowley & Lunt, *Exeter, Newmarket, & N. H. Coast Directory* (Beverly: Crowley & Lunt, Publishers, 1924), p. 119.

Larry C. Winterburn, courtesy of Robert H. Ackerman, 22 Mar. 2000. Mr. Winterburn cites his source as an 1890-1893 Chicago city directory.]

ACKERMAN, GERALD MARTIN - b1928; res: US; occ: author of nonfiction. [Havlice, Patricia Pate, *Index to Literary Biography: first supplement. Volume I: A-K.* Metuchen: The Scarecrow Press, Inc., 1983, p. 5.]

ACKERMAN, GERALD R - alive 1940; mil: drafted for World War II; res: Humboldt Co CA. [----, "Humboldt County, World War II," *Redwood Researcher*, Vol. XXXII #2, November 1999, p. 16]

ACKERMAN, GERRET J - alive 1816; m Anna Hogenkamp; ch: Gerret b 9 Apr 1816 & bapt 5 May 1816. [Durie, Howard I., "Pascack Reformed Dutch Church Baptisms 1814-1850," *The American Genealogist*, Vol. 47 #3 (July 1971), p. 177.]

ACKERMANN, GERTRUDE - author of the article "Joseph Renville of Lac qui Parle" which appeared in *Minn. Hist.*, date unknown but 1935 or earlier. [Kellogg, Louise Phelps, *The British Regime in Wisconsin and the Northwest.* Madison: State Historical society of Wisconsin, 1935, p. 243.]

ACKERMAN, GOODY - occupied a pew fronting the pulpit in the Meeting House. [Brewster, Charles W., *Rambles About Portsmouth: first series.* ----: Charles W. Brewster, 1859. Facsimile reprint of second edition published 1873 Somersworth: New Hampshire Publishing Company, 1971, p. 67.]

ACKERMAN, GOTTLEIB - m ----; res: 142 Clay for 24y; race: white; d 6 Sep 1866, age 65, cause: old age. [Hughes, Lois E., *Hamilton County, Ohio, Death Records, 1865-1869, Volume I.* Bowie: Heritage Books, Inc., 1992, p. 1.]

ACKERMANN, GREGOR - b1852 Prussia; m Mary E ---- d 16 Dec 1927; ch: Karl, Dora Brill, Oscar W, Clare Cummins, Ida M Hutchinson; edu: graduated from medical school in Switzerland; arrived in the US in 1880; res: 2319 Chapline Street, Wheeling (Ohio Co) WV; d 18 Jan 1928. "This is one of the most elegant and richly detailed houses on Chapline Street. ... The use of elaborate decoartive embellishments affirmed the success and prominence of Dr. Ackermann in the Wheeling community." "[A]s a surgeon, he has few compeers in this region [i.e., Wheeling area], and as a general practitioner, has the confidence of the community in a remarkable degree." [Historic American Buildings Survey/Historic American Engineering Record at memory.loc.gov.]

ACKERMANN, GRETJE JURGENS - b 9 Sep 1817 Strackholt GE; d/o Jurgen Eden Ackermann & Trientje Eilers; m 27 Apr 1844 in Strackholt GE to Willm Focken Fockenga; d 11 Nov 1892 Strackholt GE. [Correspondence dated 1 Oct. 2000 from Eddie Dirks.]

ACKERMAN, GUSTAVE ADOLPH - alive 1927; m Ethel Huffman; ch: Gustave Adolph b 23 Nov 1927 qv. [Debus, Allen G., *World Who's Who in Science: a biographical dictionary of notable scientists from antiquity to the present.* Chicago: Marquis-Who's Who, Inc., 1968, p. 8.]

ACKERMAN, GUSTAVE ADOLPH - b 23 Nov 1927; s/o Gustave Adolph Ackerman & Ethel Huffman; m 1 Sep 1956 Ellen Bomar Harris; ch: Carlyle Adolph, Sue Ellen; res: Worthington OH; occ: histologist, anatomist; edu: PhD Ohio state 1954. [Debus, Allen G., *World Who's Who in Science: a biographical dictionary of notable scientists from antiquity to the present.* Chicago: Marquis-Who's Who, Inc., 1968, p. 8.]

AKERMAN, GUSTAVUS L - mc 6 Dec 1847 in Portsmouth to Martha A Hanscom of Portsmouth; res: Boston. [Chipman, Scott Lee, *New England Vital Records from the "Exeter News-Letter," 1847-1852.* Camden: Picton Press, 1994, p. 33.]

AKERMAN, GUSTAVUS L - bc1822 [based on age at death]; s/o Leonard Akerman & ----; dc 24 Dec 1849 Portsmouth, age 27. [Chipman, Scott Lee, *New England Vital Records from the "Exeter News-Letter," 1847-1852.* Camden: Picton Press, 1994, p. 107.]

ACKERMAN, H E - (male); alive 1916; rel: admitted to the Harlem Ave Christian Church sometime between 1916 & 1921. [McElroy, Dorothy E. and Charles A. Earp, *The History and Roster of the First Christian Church (Disciples of Christ) of Baltimore, Maryland, 1810-1996.* Bowie: Heritage Books, Inc., 1996, p. 21.]

ACKERMAN, H W - alive 1855. Granted Richard Risher property on Horse Pen Bay, St. Bartholomew's Parish. Date of instrument: 2 Apr 1855; date of record: 24 Sep 1870; kind of instrument: title. [For the full record, see Book D p. 341 of the Direct Index to Deeds, 1865-1974, for Colleton County SC.][74] This is probably the same H W Ackerman who received property at Horse Pen Bay from from Richard Risher. Date of instrument: 1 Sep 1857; date of record: 24 Sep 1870; kind of instrument: conveyance. [For the full record, see Book D p. 342 of the Direct Index to Deeds, 1865-1974, for Colleton County SC.][75]

AKERMAN, HANNAH - bapt 6 Nov 1720 North Church, Portsmouth NH. [Baptized as an adult?] [Tibbetts, Charles W., *The New Hampshire Genealogical Record. An illustrated quarterly magazine devoted to genealogy, history and biography. Vol. IV, January 1907 - October 1907.* Dover: Charles W. Tibbetts, 1907. Facsimile reprint Bowie: Heritage Books, Inc., 1988, p. 104.]

AUCKERMAN, HANNAH - b 29 Aug 1830; d/o John Auckerman & Annie Dorrathea Shaver; m 4-10-1847 in Lawrence Co OH to David Rollins. [Correspondence dated 3 Sep. 2000 from Dorothy Pray Wilson.]

ACKERMAN, HANNAH O - b 28 May 1824 Dover; d/o Peter Ackerman & Bessie Cate; m Jonathan E Sleeper b 16 Feb 1813, s/o Nathan Sleeper & ----, d 10 May 1868 age "55-2-24;" d 12 May 1855 Bristol, age "30-11-14." [Musgrove, R. W., *History of the Town of Bristol, New Hampshire.* ----: Richard W. Musgrove, 1904. Reprint with a new foreword by Charles E. Greenwood, Somersworth: New Hampshire Publishing Company, 1976, p. 400 (Volume II).]

ACKERMAN, HANS - b 16 Nov 1907; m Helma Ackerman b 18 May 1908, d 15 Jun 1989, bur: Beth Ahm in Windsor (Hartford Co) CT; d 18 Feb 1989; bur: Beth Ahm, Windsor, Hartford Co CT. [Cohen, Edward A. & Lewis Goldfarb, *Jewish Cemeteries of Five*

---

[74] McElligott, Carroll Ainsworth and Ronald J. McElligott II, *A Guide to the Pre-Civil War Land Records of Colleton County, South Carolina* (Bowie: Heritage Books, Inc., 2000), p. 3.
[75] Ibid., p. 92.

*Counties of Connecticut, Volume 2.* Bowie: Heritage Books, Inc., 1998, p. 2.]

ACKERMANN, HANS GEORG - alive 1703; m Anna Maria Gerlach; ch: Johann Wendel b 5 Jan 1703 qv. [----, "Immigrant Ancestor Register," *The Palatine Immigrant*, vol. XXIV #1 (1998), p. 34.]

ACKERMAN, HARRIET - bc1825 [based on age at death]; m 14 Sep 1853 Anson B Hoyt b 28 Oct 1823 Yonkers, s/o Belding Hoyt & Rebecca ----; res: Yonkers NY; d 18 Sep 1854 age 29. [Is Harriet sis/o Amanda Ackerman m1 Mar 1854?] [Hoyt, David W., *A Genealogical History of the Hoyt, Haight, and Hight Families: with some account of the earlier Hyatt families, a list of the first settlers of Salisbury and Amesbury, Mass., etc.* ----: ----, 1871. Facsimile reprint Bowie: Heritage Books, Inc., 1992, p. 459.]

ACKERMAN, HARRIET - mc 24 Sep 1872 in Argyle NY to James B Ball of Boston MA; res: Boston MA. [Jackson, Mary S. and Edward F. Jackson, *Marriage Notices from Washington County, New York, newspapers, 1799-1880.* Bowie: Heritage Books, Inc., 1995, p. 91.]

ACKERMAN, HARRY - m ----, alive 1949. [Rodabaugh, James H., *The Ohio State Archaeological and Historical Quarterly*, Vol. 58 #1 (January 1949), p. 110.]

ACKERMAN, HARRY - alive 1967; occ: producer or director for ABC-TV. [----, *Who's Who in Show Business.* New York: Who's Who in Show Business, Inc., 1968, p. 242.]

ACKERMAN, HARRY - alive 1970; occ: producer or director for Screen Gems. [----, *Who's Who in Show Business.* New York: Who's Who in Show Business, Inc., 1971, p. 370.]

ACKERMAN, HARVEY - alive 1871; s/o John Harvey Ackerman & Anna Wallace; m Mary Elizabeth Manvel; ch: Charles Nelson b 7 Dec 1871 qv. [----, *The National Cyclopaedia of American Biography... Vol. XLIV.* New York: James T. White & Company, 1962., p. 326.]

ACKERMAN, HARVEY - alive 1886; res: road 2 in Alexandria (Grafton Co) NH; occ: farmer with 25 acres. [Child, Hamilton, *Business Directory of Grafton County, N. H., 1885-1886*. Syracuse: The Syracuse Journal Company, Printers and Binders, c1886, p. 3.]

ACKERMAN, HAZEL - alive 1919; was a witness to the will of Emma E Lynn written on 22 Dec 1919. [Sanderson, Ruth Bennett, "Johnson County, Kansas, Will Books," *The Johnson County, Kansas, Genealogist*, vol. 27 #3, September 1999, p. 95]

ACKERMAN, HAZEL - alive 1921; granddaughter of Mary S. Taggart, who bequeathed money (in her will) to Hazel. [Sanderson, Ruth Bennett, "Johnson County, Kansas, Will Books," *The Johnson County, Kansas, Genealogist*, Vol. 28 #1 (March 2000), p. 17.]

ACKERMAN, HELEN - m Foreman Rose. [Lee, Francis Bazley, *Genealogical and Personal Record of Mercer County, New Jersey*. New York: The Lewis Publishing Company, 1907. Facsimile reprint Bowie: Heritage Books, Inc., 1989, p. 652.]

ACKERMAN, HELEN A - b 30 Aug 1850 Coeymans NY; m 4 Jul 1871 in Greenbush NY to Henry E Lowell b 26 Oct 1847 Troy NY, s/o Ezra Lowell & Jane Campbell; res: Chatham NY. [Lowell, Delmar R., *The Historic Genealogy of the Lowells of America from 1639 to 1899*. Rutland: Delmar R. Lowell, 1899. Reprint Bowie; Heritage Books, Inc., 2000, p. 245.]

ACKERMAN, HELEN J - b 12 Jun 1918; m Charles Leonard Schiefer b 28 Apr 1918, d1954. [Scholl, Allen W., *Descendants of Moses and Isabell (Clark) Crawford of Bucks County, Pennsylvania*. Bowie: Heritage Books, Inc., p. 507.]

ACKKERMAN, HENDRICK - alive 1779; m Rebekke Halenbeek; ch: Johannis b 10 Sep 1779 & bapt 15 Oct 1779, Edwart b 2 May 1781 & bapt 3 Aug 1781. [Versteeg, Dingman and Thomas E. Vermilye, Jr., *Bergen Records. Records of the Reformed Protestant Dutch Church of Bergen in New Jersey, 1666 to 1788*. Originally published in the *Year Book of the Holland Society of New York*, 1913. Reprint Baltimore: Clearfield Publishing Co., Inc., 1990, p. 99, 101.]

AKERMAN, HENRIETTA P - d/o Leonard Akerman & ----; mc 18 Jun 1849 in Portsmouth to George S Kelt of Boston. [Chipman, Scott Lee, *New England Vital Records from the "Exeter News-Letter," 1847-1852.* Camden: Picton Press, 1994, p. 85.]

ACKERMAN, HENRY - listed as an original land owner (025) in Shiawassee Co MI but no dates are given. [----, "Original Land Owners: Shiawassee Co., Michigan," *Shiawassee Steppin' Stones,* Vol. 27 #2 (February 1998), p. 7]

ACKERMAN, HENRY - m ---- d 28 Jan 1920. [Prather, Geraldine, "Brownstown Newspaper Obituary Index, 1910-1923," *Genealogy Jottings,* Vol. 17 #3 (September 1998), p. 31]

ACARMAN, HENRY - alive 1601; ch: Margert chr 29 Nov 1601 at St Giles Cripplegate (London). [Correspondence (undated) from Bob G.[?], courtesy of Robert H. Ackerman, 22 Mar. 2000.]

AKERMAN, HENRY - alive 1790; res: Lower Mount Bethel Twp in Northampton Co. Free white males 16+ years old = 1, free white females = 3. [----, *Heads of Families at the First Census of the United States Taken in the Year 1790: Pennsylvania.* Baltimore: Genealogical Publishing Company, 1966, p. 173.]

AKERMAN, HENRY - alive 1850; res: Portsmouth, Rockingham Co NH. [See page 48 of the original census for full record.] [Jackson, Ronald Vern and Gary Ronald Teeples, *New Hampshire 1850 Index Census.* Bountiful: Accelerated Indexing Systems, Inc., 1978, p. 3.]

ACKERMAN, HENRY - alive 1856; res: OH Co WV. Plaintiff in a case against Marshall & OH Turnpike Co in 1856. [For original records, see order book volume 35, pages 50, 69, 94, 108, 176, 248, 272, 321, 385, 411, 393, 435, 447, 504.] [Craft, Kenneth Fischer Jr., *Ohio County (WV) Index, Volume 3: index to county court order books (part 3), 1777-1881.* Bowie: Heritage Books, Inc., 1999, p. 493.]

ACKERMAN/ACHERMAN/AKERMAN, HENRY - aged 7 years in register dated 1870-1871. Aged 8 years in c1870-1871 [register undated but appears to fall into place here]. Aged 9 years in register dated Feb 1872. Aged 10 years in register dated 9 Dec 1872 to 15

Mar 1873.[76] Aged 10 years c1873 [register undated]. Aged 10 years in register dated 8 Apr 1873 to 25 Jul 1873. Aged 11 years in register dated 3 Nov 1873 to 19 Feb 1874.[77]

ACKERMAN, HENRY - alive 1873; res: OH Co WV. Plaintiff in a case against Frederick Reichter. [For full record, see order book volume L1, page 78.] [Craft, Kenneth Fischer Jr., *Ohio County (WV) Index, Volume 3: index to county court order books (part 3), 1777-1881*. Bowie: Heritage Books, Inc., 1999, p. 493.]

ACKERMAN, HENRY - alive 1874; owned lot #2 (36 acres, valued at $6,480.00) in Boardman School District, Beaver Twp, Mahoning Co OH. [----, "List of the Real Estate Owners, Beaver Township, Mahoning County," *Mahoning Meanderings*, Vol. 22 (September 1998), p. 67]

ACKERMAN/ACKERMANN, HENRY - alive 1875; m Sophie Albers; ch: Henry b 10 Oct 1875; res: 118 Hunt or Hand or Hamilton. [Hughes, Lois E., *Hamilton County, Ohio, Birth Records, 1874-1875, Volume I, Book A, A-K*. Bowie: Heritage Books, Inc., 1994, p. 1.]

ACKERMAN, HENRY - b1878; d 1 Feb 1907; bur: Agudater Achim Cem Assoc on Zion St in Hartford CT. [Cohen, Edward A. & Lewis Goldfarb, *Jewish Cemeteries of Hartford, Connecticut, Volume 1*. Bowie: Heritage Books, Inc., 1995, p. 1.]

ACKERMAN, HENRY A - alive 1855; res: OH Co WV. Plaintiff in a case against Marshall & OH Turnpike Co in 1855. [For original records, see order book volume 34, pages 268, 306, 330, 392.] [Craft, Kenneth Fischer Jr., *Ohio County (WV) Index, Volume 3: index to county court order books (part 3), 1777-1881*. Bowie: Heritage Books, Inc., 1999, p. 493.]

ACKERMAN, HENRY F - b 26 Dec 1937; edu: professional degree; mil: permanent grade of Captain received 6 Jul 1966.[78] This appears

---

[76] Henry Ackerman/Acherman/Akerman's age seems to progress logically through the years so this is probably the same student. Fry, Georgene, "White's Common School Register, [Beaver Township, Mahoning County, Ohio]" *Mahoning Meanderings*, Vol. 21 (October 1997), p. 79. See also Ibid., Vol. 22 (January 1998), p. 7.

[77] Fry, Georgene, "White's Common School Register, [Beaver Township, Mahoning County, Ohio]" *Mahoning Meanderings*, Vol. 21 (November 1997), p. 89.

to be the same Henry F Ackerman[n?] who went on to receive a permanent rank of Major on 6 Jul 1973.[79]

ACKERMANS, HENRY OY - alive 1571. "By the keeper of the Great Seal by virtue of the Queen's warrant; for 13s. 4d. in the hanaper.
"The life for the following, for the undermentioned fines in the Hanaper., - (m.35) [:]
"1500.) 5 Feb. 1571. Henry oy Ackermans, subject of the Emperor. 10 [shillings]." [----, *Calendar of the Patent Rolls...Elizabeth I. Vol. V. 1569-1572.* London: Her Majesty's Stationery Office, 1966, p. 186.]

ACKERMAN, HERBERT - alive 1886; res: road 2 in Alexandria (Grafton Co) NH; occ: farmer with 25 acres. [Child, Hamilton, *Business Directory of Grafton County, N. H., 1885-1886.* Syracuse: The Syracuse Journal Company, Printers and Binders, c1886, p. 3.]

ACKERMAN, HERBERT S - author of a book on the Bogert family, no publication date available. [----, *Everton's Genealogical Helper,* Vol. 52 #6 (1998), p. 176.]

ACKERMAN, HERBERT STEWART - alive 1947; author of *The Hooper Family* also titled *Descendants of Andries Hopper of 1653.* [Hopper, Maria Jean Pratt, "Who Was Cornelia Hopper's Mother?", *The Genealogical Magazine of New Jersey,* Vol. 73 #3 (September 1998), p. 97, 99.]

ACKERMANN, HERMAN - m1845 ----. [Hughes, Lois E., *Hamilton County, Ohio, Marriage index, 1817-1845, Volume I.* Bowie: Heritage Books, Inc., 1994, p. 1.]

ACKERMAN, HERMAN E - res: 88 Woodward; race: white; d 11 Jan 1872, age 6m, cause: convulsions; bur: St Joseph. [Hughes, Lois E., *Hamilton County, Ohio, Death Records, 1870-1873, Volume II, Book A, A-K.* Bowie: Heritage Books, Inc., 1992, p. 2.]

---

[78] ----, *U. S. Army Register, Volume 1: regular army active list, 1 January 1970* (Washington: U. S. Government Printing Office, 1970), p. 1
[79] ----, *U. S. Army Register, Volume 1: regular army active list, 1 January 1974* (Washington: U. S. Government Printing Office, 1974), p. 1.

ACKERMANN, HILKE JURGEN - b 6 Feb 1825 Strackholt GE; d/o Jurgen Eden Ackermann & Trientje Eilers; m 22 May 1847 in Strackholt GE to Class Anthon Kloppenburg; d 27 Jun 1905 Strackholt GE. [Correspondence dated 1 Oct. 2000 from Eddie Dirks.]

ACKERMAN, HORACE H - m 12 Oct 1897 in Hudson NH to Carrie E McKusick. [Nash, Gerald Q. et al, *The Vital Records of Hudson, New Hampshire, 1734-1985*. Bowie: Heritage Books, Inc., 1997, p. 245.]

ACKERMAN, IRENE - bc1871 [based on age at death]; res: US; occ: actress; d1916, age 45. [Waring, J. P., *American and British Theatrical Biography: a directory*. Metuchen: The Scarecrow Press, Inc., 1979, p. 14.]

ACKERMAN, IRVIN A - alive 1935; mil: service #1914855. [For full record, see *Survey of World War Veterans of Somerset County, Pennsylvania* completed by the Works Progress Administration in 1936.] [----, "World War I Veterans of Somerset County," *Laurel Messenger*, Vol. XLI #1 (February 2000), p. 442.]

ACKERMAN, IRVING - bc1885 [based on age at death]; occ: theatre owner; d1970, age 85. [Waring, J. P., *American and British Theatrical Biography: a directory*. Metuchen: The Scarecrow Press, Inc., 1979, p. 14.]

AKERMAN, ISAAC - alive 1762; m Henriette ----; ch: Maria chr 12 Mar 1762 at St Benet Grace Church (London). [Correspondence (undated) from Bob G.[?], courtesy of Robert H. Ackerman, 22 Mar. 2000.]

ACKERMAN, ISAAC - m 3 Feb 1828 Sarah Hahn. [Kieffer, Henry Martyn, *Some of the First Settlers of "The Forks of the Delaware" and Their Descendants. Being a translation from the German of the record books of the First Reformed Church of Easton, Penna. From 1760 to 1852*. Easton: ----, 1902. Facsimile reprint Bowie: Heritage Books, Inc., 1995, p. 376.]

ACKERMAN, J - alive 1857. [Tiberi, Dee, "Account Book, 1853-1857," *The Delaware Genealogist*, Vol. 15 #3 (Fall 1999), p. 44.]

ACKERMAN, J C - s/o Laurence Ackerman & ----; res: Mobile; d by 2 Oct 1870. [Kelsey, Michael et al, *"The Southern Argus:" obituaries, death notices, and implied deaths June 1869 through June 1874.* Bowie: Heritage Books, Inc., 1996, p. 71.]

ACKERMAN, J MARK - b1939; res: US; occ: author of nonfiction. [Havlice, Patricia Pate, *Index to Literary Biography: first supplement. Volume I: A-K.* Metuchen: The Scarecrow Press, Inc., 1983, p. 5.]

ACKERMAN, J P - res: [LaGrange?]; dc 6 Dec 1867 [of yellow fever?]. [Kelsey, Michael et al, *Miscellaneous Texas Newspaper Abstracts - Deaths, Volume 2.* Bowie: Heritage Books, Inc., 1997, p. 178.]

ACKERMANS, J W - bc1826 [based on age at death] NY; d 5 Mar 1903 Green Lake, age 77. [South King County Genealogical Society, *King County, Washington, Deaths, 1891-1907.* Bowie: Heritage Books, Inc., 1996, p. 1.]

ACKERMAN, JACK - alive 1951; m Estelle Kuchlik; ch: Roy Alan b 9 Sep 1951 qv. [----, *Who's Who in Frontier Science and Technology.* Chicago: Marquis Who's Who, Inc., 1984, p. 4.]

ACKERMAN, JACKSON - bc1820 KY [based on his age of 30y in the 1850 census]; m Sarah A ---- b KY; ch: Mary E b KY & age 7 in 1850, William H b KY & age 5 in 1850. [Lawson, Rowena, *Nelson County, Kentucky, 1850 Census.* Bowie: Heritage Books, Inc., 1985, p. 69.]

ACKERMAN, JACOB - m Anna Brundage, alive 1875; res: Waterloo NY. [Jackson, Mary S. and Edward F. Jackson, *Death Notices from Steuben County, New York, Newspapers, 1797-1884.* Bowie: Heritage Books, Inc., 1998, p. 294, 303.]

ACKERMAN, JACOB - alive 1793; res: Frederick Co MD; owned no taxable property or land. [----, "1793 Tax, Unity and Burnt House Woods Hundred," *Western Maryland Genealogy*, Vol. 13 #2, p. 80]

ACKERMAN, JACOB - m 2 Sep 1798 in "Shawangunk Dutch Ref Ch" (Orange Co NY) to Mary Pride. [Weller, Ralph H., "Orange

County, New York, Early Marriages," *The Orange County Genealogical Society Quarterly*, Vol. 30 #3 (August 2000), p. 22.]

ACKERMAN, JACOB - m 24 Jan 1813 Elisabeth Koechlein.[80] The following children are probably all by this couple: Anna Elis b 24 Nov 1813 & bapt 26 Dec 1813.[81] Rebecca b 20 Nov 1818 & bapt 29 May 1819.[82] ---- b 9 Feb 1820 & bapt 5 Mar 1820.[83] William Henry b 18 Jul 1821 & bapt 18 Mar 1822.[84] Mary b 18 Oct 1822 & bapt 16 Mar 1823.[85]

ACREMAN, JACOB - alive 1813. "George Quattlebaum to Jacob Acreman, 9 December 1816, Two hundred fifty Dollars, 90 acres on Sleepy Creek, it being part of land granted to John Quadlebum Senr. ... Proven 22 January 1814 by Jacob Harling. Rec 16 December 1816." [For full record, see p. 238 of Deed Book 33.][86] This is probably the same man: "George Quattlebaum to Jacob Acreman, Deed, 18 October 1815, Five hundred Dollars, 149 acres on [lost in binding]py Creek, being part of land granted to sd George Quattlebaum 2 February 1795. ... Proven 10 February 1816 by James Head; Jesse Blocker JQ. Rec 13 Feb 1816." [For full record, see p. 486 of Deed Book 32.][87]

AUCKERMAN, JACOB - b 4-6-1814; s/o John Auckerman & Annie Dorrathea Shaver; m 21 Apr 1836 in Lawrence Co OH to Rachel Robbins b 3-6-1816, d 2-8-1870; bur: Kelley-Collins Cem. [Correspondence dated 3 Sep. 2000 from Dorothy Pray Wilson.]

ACKERMAN, JACOB - dc 18 May 1834, age 3y 2m 2d. [Kieffer, Henry Martyn, *Some of the First Settlers of "The Forks of the Delaware" and Their Descendants. Being a translation from the German of the record books of the First Reformed Church of Easton,*

---

[80] Kieffer, Henry Martyn, *Some of the First Settlers of "The Forks of the Delaware" and Their Descendants. Being a translation from the German of the record books of the First Reformed Church of Easton, Penna. From 1760 to 1852.* (Easton: ----, 1902. Facsimile reprint Bowie: Heritage Books, Inc., 1995), p. 362.
[81] Ibid., p. 224.
[82] Ibid., p. 257.
[83] Ibid., p. 260.
[84] Ibid., p. 268.
[85] Ibid., p. 273.
[86] Wells, Carol, *Edgefield County, South Carolina: deed books 32 and 33* (Bowie: Heritage Books, Inc., 2000), p. 120.
[87] Ibid., p. 69.

*Penna. From 1760 to 1852.* Easton: ----, 1902. Facsimile reprint Bowie: Heritage Books, Inc., 1995, p. 332.]

ACKERMAN, JACOB - alive 1835; m Sarah Hall; ch: Jacob Hanson b 12 Dec 1835 qv. [Musgrove, R. W., *History of the Town of Bristol, New Hampshire.* ----: Richard W. Musgrove, 1904. Reprint with a new foreword by Charles E. Greenwood, Somersworth: New Hampshire Publishing Company, 1976, p. 2 (Volume II).]

ACKERMAN, JACOB - m 12 Apr 1840 Lyddia Hahn. [Kieffer, Henry Martyn, *Some of the First Settlers of "The Forks of the Delaware" and Their Descendants. Being a translation from the German of the record books of the First Reformed Church of Easton, Penna. From 1760 to 1852.* Easton: ----, 1902. Facsimile reprint Bowie: Heritage Books, Inc., 1995, p. 390.]

ACKERMAN, JACOB - m 9 Mar 1841 Luisa Fraess. [Kieffer, Henry Martyn, *Some of the First Settlers of "The Forks of the Delaware" and Their Descendants. Being a translation from the German of the record books of the First Reformed Church of Easton, Penna. From 1760 to 1852.* Easton: ----, 1902. Facsimile reprint Bowie: Heritage Books, Inc., 1995, p. 391.]

ACKERMAN, JACOB - bc 1847 [based on mustering in age] GE; mil: at age 18, he mustered in as a private in the 149th IL Inf Reg, Co B on 11 Feb 1865; unm; occ: engineer. [Halpin, Cathryn, "149th Illinois Infantry Regiment, Company B," *St. Clair County Genealogical Society Quarterly*, Vol. 22 #4 (1999), p. 159]

ACKERMAN, JACOB - alive 1865; res: Beaver Twp, Mahoning Co, OH. Listed as being liable for military duty. [Pletcher, Pamela, "Mahoning County Commutation Book for 1865 Entitled *Duplicate List of persons Liable to Military Duty*," *Mahoning Meanderings*, Vol. 23 (February 1999), p. 13.]

ACKERMANN, JACOB - alive 1866; naturalized 6 Nov 1866, #542. [Cahill, Melinda Morgenstern & Diane Renner Walsh, "Naturalization Record Index of the County Court, St. Clair Co., IL, 1864-1906, A-J," *St. Clair County Genealogical Society Quarterly*, Vol. 21 #1 (1998), p. 2. According to the introduction to the index, this data is all that is available in the original source.]

ACKERMANN, JACOB - alive 1880, age 35; res: Lebanon City (St Clair Co) IL 1880. Also in his household in 1880: Mary aged 26, Lena aged 7, Julia aged 5, & Christina aged 3. [Tilton, Allyson Monroe, "1880 Federal Census - Lebanon City," *St. Clair County Genealogical Society Quarterly*, Vol. 22 #2 (1999), p. 47.]

ACKERMAN, JACOB HANSON - b 12 Dec 1835 Farmington; s/o Jacob Ackerman & Sarah Hall; m 15 May 1862 in Alexandria to Mary D Welton b 20 Nov 1841, d/o Heman J Ackerman & Abigail Gray; ch: Annette Mary b 14 Apr 1863 qv, Frank Leslie b 14 May 1865 qv; res: Farmington, Alexandria, Bristol 1891; d 22 Oct 1902, age "66-9-10." "In the spring of 1891, he purchased the J. Martin Sleeper farm in Bristol where he resided" until his death. [Musgrove, R. W., *History of the Town of Bristol, New Hampshire.* ----: Richard W. Musgrove, 1904. Reprint with a new foreword by Charles E. Greenwood, Somersworth: New Hampshire Publishing Company, 1976, p. 2 (Volume II).]

ACKERMANN, JACOB FIDELIS - b1765; res: GE; d1815. [Gascoigne, Robert Mortimer, *A Historical Catalogue of Scientists and Scientific Books from the earliest times to the close of the nineteenth century.* New York: Garland Publishing, Inc., 1984, p. 892.]

ACKERMAN, JACOB H - alive 1886; res: road 22 in Alexandria (Grafton Co) NH; occ: farmer with 100 acres. [Child, Hamilton, *Business Directory of Grafton County, N. H., 1885-1886.* Syracuse: The Syracuse Journal Company, Printers and Binders, c1886, p. 3.]

ACKERMANN, JAKOB - alive 1838; m Elizabeth Oberuck; ch: Genovefa b1838 qv; res: possibly Fuhrbach GE. [Correspondence dated 30 July 2000 from Carl W. Weil.]

ECKERMANN, JAKOB CHRISTOPH RUDOLPH - b1754; res: GE; occ: theologian; d1837. [Hyamson, Albert M., *A Dictionary of Universal Biography of All Ages and All Peoples.* London: ----, 1916. Reprint Clearfield Company, Inc., 1995, p. 190.]

ACREMAN, JAMES - alive 1691; m Mary ----; ch: Margaret chr 15 Jul 1691 at St Dionis Back Church (London). [Correspondence (undated) from Bob G.[?], courtesy of Robert H. Ackerman, 22 Mar. 2000.]

AKERMAN, JAMES - s/o John Akerman & ----; m1813 Elizabeth Long of Chappenham, d Jan 1877 Marazion; ch: John William b 16 Aug 1825 qv, James m1840 qv, Elizabeth m1849 Rev Dr Stantial, Mary m1849 J T Polkinghome; res: Bromham, Wilts[hire] EN; d Apr 1848 Penzance. [Burke, Bernard, *A Genealogical and Heraldic History of the Colonial Gentry.* Baltimore: Genealogical Publishing Company, 1970, p. 779.]

AKERMAN, JAMES - s/o James Akerman & Elizabeth Long; m1840 Mary Bracher of Salisbury; ch: William, Henry, Mary. [Burke, Bernard, *A Genealogical and Heraldic History of the Colonial Gentry.* Baltimore: Genealogical Publishing Company, 1970, p. 779.]

AKERMAN, JAMES - alive 1856; engineer of the Eastern Railroad train that derailed c 4 Feb 1856 near Wenham. [Chipman, Scott Lee, *New England Vital Records from the "Exeter News-Letter," 1853-1858.* Camden: Picton Press, 1994, p. 148.]

AUKERMAN/ACKERMAN, JAMES A - m 9 May 1888 in Richfield KS to Fanny C Long; res: Morton Co KS. At time of marriage, he was 28 and she was 18. [Gnagey, Ruth Failing, "Morton County, Kansas, Marriages, Book A, 18 March 1887 to 23 March 1925," *The Treesearcher,* Vol. 40 #1 (1998), p. 12.]

ACKERMAN, JAMES ARTHUR - b 18 Feb 1878; s/o Edwin D Ackerman & Anna Lord; m 4 Mar 1899 in Rye to Etta F Colby b1878; occ: railroad employee. [Locke, Arthur H., *A History and Genealogy of Captain John Locke (1627-1696) of Portsmouth and Rye, N. H., and His Descendants. Also of Nathaniel Locke of Portsmouth and a short account of the history of the Lockes in England.* ----: ----, ----. Facsimile reprint Bowie: Heritage Books, Inc., 1993, p. 522.]

AKERMAN, JAMES D - mc 16 Jan 1854 in Portsmouth to Anna Dearborn. [Chipman, Scott Lee, *New England Vital Records from the "Exeter News-Letter," 1853-1858.* Camden: Picton Press, 1994, p. 44.]

AKERMAN, JAMES H - b 18 Sep 1893 GA; mil: $2^{nd}$ Lt of cavalry 26 Oct 1917, $1^{st}$ Lt 19 Dec 1918, Captain 1 Jul 1920, retired from active duty 31 Dec 1922 "disability in line of duty." [----, *Official Army Register January 1, 1925*. Washington: U. S. Government Printing Office, 1925, p. 673.]

ACKERMAN, JAMES P - m 14 Nov 1857 in Bath NY to Amelia M Decker; res: Bath NY. [Jackson, Mary S. and Edward F. Jackson, *Marriage Notices from Steuben County, New York, Newspapers, 1797-1884*. Bowie: Heritage Books, Inc., 1998, p. 124.]

ACKERMAN, JAMES R JR - b 10 Nov 1942; edu: college graduate; mil: permanent grade $2^{nd}$ Lt. [----, *U. S. Army Register, Volume II: army, NGUS, USAR, and other active lists, 1 January 1970*. Washington: U. S. Government Printing Office, 1970, p. 3.]

ACKERMAN, JAMES S(LOSS) - m1947 ----; edu: BA Yale 1941, MA NY University 1947 & PhD (fine arts) 1952; occ: assoc prof 1956- . [Cattell, Jaques, *Directory of American Scholars: a biographical directory, $3^{rd}$ edition*. New York: R. R. Bowker Company, 1957, p. 2.]

ACKERMAN, JANET - alive 1994; granddaughter of Robert V Bruckshaw who died 17 Sep 1994; res: Norwalk OH. [Timman, Henry R., "Obituaries," *The Firelands Pioneer*, 3rd series, Vol. XIII, p. 107.]

ACKERMAN, JEREMY - alive 1562. [..."to pay customs as an alien and not to live in Berwike or Potesmouthe"] "Jeremy Ackerman, Spanish subject.    No fine." [----, *Calendar of the Patent Rolls...Elizabeth.    Vol. II.    1560-1563*.    London: Her Majesty's Stationery Office, 1948. Reprint Germany: Kraus Reprint, 1976, p. 457.]

ACKERMAN, JOAN ELIZABETH - b 6 Sep 1937; d/o Clinton W Ackerman & Ethel C Leonard; m Fred Frey b 1 Aug 1937. [Scholl, Allen W., *Descendants of Moses and Isabell (Clark) Crawford of Bucks County, Pennsylvania*. Bowie: Heritage Books, Inc., p. 511, 512.]

ACKERMAN, JOB N - alive 1886; res: road 9 in Alexandria (Grafton Co) NH; occ: farmer with 250 acres. [Child, Hamilton, *Business Directory of Grafton County, N. H., 1885-1886.* Syracuse: The Syracuse Journal Company, Printers and Binders, c1886, p. 3.]

ACKERMANN, JOHAN BERNARD HERM - d 16 Jul 1849, age 1y; bur: 17 Jul 1849, Old St Mary Roman Cath Ch, Hamilton Co OH. [Hamilton County Chapter of the Ohio Genealogical Society, *Hamilton County, Ohio, Church Death Records, 1811-1849.* Bowie: Heritage Books, Inc., 2000, p. 1.]

AKERMANN, JOHAN HERMAN - m Margaretha Akermann; ch: Maria Catharina d age 6m & bur: 27 Aug 1845 in Holy Trinity Roman Cath Ch in Hamilton Co OH. [Hamilton County Chapter of the Ohio Genealogical Society, *Hamilton County, Ohio, Church Death Records, 1811-1849.* Bowie: Heritage Books, Inc., 2000, p. 2.]

ACKERMANN, JOHANN - alive 1846; res: Stettin [GE?], TX. Immigrated in 1846. [Dalum, Gerald, "Pomeranians and Others to Texas," *Die Pommerschen Leute*, Band 21 (Winter 1998), p. 80.]

ACKERMANN, JOHANN ADAM - b1780; res: GE; occ: landscape painter; d1853. [Hyamson, Albert M., *A Dictionary of Universal Biography of All Ages and All Peoples.* London: ----, 1916. Reprint Clearfield Company, Inc., 1995, p. 4.]

ACKERMANN, JOHANN CHRISTIAN GOTTLIEB - b Feb 1756 Zeulenroda GE; s/o Johann Samuel Ackermann & Eva Rosine Steinmuller; m Eleanore Friedrike von Wolfersdorff; ch: 9; occ: physician; edu: MD University of Gottingen 1775; d 9 Mar 1801. "Pioneer in army hygiene."[88]

ACKERMANN, JOHANN FRIEDRICH - b1726; res: GE; d1804. [Gascoigne, Robert Mortimer, *A Historical Catalogue of Scientists and Scientific Books from the earliest times to the close of the*

---

[88] Debus, Allen G., *World Who's Who in Science: a biographical dictionary of notable scientists from antiquity to the present* (Chicago: Marquis-Who's Who, Inc., 1968), p. 8, 9. Johann Christian Gottlieb Ackermann is also listed as a medical writer. Hyamson, Albert M., *A Dictionary of Universal Biography of All Ages and All Peoples* (London: ---, 1916. Reprint Clearfield Company, Inc., 1995), p. 4.

*nineteenth century.*  New York: Garland Publishing, Inc., 1984, p. 256.]

ECKERMANN, JOHANN PETER - b1792; res: GE; occ: poet, essayist; d1854.  [Hyamson, Albert M., *A Dictionary of Universal Biography of All Ages and All Peoples.*  London: ----, 1916.  Reprint Clearfield Company, Inc., 1995, p. 190.]

ACKERMANN, JOHANN SAMUEL - alive 1756; m Eva Rosine Steinmuller; ch: Johann Christian Gottlieb b Feb 1756 qv.  [Debus, Allen G., *World Who's Who in Science: a biographical dictionary of notable scientists from antiquity to the present.*  Chicago: Marquis-Who's Who, Inc., 1968, p. 8.]

ACKERMANN, JOHANN WENDEL - b 5 Jan 1703 Neckarbischofsheim, Baden-Wurttemberg; s/o Hans Georg Ackermann & Anna Maria Gerlach; m 4 Sep 1725 in Neckarbischofsheim to Anna Maria Schick d/o Johann Georg Schick; ch: Johann Heinrich, Johann Georg m Catharina Danninger, Johann Leonard d young, Maria Barbara m Johann Georg Federhaaf, Georg Balthasar m Christina ---- & m Mrs Elisabeth Albrecht, Maria Christina m Abraham Myer; occ: blacksmith, farrier, armorer; d 31 Mar 1864 Lancaster PA.  Arrived in Philadelphia on board *Osgood* on 29 Sep 1750.[89]

ACKERMAN, JOHANNES - b1725; mil: private in Colonel Theunis Dey's Regiment Bergen Co NJ Militia.  [----, *Year Book of the Society of Sons of the Revolution in the State of New York.*  New York: Francis E. Fitch, 1899, p. 256.]

ACKERMAN, JOHANNES - b 16 Dec 1790 near Bethabara, Stokes Co NC; m1818 Anna Johanna Spaugh b 27 Mar 1796 Friedberg (Rowan Co) NC; ch: Allen m Ridelphia Kearney, Sophia b 23 Jan 1837 qv, Romulus Alexander b 31 Jan 1821 qv, William qv, Emma, Edward Edwin b 4 Jan 1830 qv; d 14 Mar 1864.  [Tesh, Peggy J., "Heinrich Peter Tesch and His Descendants," *The Forsyth County*

---

[89] ----, "Immigrant Ancestor Register," *The Palatine Immigrant*, Vol. XXIV #1 (1998), p. 34.  The death date for Johann Wendel Ackermann was given as 31 Mar 1764 in ----, "Immigrant Ancestor Register," *The Palatine Immigrant*, Vol. XXIV #2 (March 1999), p. 63.

ACKERMAN, JOHN - m Catharine ----; res: NJ, PA; bur: Knox Co OH. [Correspondence dated 3 Sep. 2000 from Dorothy Pray Wilson.]

ACREMAN, JOHN - m Mary ----; res: Bristol; occ: mariner. Mary was bound to Henry Bankes in 1659 "to serve 4 years in Barbadoes." [Coldham, Peter Wilson, *The Complete Book of Emigrants, 1607-1660. A comprehensive listing compiled from English public records of those who took ship to the Americas for political, religious, and economic reasons; of those who were deported for vagrancy, roguery, or non-conformity; and of those who were sold to labour in the new colonies.* Baltimore: Genealogical Publishing Co., Inc., 1988, p. 420.]

AKERMAN, JOHN - m Nellie ----, alive 1924 & residing on Highland Ave (rural delivery 1) in Hampton NH; d by 1924. [Crowley & Lunt, *Exeter, Newmarket, & N. H. Coast Directory.* Beverly: Crowley & Lunt, Publishers, 1924, p. 166.]

ACREMAN, JOHN - alive 1330. "Writ for aid for Francis Isumberd, the king's serjeant-at-arms, and James de Bruges, king's yeoman, appointed to arrest John Skynkel, John Acreman,... and other men of Flanders, to convey them to Windsor Castle, there to be kept in safe custody, and to take into the king's hands their goods wherever found." Dated 12 Aug. 1330, Bourne. [----, *Calendar of the Patent Rolls... Edward IV. A.D. 1327-1330.* ---: ---, 1893. Reprint Germany: Kraus Reprint, 1972, p. 573.]

LE AKURMAN, JOHN - alive 1331. "Licence for the alienation in mortmain by John le Akurman of Rongeton to the prior and convent of Briweton (Bruton), in part satisfaction of the 10 [pounds] in land and rent which they have the king's licence to acquire, of 4 acres of land in Rongeton held of the priory by the rent of 12 [pence], and of the clear yearly value of 2 [shillings] as appears by the inquisition." Witness: John de Eltham. Dated 12 Apr 1331, Eltham. [----, *Calendar of the Patent Rolls... Edward III. A.D. 1330-1334.* ---: ---, 1893. Reprint Germany: Kraus Reprint, 1972, p. 101.]

ACREMAN, JOHN - alive 1339. "Grant to John Acreman of Bruges of 10 [pounds] yearly out of the customs in the port of Kyngeston-upon-Hull, for life or until he receive 10 [pounds] yearly of land and rent." Dated 26 Jun 1339, Vilvorde. [----, *Calendar of the Patent Rolls...Edward III. A.D. 1338-1340.* ---: ---, 1895. Reprint Germany: Kraus Reprint, 1972, p. 387.]

AKERMAN, JOHN - alive 1353. "Commission of oyer and terminer to William de Shareshull,...on complaint by John de Shareshull, clerk, that...John Akerman...and others, at Brampton, co. Oxford, assaulted and imprisoned him, carried away his goods and assaulted his men and servants, whereby he lost their service for a great time." Dated 10 Jun 1353, Wesminster. [---, *Calendar of the Patent Rolls...Edward III. Vol. IX. A.D. 1350-1354.* ----: ----, 1907. Reprint Germany: Kraus Reprint, 1971, p. 507.]

AKURMAN, JOHN - alive 1405. "Presentation of John Akurman, parson of the church of Huccham, in the diocese of Lincoln, to the church of Thorle, in the diocese of London, on an exchange of benefices with John Berton." Dated 18 May 1405, Wesminster. [---, *Calendar of the Patent Rolls...Henry IV. Vol. III. A.D. 1405-1408.* ----: ----, 1907. Reprint Germany: Kraus Reprint, 1971, p. 17.]

ACREMAN, JOHN - b Maughelyn in Brabant; res: 18 Apr 1436. He is permitted "to inhabit the realm peaceably and enjoy his goods" because he "has taken an oath of fealty." [----, *Calendar of the Patent Rolls...Henry VI. Vol. II. A.D. 1429-1436.* ----: ----, Reprint Germany: Kraus Reprint, 1971, p. 564.]

AKERMAN, JOHN - alive 1460. "The life to John Akerman to purvey wheat, wood and all other things necessary to the bakery, and carriage therefor, until 20 February next." Dated 18 Aug 1460, Westminster.[90] This is probably the same "John Akerman to purvey wheat, wood and all other things necessary to the bakery, and carriage therefor, until 12 August next." Dated 11 Feb 1461. [The index lists John Akerman as "purveyor of the household" - presumably for the king.][91]

AKERMAN, JOHN - bc1690; occ: farmer; res: Bromham, Wilts[hire] EN; ch: Robert qv. [Burke, Bernard, *A Genealogical and Heraldic History of the Colonial Gentry.* Baltimore: Genealogical Publishing

---

[90] ----, *Calendar of the Patent Rolls...Henry VI. Vol. VI. A.D. 1452-1461* (----: ----, 1910. Reprint Germany: Kraus Reprint, 1971), p. 601.
[91] Ibid., p. 628.

Company, 1970, p. 779.]

AKERMAN, JOHN - b1747; s/o Robert Akerman & ----; res: Bromham, Wilts[hire] EN; ch: James m1813 qv. [Burke, Bernard, *A Genealogical and Heraldic History of the Colonial Gentry.* Baltimore: Genealogical Publishing Company, 1970, p. 779.]

ACKERMAN, JOHN - b 24 Dec 1757 Bergen Co or Middlesex Co NJ; m1 ----; m2 Feb 1803 in Bedford Co PA to Amy ----, d 12 Sep 1850 aged 75y 24d; ch: 4; res: N. Brunswick (Middlesex Co) NJ, Bedford Co PA in 1790, Knox Co OH in 1810; mil: "S16028, New Jersey Service, Ohio Agency; Cert. 19611 issued 8 August 1833, at $70 per annum, from 4 March 1831, Act of 7 June 1832;" d 8 Sep 1841, age 83y 9m 16d.
    "John Ackerman, resident of Middlebury Twp., Knox Co., Ohio, 28 Sept. 1832, 75 years, applied for benefit Act 7 June 1832; declares he entered Revolutionary army 18 May 1778 with Christopher Van Deventer, Gorline Ackerman, Enoch Dunham, John Avert (or Ovest), George Avert (or Ovest), John Freeland, Isaac Blanchard, and Garret Nephis; in New Jersey regiment, N. J. line, under Col. Ogden, Maj. Aaron Ogden (Governor elect of N. J.), Adj. Jacob Piatt, Capt. Peter Van Voris, and Orderly Sgt. Burlock; left service 18 Feb. 1779; resided all during service in New Brunswick, Middlesex Co., N. J.; in Battle of Monmouth, stationed in left wing of army on Sunday 20th of June; his regiment ordered to retreat which was affected by passing through a morass in which he lost his shoes; they came to a road just as General Washington in immediate command halted his troops; General Washington asked the retreating troops if they could fight and they answered with three cheers; after the battle his regiment marched to Englishtown, thence to Elizabeth Town where he remained until discharged completing his nine months' service; enlisted second time in 1779 with James Van Voris and Amonch (?) Pherry or Ferry; the first month he substituted for Jacob Stults; enlisted in person Sept. 1779 until Dec. 1779; stationed at Elizabeth Town during this service keeping guard; previously in 1776 and 1777 served terms in militia of N. J. under Col. Dyken, Capt. John Wagoner, Lt. Wm. Cheesman, and Lt. David Sarves; he saw British in possession of Staten Island when at Perth Amboy; states Col. John Nelson, Lt. Col John Taylor, Maj. John Van Emberrak, Capt. James Johnson, Capt. John Wolgan stationed in Cranberry when British were in possession of Brunswick; other service under Capt. John Dy

(or Die); he was born in 1757 Bergain (Bergen) Co., N. J., record in family bible at his hom [sic]; living in N. Brunswick, Middlesex Co., N. J., during Revolution; moved in 1790 to Bedford Co., Pa.; moved in 1810 to Knox Co., Ohio, when he then lived; stated his name was frequently pronounced Ockerman or Ocermon; stated following had belief in his Revolutionary War service: Benjamin Green, William Levering, John Levering, and Abraham Blair." [Baer, Mabel Van Dyke, "Abstract of Pension Record of John Ackerman," *Chips from Many Trees and Growing Roots*, Vol. 2 (Summer 1998), p. 15-17]

AKERMAN, JOHN - alive 1775. The 4th Provincial Congress met on 22 May 1775 & "Voted That John Akerman be bro't before this Body for Examination.

"Voted, That the examination of John Akerman, Benjamin Hart and John Peirce be referred to the Committees of Portsmouth, Greenland and Rye, and that if they find any thing worthy of notice they would report to this Body as soon as may be.

"Voted, That John Akerman be committed to Goal and there remain until to morrow morning.

"Portsmouth, 23d May, 1775. This certifies that the bearer, Mr. John Folsom bro't a prisoner, viz. John Akerman from the Provincial Congress at Exeter, before the Comtee [Committee] of Safety for the Town of Portsmo[uth], who ordered a guard to be kept on him, till examination to morrow 10 o'clock, A.M. [signed] Neal McIntyer, Secy. Committee Hall, Tuesday, 4 o'clock, P.M."

"Report of abovesaid Committees in Relation to John Akerman. [Copied from MS. State Pap. Revn Vol. I., p. 173.]

"Rockingham SS.

"At a meeting of the Committees of Safety of the Town of Portsmouth, Greenland and Rye concerning the Examination of one John Akerman upon a suspicion of said John Akerman's being Injurious to the Liberties and Privileges of this Country, suspected to be giving and receiving Intelligences from the British Troops, for which purpose of Enquiry the said Akerman was sent from the Provincial Congress in Exeter to these Committees, And after a thorough examination of the said Akerman, Benjamin Hart and John Peirce who were represented to them by said Congress as having sent the said Akerman into the country, It appears to the said Committees that the said Akerman was sent into the country as afresaid for Personal safety, to give intelligence of any armed men coming to Portsmouth as the Peculiar stations of some persons gave suspicion of some design against them, and that it was for no other end that the said Akerman was sent as appears from their particular Examinations upon oath, had Before us the said Committees, and they were accordingly dismissed. [dated] Portsmouth, May 24th 1775. By order of the Committee for Portsmo.[,] H. Wentworth, Chairman. By order of the Comte for Greenland, John Haven, Chairman. By order of the Comte for Rye, Joseph Parsons, Chairman." [Bouton, Nathaniel, *Provincial Papers. Documents and Records Relating to the Province of New-Hampshire, from 1764 to 1776; including the whole administration of Gov. John Wentworth; the events immediately preceding the Revolutionary War; the losses at the Battle of Bunker Hill, and the record of all proceedings till the end of our provincial history. Volume VII.* Nashua: Orren C. Moore, State Printer, 1873, p. 478, 479.]

AKERMAN, JOHN - alive 1776; res: Portsmouth. [Batchellor, Albert Stillman, *Miscellaneous Revolutionary Documents of New Hampshire including the association test, the pension rolls, and other important papers. Vol. 30.* Manchester: The John B. Clarke Co., 1910, p. 114.]

ACKERMAN, JOHN - alive c1776. [Leiby, Adrian C., *The Revolutionary War in the Hackensack Valley: the Jersey Dutch and the neutral ground, 1775-1783.* New Brunswick: Rutgers University Press, 1962, p. 109.]

AKERMAN, JOHN - alive 1776; signed Association Test of 1776 in which he agreed to "oppose the Hostile Proceedings of the British Fleets, and Armies, against the United American Colonies." [Brewster, Charles W., *Rambles About Portsmouth: first series.* ----: Charles W. Brewster, 1859. Facsimile reprint of second edition published 1873 Somersworth: New Hampshire Publishing Company, 1971, p. 215.]

ACKKERMAN, JOHN - alive 1776; m Antie Demsei; ch: John b 20 Nov 1776 & bapt 1 Jan 1779. [Versteeg, Dingman and Thomas E. Vermilye, Jr., *Bergen Records. Records of the Reformed Protestant Dutch Church of Bergen in New Jersey, 1666 to 1788.* Originally published in the *Year Book of the Holland Society of New York*, 1913. Reprint Baltimore: Clearfield Publishing Co., Inc., 1990, p. 97.]

AKERMAN, JOHN - alive 1777; mil: entered the American Revolutionary naval service on board the Continental frigate *Raleigh* on 25 Jan 1777; res: Portsmo[uth]. Information taken from the *Ship Raleigh's Book* identifies him as "Ordinary" [suggesting he was a sailor but not worthy of the title "Seaman"?], gives his height as 5 feet 5.5 inches & his complexion as "red," and his nationality as American; his wages per month were to be "D," a designation that is not explained [if it means "ditto" then his wages would have been $7 1/3 per month]. [For a description of the ship's activities, see pages 177-180 in the source.] [Tibbetts, Charles W., *The New Hampshire Genealogical Record. An illustrated quarterly magazine devoted to genealogy, history and biography. Vol. II, July 1904 - April 1905.* Dover: Charles W. Tibbetts, 1905. Facsimile reprint Bowie: Heritage Books, Inc., 1988, p. 186.]

ACREMAN/ACKERMAN, JOHN - alive 1780; mil: served in Capt. Wagoner/Weegner's Company from Springfield Twp. [Egle, William Henry, *Pennsylvania Archives: 3rd Series, Vol. VI.* Harrisburg: Clarence M. Busch, Printer, 1896, p. 27, 30, 137, 138.]

ECKERMAN, JOHN - alive 1780. [Egle, William Henry, *Pennsylvania Archives: 3rd Series, Vol. VI.* Harrisburg: Clarence M. Busch, Printer, 1896, p. 34.]

AUCKERMAN, JOHN - b 5-11-1786; s/o Stofel Auckerman & Elizabeth ----; m 22 Aug 1810 Annie Dorrathea Shaver d 25 Sep 1846; ch: William b30 Apr 1811 qv, Mary Catherine b 17 Nov 1812 qv, Jacob b 4-6-1814 qv, Mary b 2-4-1816 qv, Sarah b 11-1-1818, Solomon b 18 Dec 1819, John b 18 Dec 1821 qv, Samuel b 11-12-1823, David b 19 Apr 1825 qv, Elizabeth b 9-1-1826, Julianna b 7-9-1828 qv, Hannah b 29 Aug 1830 qv, Rebecca b 23 Jan 1833 in Lawrence Co OH, Daniel b 3-4-1835 in Lawrence Co OH, Joel b 6-10-1837 in Lawrence Co OH & d 6-2-1842 in Lawrence Co OH. [Correspondence dated 3 Sep. 2000 from Dorothy Pray Wilson.]

AKERMAN, JOHN - alive 1790; res: Bucks Co. Free white males 16+ years old = 3, free white males less than 16 = 4, free white females = 1. [----, *Heads of Families at the First Census of the United States Taken in the Year 1790: Pennsylvania.* Baltimore: Genealogical Publishing Company, 1966, p. 59.]

ACKERMAN, JOHN - bc1790-1800 NY; m Elizabeth Douglas bc1799-1805; ch: John Douglas, Samuel, Charles Holmes, William E, James B[radford?]; res: Plymouth MA 1830. [Query submitted by Roger D. Joslyn to *The American Genealogist*, Vol. 64 #1 (January 1989), p. 206.]

AKERMAN, JOHN - alive c1800?; erected a rope walk c1800 on Middel Street, extending south from Wibird's hill. [Brewster, Charles W., *Rambles About Portsmouth: first series.* ----: Charles W. Brewster, 1859. Facsimile reprint of second edition published 1873 Somersworth: New Hampshire Publishing Company, 1971, p. 171.]

AKERMAN, JOHN - alive 1800; res: Portsmouth. Free white males under 10y = 0, 10-16y = 0, 16-26y (including heads of households) = 1, 26-45y (including heads of households) = 0, 45y & upwards (including heads of households) = 1. Free white females under 10y = 1, 10-16y = 0, 16-26y (including heads of households) = 0, 26-45y (including heads of households) = 0, 45y & upwards (including heads of households) = 1. [----, *Heads of Families at the Second Census of the United States Taken in the Year 1800: New Hampshire.* Madison: John Brooks Threlfall, 1973, p. 144.]

ACKERMAN, JOHN - alive 1800; res: Portsmouth. Free white males under 10y = 1, 10-16y = 0, 16-26y (including heads of households) = 1, 26-45y (including heads of households) = 0, 45y & upwards (including heads of households) = 0. Free white females under 10y = 3, 10-16y = 0, 16-26y (including heads of households) = 1, 26-45y (including heads of households) = 0, 45y & upwards (including heads of households) = 0. [----, *Heads of Families at the Second Census of the United States Taken in the Year 1800: New Hampshire.* Madison: John Brooks Threlfall, 1973, p. 145.]

ACKERMAN, JOHN - bc1814 [based on age at death]; dc 12 Dec 1837, age 23y 9m 28d. [Kieffer, Henry Martyn, *Some of the First Settlers of "The Forks of the Delaware" and Their Descendants. Being a translation from the German of the record books of the First Reformed Church of Easton, Penna. From 1760 to 1852.* Easton: ----, 1902. Facsimile reprint Bowie: Heritage Books, Inc., 1995, p. 337.]

AKERMAN, JOHN - alive 1818; m Elizabeth Ann ----; ch: Joseph chr 9 Feb 1818 at St Sepulchre (London). [Correspondence (undated) from Bob G.[?], courtesy of Robert H. Ackerman, 22 Mar. 2000.]

AUCKERMAN, JOHN - b 18 Dec 1821; s/o John Auckerman & Annie Dorrathea Shaver; m Anna Marie ---- b 27 Dec 1821, d 7 Jul 1880; d 12-10-1896; bur: Kelley-Collins Cem. [Correspondence dated 3 Sep. 2000 from Dorothy Pray Wilson.]

ACKERMAN, JOHN - m 24 Dec 1822 Sus Metz. [Kieffer, Henry Martyn, *Some of the First Settlers of "The Forks of the Delaware" and Their Descendants. Being a translation from the German of the record books of the First Reformed Church of Easton, Penna. From 1760 to 1852.* Easton: ----, 1902. Facsimile reprint Bowie: Heritage Books, Inc., 1995, p. 372.]

ACKERMAN, JOHN - alive 1834; m Abigail Gray; ch: Mary Jane b 30 Nov 1834 qv. [Musgrove, R. W., *History of the Town of Bristol, New Hampshire.* ----: Richard W. Musgrove, 1904. Reprint with a new foreword by Charles E. Greenwood, Somersworth: New Hampshire Publishing Company, 1976, p. 382 (Volume II).]

ACKERMAN, JOHN - d 9 Jul 1849 "in this village" [Saugerties?]. [Klinkenberg, Audrey M., *Obituaries, Death Notices and Genealogical Gleanings from "The Saugerties Telegraph," Volume 1: 1848-1852.* Bowie: Heritage Books, Inc., 1989, p. 20.]

AKERMAN, JOHN - alive 1850; res: Alexandria, Grafton Co NH. [See page 155 of the original census for full record.] [Jackson, Ronald Vern and Gary Ronald Teeples, *New Hampshire 1850 Index Census.* Bountiful: Accelerated Indexing Systems, Inc., 1978, p. 3.]

ACKERMANN, JOHN - alive 1852; age 24; res: Bavaria. Immigrated through Havre & arrived at New Orleans on 17 Oct 1852. Made his declartion of intention on 23 Mar 1858 but no naturalization record is listed. [Hughes, Lois E., *Hamilton County, Ohio, Citizenship Record Abstracts, 1837-1916.* Bowie: Heritage Books, Inc., 1991, p. 1.]

ACKERMAN, JOHN - bc1856 [based on age at death] Cincinnati; unm; occ: cigar maker; res: Corryville; race: white; d 21 Jan 1874, age 18, cause: consumption; bur: Carthage Rd. [Hughes, Lois E., *Hamilton County, Ohio, Death Records, 1874-1877, Volume III, Book A, A-K.* Bowie: Heritage Books, Inc., 1992, p. 1.]

AKERMAN, JOHN - alive 1859; occ: deputy sheriff for Newburyport [MA]. [Adams, Sampson, & Co., *The Salem Directory, containing the names of the citizens, city officers, a business directory, general events of the years 1856 and 1857, and an almanac for 1859. Also, a business directory of South Danvers.* Salem: Henry Whipple & Son, 1859, p. 248.]

ACKERMANN, JOHN - b GE; alive 1862; mil: US Service 12th [MO?] Vols; res: West Belleville, St Clair Co IL. The military census listed able-bodied men between the ages of 18 & 45 yrs. [Biehl, Robert, "Military Census, 1862, St. Clair County, Illinois: West Belleville and North Belleville," *St. Clair County Genealogical Society Quarterly*, Vol. 21 #2 (1998), p. 80]

ACKERMAN, JOHN - alive 1870; res: Lafayette Co MO. Naturalized 10 Oct 1870 in Lafayette Co MO. [----, "Lafayette County, Missouri, Naturalizations, 1870-1879," *The Kansas City Genealogist*, Vol. 39 #3 (Winter 1999), p. 118.]

ACKERMAN, JOHN - alive c1872; edu: age 10 in White's Common School Register, undated, Beaver Twp, Mahoning Co OH. [----, "White's Common School Register," *Mahoning Meanderings*, Vol. 22 (January 1998), p. 7.]

ACKERMAN/AKERMAN, JOHN - aged 15 years in register dated 1870-1871. Aged 16 years in register dated 9 Dec 1872 to 15 Mar 1873.[92] Aged 17 years in register dated 3 Nov 1873 to 19 Feb 1874.[93]

ACKERMAN, JOHN - alive 1889; res: Finley Twp, Douglas Co MO. He is recorded as taking up a stray animal in Jan 1889. [----, "Douglas County Stray Records, 1885-1906," *Ozar'kin*, Vol. XX #1 (Spring 1998), p. 9.]

---

[92] Georgene Fry, "White's Common School Register, [Beaver Township, Mahoning County, Ohio]" *Mahoning Meanderings*, (Vol. 21, October 1997), p. 79.
[93] Georgene Fry, "White's Common School Register, [Beaver Township, Mahoning County, Ohio]" *Mahoning Meanderings*, (Vol. 21, November 1997), p. 89.

ACKERMAN, JOHN - dc1940; bur: Dade Co FL. [Burnsad, Cathy, "Veteran's Graves Registration Project," *The Florida Genealogist*, Vol. XXII #3 (Fall 1999), p. 94.]

ACKERMAN, JOHN - b 15 Oct 1945; edu: college graduate; mil: permanent grade 2nd Lt. [----, *U. S. Army Register, Volume II: army, NGUS, USAR, and other active lists, 1 January 1970.* Washington: U. S. Government Printing Office, 1970, p. 3.]

AKARMAN, JOHN SR - alive 1679. "Petition, dated Burlington, signed by John Budd, John Mifflin, and others [including John Akarman Sr and John Akerman Jr] from Old England, for grants of land.

"Honerble Sir[:] Wee whose names ar here vnder subscribed lately come ffom old England with Intent to inhabitt in this contry And if yor. Honor. Please to grant vs an order vnder yor hand too setle between Mr. Pitter Alderridges Plantation & the ffalls of Dellowar River we shall bee willing to Imbrace it & to hold it according to the custom of the contry being a ffitt Place for Husbandmen: wee may haue land in Jersie side but we ar willing to become Tennants to his Highness the Duke of yourke, if yor. Honor. Please to giue vs the grant and cleer the Indians that now............to send for the Rest of or ffamilys use thereof of or o[u]r relations which Looke for a Returne from vs soe desiring yor. Answere by this barrer wee shall waite for it before we settle & shall Rest Your Humble Servants although vnknown [list of signers follows, dated] Burlington June ye 23[rd] 1679." [Fernow, B., *Documents Relating to the History of the Dutch and Swedish Settlements on the Delaware River.... Vol. XII.* Albany: The Argus Company, Printers, 1877, p. 623, 624.]

ACKERMAN, JOHN A - alive 1845; m Sally Delamarter; ch: Abraham b 27 Sep 1845 & bapt 23 Nov 1845, Garret b & bapt 1849. [Durie, Howard I., "Pascack Reformed Dutch Church Baptisms 1814-1850," *The American Genealogist*, Vol. 48 #2, p. 114, 115.]

ACKERMAN, JOHN B - alive 1868; occ: carpenter; residence or business: "Madison Ave.n.Union," Flushing NY. [----, "Flushing Directory, 1868, Part 1," *Queens Genealogy Workshop*, Vol. 1 #1 (Spring 2000), p. 3.]

ACKERMAN, JOHN B - b 29 Apr 1909 NY; mil: Captain 10 Jun 1942. [----, *Official Army Register January 1, 1945*. Washington: U. S. Government Printing Office, 1945, p. 8.]

ACKERMAN, JOHN B - alive 1947; m Anne Faith Donaldson; ch: Allan Douglas b 13 Jun 1947 qv. [----, *Who's Who in Frontier Science and Technology*. Chicago: marquis Who's Who, Inc., 1984, p. 3.]

AKERMAN, JOHN C - bc1825 NH [based on his age of 35 in the 1860 census]; m Charlotte A ---- b NH; ch: Charlotte W b NH & age 11 in 1860, Josephine A b NH & age 3 or 5 in 1860 census; occ: shoemaker; res: Hampton Falls. According to the 1860 census, they were family #35 in dwelling #30; John C Akerman had real estate valued at 500 & a personal estate valued at 100.[94] According to the 1870 census, they were family #63 in dwelling #50 in Hampton Falls NH. John C Akerman gave his occupation as farmer; he had real estate valued at 1500 and a personal estate valued at 200. His wife, Charlotte A, is 43y; ch: Charlotte W is 20y & at home, Josephine A is 13y & attending school, John E is [5?] b NH.[95] John C Akerman may have been dead by 1900. In that year, his wife appears as head of the household but identifies herself as married; she lives with her grandson, Charles I Akerman b May 1879 qv. She was born in June 1827 in NH and gives her age as 72 in 1900. John C and Charlotte A Akerman had four children, none of whom were living by 1900.[96]

ACKERMAN, JOHN D - m 27 Jan 1875 in Bath NY to Deborah M Morrow; res: Cameron NY. [Jackson, Mary S. and Edward F. Jackson, *Marriage Notices from Steuben County, New York, Newspapers, 1797-1884*. Bowie: Heritage Books, Inc., 1998, p. 200.]

ACKERMAN, JOHN F - alive 1890; m Mary Allice Eggemeyer; ch: Carl William b 16 Jan 1890 qv. [Ohles, Frederik, et al, *Biographical Dictionary of Modern American Educators*. Westport: Greenwood Press, 1997, p.1]

---

[94] *Rockingham County, New Hampshire, 1860 Census*, p. 76.
[95] *Rockingham County, New Hampshire, 1900 Census*, p. 235.
[96] See dwelling 3, family 4 in Hampton Falls, *Rockingham County, New Hampshire, 1900 Census*.

ACKERMAN, JOHN HARVEY - m Anna Wallace; ch: Harvey alive 1871 qv. [----, *The National Cyclopaedia of American Biography... Vol. XLIV.* New York: James T. White & Company, 1962, p. 326.]

ACKERMAN, JOHN JOH - alive 1831; m Jane Ackerman; ch: John b 25 Oct 1831 & bapt 27 Nov 1831. [Durie, Howard I., "Pascack Reformed Dutch Church Baptisms 1814-1850," *The American Genealogist*, Vol. 47 #4, p. 251.]

ACKERMAN, JOHN L - res: NY City NY; dc 30 Nov 1864 (will filed on this date). No Ackermans are listed among the executors and beneficiaries. [See case #8837 in box #18 for full record.] [Hughes, Lois E., *Wills Filed in Probate Court, Hamilton County, Ohio, 1791-1901: Volume 1, A-K.* Bowie: Heritage Books, Inc., 1991, p. 1.]

ACKERMAN, JOHN L - alive 1927; m Marian Freeland; ch: Floyd Freeland b 1 May 1927 qv. [Rigdon, Walter, *The Biographical Encyclopaedia & Who's Who of the American Theatre.* New York: James H. Heineman, Inc., 1966, p. 231.]

ACKERMAN, JOHN M - b 27 Sep 1949; mil: permanent rank of $2^{nd}$ Lt received 9 Jun 1971; edu: less than 2y of college. [----, *U. S. Army Register, Volume 1: regular army active list, 1 January 1974.* Washington: U. S. Government Printing Office, 1974, p. 1.]

ACKERMAN, JOHN NORMAN - b 7 Feb 1932; s/o Clinton W Ackerman & Ethel C Leonard; m 9 Jul 1960 Dorothy Bower b 8 Feb 1927. [Scholl, Allen W., *Descendants of Moses and Isabell (Clark) Crawford of Bucks County, Pennsylvania.* Bowie: Heritage Books, Inc., p. 511.]

AKERMAN, JOHN S - m Mary E ---- bc1814 [based on age at death], dc 27 Mar 1838 Portsmouth, age 24. [Chipman, Scott Lee, *New England Vital Records from the "Exeter News-Letter," 1831-1840.* Camden: Picton Press, 1993, p. 152.]

AKERMAN/AKORMAN, JOHN S - bc1811 NH [based on age of 39y in 1850 census]; m ---- [unreadable] b NH & age 31 in 1850 census; ch: John F [b NH?] & age 14 in 1850 census, Anne Mary[?] b NH & age 10 in 1850 census, Sarah B[?] b NH & age 9 in 1850 census, Charles M[?] b NH & age 7 in 1850 census; occ: painter; res: Portsmouth, Rockingham Co NH. They are family #378 in dwelling #295.[97] This is probably the same John S Akerman whose child John F dc 15 Jan 1855 Portsmouth (age 10).[98]

ACKERMANN, JOHN W - alive 1889; occ: architect at 78 Ashland, Chicago IL; res: 44 Beethoven Pl, Chicago IL. [Is he related to Albert G Ackerman who resided at the same place?][99] John W Ackermann worked as an architect at 160 Lasalle.[100]

ACKERMAN, JOHN WALTER - alive 1905; m Bertha Vedder; ch: Lauren Vedder b 12 Mar 1905 qv. [Debus, Allen G., *World Who's Who in Science: a biographical dictionary of notable scientists from antiquity to the present.* Chicago: Marquis-Who's Who, Inc., 1968, p. 8.]

AKERMAN, JOHN WILLIAM - b 16 Aug 1825 Plymouth; s/o James Akerman & Elizabeth Long; m1 28 Jun 1850 Jane Stantial of Corsham, d/o C Stantial; m2 3 Jan 1878 Emma Elizabeth Brumby of Bath, d/o W H Brumby; ch of Jane Stantial: James b1852 & d in infancy, Susan b1854 & d in infancy, Elizabeth Charlotte b 16 Oct 1855 qv, Catherine b1856 & d in infancy; ch by Emma Elizabeth Brumby: Conrad b 8 Oct 1878; res: Pietermaritzburg, Natal, South Africa; occ: Speaker of the Legislative Council at Natal. John William Akerman "embarked at Plymouth in the *British Tar* bound for Natal, and arrived there in September, 1850, and is one of the few survivors of the English colonists of that early period, the real founders of the colony's fortunes. He took up his abode amongst the Dutch inhabitants of the upper districts of the colony for the purpose of acquiring a knowledge of their method of farming, their language, and their modes of thought, an acquisition which proved of great use to him in after years. In 1855, he removed to Pietermaritzburg, and turned his attention to the profession in which he had been trained for eleven years in the mother country, where he was one of the

---

[97] *New Hampshire 1850 Census*, p. 26 at familytreemaker.com, accessed 27 August 2000.
[98] Chipman, Scott Lee, *New England Vital Records from the "Exeter News-Letter," 1853-1858* (Camden: Picton Press, 1994), p. 96.
[99] Correspondence dated 18 Dec. 1979 from Larry C. Winterburn, courtesy of Robert H. Ackerman, 22 Mar. 2000. Mr. Winterburn cites his source as an 1889 Chicago city directory.
[100] Ibid. Mr. Winterburn cites his source as an 1890-1893 Chicago city directory.

foundation associates of the Pharmaceutical Society of Great Britain. He retired from business in 1875, and devoted himself entirely to public life. He sat from 1857 to 1862 as member of the Municipal Corporation of Pietermaritzburg, and was mayor of that city for one year, when he founded the Alexandra Park, and carried out other important town improvements. He sat for Pietermaritzburg in the Legislative Council almost continuously from 1862 to 1892, and was one of its most active members and a leader of a large party in that house, and is identified with all the great legislative measures of those years. In 1870 he was summoned to the Executive Council, and was the first elective member so honored. He was appointed justice of the peace in 1863 for Pietermaritzburg, and subsequently for the whole colony. In October, 1880, he was elected Speaker, and was re-elected on four other occasions. His tenure of this office extended to nearly twelve years. He represented Natal at the Colonial and Indian Exhibition in 1886, and was created K.C.M.G. in the following year, being the first Natal colonist, holding only an elective office, so honored by Her Majesty. Sir John has been president, vice-president, or committe-man in most of the public institutions of the colony, including the Natal Society, the Natal Rifle Association, the Botanic Society, and many others. He has served on almost all the important commissions of his colony. Sir John started, during the war, the 'Zulu War Relief Fund' and the 'Sick and Wounded Fund,' and succeeded in collecting nearly 8000 [pounds] from Natal, the adjacent states, and Mauritius, where his name was well-known. In April 1892, he resigned his office, owing to ill-health, after a residence of forty years, in the colony, thirty-five of which had been devoted to an acitve and unremitting public life." [Burke, Bernard, *A Genealogical and Heraldic History of the Colonial Gentry.* Baltimore: Genealogical Publishing Company, 1970, p. 778, 779.]

ACKERMAN, JONA C - ch: Mary S m 3 Feb 1870 qv; res: New Brunswick NJ. [Hoyt, David W., *A Genealogical History of the Hoyt, Haight, and Hight Families: with some account of the earlier Hyatt families, a list of the first settlers of Salisbury and Amesbury, Mass., etc.* ----: ----, 1871. Facsimile reprint Bowie: Heritage Books, Inc., 1992, p. 180, 459, 562.]

ACKERMAN, JONATHAN - bc1823 [based on his age of 27 in 1850]; m [Ninooh?] b NH & age 21y in 1850 census; ch: [Ninooh?] A b NH & age 11/12 in 1850 census res: Alexandria, Grafton Co NH.

[*New Hampshire 1850 Census*, p. 157, at familytreemaker.com, accessed 27 August 2000.]

ACKERMAN, JONATHAN B - d 21 Aug 1826. [----, *Ancestors of the Colonists of Londonderry, from the earliest record to the end of 1910*, p. 270, database posted at ancestry.com, accessed 15 July 2000.]

ACKERMAN, JONATHAN COMBS - m Maria Smith; ch: Caroline E m1842 qv, Warren b 27 Nov 1827 qv; occ: financier, merchant; res: New Brunswick NJ. [Ricord, F. W., *History of Union County, New Jersey*. Newark: East Jersey History Company, 1897, p. 63, 623.]

AKERMAN, JONES - m Mehetabel ---- bc1797 [based on death date], dc 1 May 1832, age 35. [Chipman, Scott Lee, *New England Vital Records from the "Exeter News-Letter," 1831-1840*. Camden: Picton Press, 1993, p. 43.]

AKERMAN, JOS - ch: Almira bc1802 qv; res: Portsmouth; d by 22 Sep 1845. [Chipman, Scott Lee, *New England Vital Records from the "Exeter News-Letter," 1841-1846*. Camden: Picton Press, 1993, p. 147.]

AKERMAN, JOS D - bc1837 [based on age at death]; dc 19 Sep 1859 Portsmouth, age 22. [Chipman, Scott Lee, *New England Vital Records from the "Exeter News-Letter," 1859-1865*. Camden: Picton Press, 1996, p. 35.]

AKERMAN, JOSEPH - owned a wall pew on the east side of North Church. [Brewster, Charles W., *Rambles About Portsmouth: first series*. ----: Charles W. Brewster, 1859. Facsimile reprint of second edition published 1873 Somersworth: New Hampshire Publishing Company, 1971, p. 328.]

AKERMAN, JOSEPH - alive 1765; m ----; the following children may all be his: Elizabeth bapt 30 Jun 1765 at North Church in Portsmouth NH,[101] John bapt 4 Aug 1765 at North Church in

---

[101] Tibbetts, Charles W., *The New Hampshire Genealogical Record. An illustrated quarterly magazine devoted to genealogy, history and biography. Vol. V, January 1908 - October 1908* (Dover: Charles W. Tibbetts, 1908. Facsimile reprint Bowie: Heritage Books, Inc., 1988), p. 183.

Portsmouth NH,[102] Joseph bapt 25 Dec 1768 at North Church in Portsmouth NH,[103] Samuel bapt 7 Apr 1771 at North Church in Portsmouth NH,[104] Amy bapt 17 Oct 1773 at North Church in Portsmouth NH.[105]

AKERMAN, JOSEPH - alive 1773; a grantee of Success Twp 12 Feb 1773. [Batchellor, Albert Stillman, *State of New Hampshire. Town Charters granted within the present limits of New Hampshire, being the continuation and conclusion of the grants of townships issued by the provincial government of New Hampshire, presented in alphabetcical arrangement, and including all subsequent to the letter E, will illustrative maps, plans, bibliographical citations and complete indexes, and an appendix containg documents relating to the most ancient towns of this State, and historical notes and monographs. Volume XXV. Town charters, Volume II.* Concord: Edward N. Pearson, Public Printer, 1895, p. 555.]

ACKERMAN/AKERMAN/ACREMAN, JOSEPH - alive 1775; mil: served in the 3rd VA Regiment Continental Line, 4th VA Regiment Continental Line.   [Gwathmey, John H., *Historical Register of Virginians in the Revolution: soldiers - sailors - marines, 1775-1783.* Richmond: The Dietz Press, Publishers, 1938, p. 2, 5.]

AKERMAN, JOSEPH - alive 1775; mil: served in the 3rd VA Regiment Continental Line, 4th VA Regiment Continental Line, 8th VA Regiment Continental Line, 12th VA Regiment Continental Line. [Gwathmey, John H., *Historical Register of Virginians in the Revolution: soldiers - sailors - marines, 1775-1783.* Richmond: The Dietz Press, Publishers, 1938, p. 5.]

AKERMAN, JOSEPH - alive 1776; res: Portsmouth.   [Batchellor, Albert Stillman, *Miscellaneous Revolutionary Documents of New Hampshire including the association test, the pension rolls, and other important papers. Vol. 30.* Manchester: The John B. Clarke Co.,

---

[102] Ibid.
[103] Ibid., p. 188.
[104] Tibbetts, Charles W., *The New Hampshire Genealogical Record. An illustrated quarterly magazine devoted to genealogy, history and biography. Vol. VI, January 1909 - October 1909* (Dover: Charles W. Tibbetts, 1909. Facsimile reprint Bowie: Heritage Books, Inc., 1988), p. 42.
[105] Ibid., p. 45.

AKERMAN, JOSEPH - alive 1776; signed Association Test of 1776 in which he agreed to "oppose the Hostile Proceedings of the British Fleets, and Armies, against the United American Colonies." [Brewster, Charles W., *Rambles About Portsmouth: first series.* ----: Charles W. Brewster, 1859. Facsimile reprint of second edition published 1873 Somersworth: New Hampshire Publishing Company, 1971, p. 215.]

AKERMAN, JOSEPH - alive 1776; m ----; ch: Benjamin bapt 18 Feb 1776 qv.[106] This may be the same Joseph Akerman who had ch: Anna bapt 2 Aug 1778 at North Church in Portsmouth NH.[107]

AKERMAN, JOSEPH - alive 1789; on the committee to prepare the reception for President George Washington's visit to Portsmouth. [Brewster, Charles W., *Rambles About Portsmouth: first series.* ----: Charles W. Brewster, 1859. Facsimile reprint of second edition published 1873 Somersworth: New Hampshire Publishing Company, 1971, p. 258.]

AKERMAN, JOSEPH - alive 1784; res: Portsmouth; occ: yoeman. Posted surety for Salome Akerman in 1784. [Evans, Helen F., *Abstracts of the Probate Records of Rockingham County, New Hampshire, 1771-1799, Volume 1.* Bowie: Heritage Books, Inc., 2000, p. 8.]

AKERMAN, JOSEPH - alive 1789; res: Portsmouth; occ: cordwainer. [Evans, Helen F., *Abstracts of the Probate Records of Rockingham County, New Hampshire, 1771-1799.* Bowie: Heritage Books, Inc., 2000, p. 720.]

AKERMAN, JOSEPH - alive 1790; res: Portsmouth Town NH. Free white males of 16y & upwards, including heads of families = 2. Free white males under 16y = 1. Free white females, including heads of families = 3. [----, *Heads of Families at the First Census of the*

---

[106] Tibbetts, Charles W., *The New Hampshire Genealogical Record. An illustrated quarterly magazine devoted to genealogy, history and biography. Vol. VI, January 1909 - October 1909* (Dover: Charles W. Tibbetts, 1909. Facsimile reprint Bowie: Heritage Books, Inc., 1988), p. 77.

[107] Ibid., p. 79.

*United States Taken in the Year 1790: New Hampshire.* Washington: Government Printing Office, 1907. Reprint Baltimore: Genealogical Publishing Company, 1966, p. 78.]

AKERMAN, JOSEPH - alive 1790; in 1790 or 1791, took a 999-year lease for a lot owned by the North Parish. [Brewster, Charles W., *Rambles About Portsmouth: first series.* ----: Charles W. Brewster, 1859. Facsimile reprint of second edition published 1873 Somersworth: New Hampshire Publishing Company, 1971, p. 48.]

AKERMAN, JOSEPH - alive 1795; res: Portsmouth; occ: yeoman. [Evans, Helen F., *Abstracts of the Probate Records of Rockingham County, New Hampshire, 1771-1799.* Bowie: Heritage Books, Inc., 2000, p. 946, 1012.]

AKERMAN, JOSEPH - alive 1798; res: Portsmouth; occ: gentleman. [Evans, Helen F., *Abstracts of the Probate Records of Rockingham County, New Hampshire, 1771-1799.* Bowie: Heritage Books, Inc., 2000, p. 348.]

AKERMAN, JOSEPH - alive 1800; res: Portsmouth. Free white males under 10y = 2, 10-16y = 2, 16-26y (including heads of households) = 2, 26-45y (including heads of households) = 0, 45y & upwards (including heads of households) = 0. Free white females under 10y = 1, 10-16y = 1, 16-26y (including heads of households) = 1, 26-45y (including heads of households) = 0, 45y & upwards (including heads of households) = 0. [----, *Heads of Families at the Second Census of the United States Taken in the Year 1800: New Hampshire.* Madison: John Brooks Threlfall, 1973, p. 145.]

AKERMAN, JOSEPH - m 9 Jan 1804 in Shoreditch, St Leonards to Sarah Collett. [Correspondence (undated) from Bob G.[?], courtesy of Robert H. Ackerman, 22 Mar. 2000.]

AKERMAN, JOSEPH - alive 1806; ch: Mary bc1806 [based on age at death] & dc 14 Jul 1845 Portsmouth (age 39); d by 14 Jul 1845. [Chipman, Scott Lee, *New England Vital Records from the "Exeter News-Letter," 1841-1846.* Camden: Picton Press, 1993, p. 141.]

ACKERMAN, JOSEPH - m 10 Feb 1810 in Seabrook NH to Charlotte Sanborn. [Jones, William Haslet, *Vital Statistics of*

*Seabrook, New Hampshire, 1768-1903.* Bowie: Heritage Books, Inc., 1998, p. 114.]

AKERMAN, JOSEPH - alive 1812; m Esther ----; ch: Charles b 27 Feb 1812 qv. [Correspondence dated August 2000 from Marjorie Jackson.]

AKERMAN, JOSEPH - alive 1814. "On January 12, 1814, true to the prediction of an Eliot 'seer,' the walk of Joseph Akerman 3d 'situated on the south road, was set on fire by an incendiary and entirely consumed, with its contents, consisting of about five tons of tarred yarns, which had been saved from the last fire by being thrown into the dock,and had been stretched in this walk to dry; of three tons of hemp and sails, which had been stored there, as a safe place of deposit. The fire was communicated to the yards at the lower end of the walk, and spread through it with great velocity, so that the whole was in flames in ten minutes. By great exertions, the buildings near the head of the rope-walk were prevented from taking fire. The loss is estimated at three thousand dollars. A prophecy had been circulated the week past, that there would be a fire at the south part of the town at half past seven o'clock on Wednesday evening. Little attention was paid to it by the reflecting part of the community, who supposed it to proceed from the dreams of some fanatic; but when the event so exactly corresponded with the prophecy, it was strongly suspected that a close connexion subsisted between the prophet and the incendiary. The selectmen offered a reward of five hundred dollars for the discovery and conviction of the person who perpetrated the atrocious offence.'" [Quoted from Adams, *Annals of Portsmouth*, p. 358, 359 in Saltonstall, William G., *Ports of Piscataqua.* ----: Harvard University Press, c. 1941. Reprint Bowie: Heritage Books, Inc., 1987, p. 175, 176.]

AKERMAN, JOSEPH - alive 1817; res: Murray's Row in Hampton Falls, Portsmouth 1814; pol: selectman 1817. [Brown, Warren, *History of Hampton Falls, N. H., Volume II: containing the church history and many other things not previously recorded.* Concord: The Rumford Press, 1918, p. 282.]

AKERMAN, JOSEPH - alive 1837; m Rebecca Maria ----; ch: Joseph chr 30 Jun 1837 at Shoreditch (St Leonards). [Correspondence (undated) from Bob G.[?], courtesy of Robert H. Ackerman, 22 Mar. 2000.]

ACKERMAN, JOSEPH - alive 1838; m Sarah ----; ch: Joseph chr 8 Jul 1838 at Westminster (St Anne, Soho). [Correspondence (undated) from Bob G.[?], courtesy of Robert H. Ackerman, 22 Mar. 2000.]

AKERMAN, JOSEPH - alive 1843; m Virtue ----; ch: Joseph Thomas chr 30 Jul 1843 at Shoreditch (St Leonards). [Correspondence (undated) from Bob G.[?], courtesy of Robert H. Ackerman, 22 Mar. 2000.]

AKERMAN, JOSEPH - alive 1856; m Rebecca Maria ----; ch: Martha chr 30 Mar 1856 at St John the Baptist (Shoreditch). [Correspondence (undated) from Bob G.[?], courtesy of Robert H. Ackerman, 22 Mar. 2000.]

ACKERMAN, JOSEPH - alive 1870; m Ann ----; ch: Joseph chr 13 Apr 1870 at Stepney (St Dunstan). [Correspondence (undated) from Bob G.[?], courtesy of Robert H. Ackerman, 22 Mar. 2000.]

AKERMAN, JOSEPH - alive 1850; res: Alexandria, Grafton Co NH. [See page 155 of the original census for full record.] [Jackson, Ronald Vern and Gary Ronald Teeples, *New Hampshire 1850 Index Census*. Bountiful: Accelerated Indexing Systems, Inc., 1978, p. 3.]

AKERMAN, JOSEPH - alive 1850; res: Hampton, Rockingham Co NH. [See page 257 of the original census for full record.] [Jackson, Ronald Vern and Gary Ronald Teeples, *New Hampshire 1850 Index Census*. Bountiful: Accelerated Indexing Systems, Inc., 1978, p. 3.]

AKERMAN, JOSEPH - alive 1850; res: Portsmouth, Rockingham Co NH. [See page 112 of the original census for full record.] [Jackson, Ronald Vern and Gary Ronald Teeples, *New Hampshire 1850 Index Census*. Bountiful: Accelerated Indexing Systems, Inc., 1978, p. 3.]

AKERMAN, JOSEPH - alive 1850. One of several men "chosen to confer with and assist the selectmen in maintaining law and order in [Newburyport]." [Currier, John J., *History of Newburyport, Massachusetts, 1764-1905*. Newburyport: author, 1906. Rperint Somersworth: New Hampshire Publishing Company, 1977, p. 175.]

ACKERMAN, JOSEPH - d before 19 Dec 1868. It was on this date that his body was removed from Chicago Catholic Cem & put in Calvary Cem. He is given the identification of "N.H. 5.13.D" but no explanation of codes is provided in the periodical. [----, "Chicago Catholic Cemetery," *Chicago Genealogist*, Vol. 32 #3 (Spring 2000), p. 75.]

ACKERMAN, JOSEPH - mil: 3rd Infantry Co F (NH), awarded Gillmore Medal; d1879 Nashua; bur: Nashua NH. [Longver, Phyllis O., *New Hampshire Civil War Death and Burial Locations*. Bowie: Heritage Books, Inc., 2000, unpaginated.]

ACKERMANN, JOSEPH - alive 1884; age 21; res: GE. Immigrated through Havre & arrived at NY City on 14 Feb 1884. Made his declaration of intention on 18 Aug 1886 but no naturalization record is listed. [Hughes, Lois E., *Hamilton County, Ohio, Citizenship Record Abstracts, 1837-1916*. Bowie: Heritage Books, Inc., 1991, p. 1.]

ACKERMAN, JOSEPH - bc1893 [based on age at death]; d 7 Jun 1971 Nashua NH, age 78. [Nash, Gerald Q. et al, *The Vital Records of Hudson, New Hampshire, 1734-1985*. Bowie: Heritage Books, Inc., 1997, p. 492.]

AKERMAN, JOSEPH JR - ch: Elizabeth mc 31 Jan 1832 qv. [Chipman, Scott Lee, *New England Vital Records from the "Exeter News-Letter," 1831-1840*. Camden: Picton Press, 1993, p. 34.]

AKERMAN, JOSEPH JR - alive 1794. Witnessed the will of Peter Man. [Evans, Helen F., *Abstracts of the Probate Records of Rockingham County, New Hampshire, 1771-1799*. Bowie: Heritage Books, Inc., 2000, p. 588.]

AKERMAN, JOSEPH JR - alive 1795; ch: Emily bapt 19 Apr 1795 at North Church in Portsmouth NH, Supply Jackson bapt 19 Apr 1795 qv. [It is assumed that these two children, identified as those of Joseph Akerman Jr., are indeed the offspring of the same man.] [Tibbetts, Charles W., *The New Hampshire Genealogical Record. An illustrated quarterly magazine devoted to genealogy, history and biography. Vol. VII, January 1910 - April 1910*. Dover: Charles W.

Tibbetts, 1910. Facsimile reprint Bowie: Heritage Books, Inc., 1988, p. 80.]

AKERMAN, JOSEPH JR - alive 1800; res: Portsmouth. Free white males under 10y = 1, 10-16y = 1, 16-26y (including heads of households) = 1, 26-45y (including heads of households) = 0, 45y & upwards (including heads of households) = 0. Free white females under 10y = 1, 10-16y = 1, 16-26y (including heads of households) = 1, 26-45y (including heads of households) = 0, 45y & upwards (including heads of households) = 2. [----, *Heads of Families at the Second Census of the United States Taken in the Year 1800: New Hampshire*. Madison: John Brooks Threlfall, 1973, p. 145.]

AKERMAN, JOSEPH JR - alive before 1813; occ: collector of taxes. [Brewster, Charles W., *Rambles About Portsmouth: second series*. ----: Lewis W. Brewster, 1869. Facsimile reprint Somersworth: New Hampshire Publishing Company, 1972, p. 224.]

AKERMAN, JOSEPH JR - alive 1815; occ: deputy sheriff. [Evans, Helen F., *Abstracts of the Probate Records of Rockingham County, New Hampshire, 1771-1799*. Bowie: Heritage Books, Inc., 2000, p. 350.]

AKERMAN, JOSEPH SR - bc1741 [based on age at death]; dc 29 Jan 1833 Portsmouth, age 92. [Chipman, Scott Lee, *New England Vital Records from the "Exeter News-Letter," 1831-1840*. Camden: Picton Press, 1993, p. 64.]

AKERMAN, JOSEPH D - alive 1850; res: Portsmouth, Rockingham Co NH. [See page 38 of the original census for full record.] [Jackson, Ronald Vern and Gary Ronald Teeples, *New Hampshire 1850 Index Census*. Bountiful: Accelerated Indexing Systems, Inc., 1978, p. 3.]

AKERMAN, JOSEPH L - bc1821 [based on mustering in age]; res: Ipswich MA; occ: postmaster 20 Jul 1865 - 3 Jan 1868; mil: mustered into Co K $2^{nd}$ MA on 9 Aug 1862, at age 41, & mustered out 4 Feb 1864 due to disability. [Waters, Thomas Franklin, *Ipswich in the Massachusetts Bay Colony, Volume II. A history of the town from 1700 to 1917*. Ipswich: The Ipswich Historical Society, 1917.

Reprint Newburyport: Parker River Researchers, 1988, p. 669, 764, 788.]

AKERMAN, JOSEPHINE - alive 1931; edu: student in Centre School, Hampton NH 1931. [Randall, Peter Evans, *Hampton, a century of town and beach, 1888-1988.* Portsmouth: Peter E. Randall, Publisher, 1989, p. 762. See photograph on page 762.]

-----

The following three entries are probably the same woman.

AKERMAN, JOSEPHINE R - alive 1935; unm; occ: housekeeper; res: boarded with C I Akerman in Hampton Falls NH. [Is this Charles I Akerman?] [Crowley & Lunt, *Exeter, Hampton, & N. H. Coast Directory.* Beverly: Crowley & Lunt, Publishers, 1935, p. 398.]

AKERMAN, JOSEPHINE R - alive 1941; unm; occ: housekeeper; res: boarded with Mrs M M Akerman in Hampton Falls NH. [Crowley & Lunt, *Exeter, Hampton, & N. H. Coast Directory.* Beverly: Crowley & Lunt, Publishers, 1941, p. 420.]

AKERMAN, JOSEPHINE R - alive 1960; occ: motel worker; res: Lincoln Ave, Hampton NH. [----, *Exeter, Brentwood, East Kingston, Greenland, Kensington, Newfield, and Stratham Directory, 1960.* New Haven: The Price & Lee Co., 1960, p. 473.]

-----

AKERMAN, JOSIAH - m Elizabeth March. [Brewster, Charles W., *Rambles About Portsmouth: first series.* ----: Charles W. Brewster, 1859. Facsimile reprint of second edition published 1873 Somersworth: New Hampshire Publishing Company, 1971, p. 129.]

AKERMAN, JOSIAH - m Mary ----; ch: Josiah (oldest son), John, George mariner of Portsmouth, Mark baker of Portsmouth, Catharine m Hiram Coffin, Elizabeth m Nathaniel Akarman, Betsy m ---- Melcher; res: Portsmouth; occ: butcher; dc 1773.[108] This is probably the Josiah Akerman who had Josiah bapt 31 May 1761 at North Church

---

[108] Evans, Helen F., *Abstracts of the Probate Records of Rockingham County, New Hampshire, 1771-1799, Volume 1* (Bowie: Heritage Books, Inc., 2000), p. 6-8.

in Portsmouth NH.[109] This is probably the Josiah Akerman who had George bapt 6 Mar 1762 [or 1763?] at North Church in Portsmouth NH.[110] This is probably the Josiah Akerman who had John bapt 4 Aug 1765 at North Church in Portsmouth NH.[111] This is probably the Josiah Akerman who had Katherine bapt 6 Dec 1767 at North Church in Portsmouth NH.[112]

AKERMAN, JOSIAH - alive 1790; res: Portsmouth Town NH. Free white males of 16y & upwards, including heads of families = 2. Free white males under 16y = 1. Free white females, including heads of families = 2. [----, *Heads of Families at the First Census of the United States Taken in the Year 1790: New Hampshire*. Washington: Government Printing Office, 1907. Reprint Baltimore: Genealogical Publishing Company, 1966, p. 78.]

AKERMAN, JOSIAH - alive 1795; occ: baker; res: Portsmouth. Administrator of estate of Josiah Akerman. [Evans, Helen F., *Abstracts of the Probate Records of Rockingham County, New Hampshire, 1771-1799, Volume 1*. Bowie: Heritage Books, Inc., 2000, p. 7.]

AKARMAN, JOSIAH - alive 1797; occ: baker; res: Portsmouth. [Evans, Helen F., *Abstracts of the Probate Records of Rockingham County, New Hampshire, 1771-1799*. Bowie: Heritage Books, Inc., 2000, p. 138, 139, 716, 1013.]

AKERMAN, JOSIAH - m1815 Nancy Locke; res: Portsmouth. [Locke, Arthur H., *A History and Genealogy of Captain John Locke (1627-1696) of Portsmouth and Rye, N. H., and His Descendants. Also of Nathaniel Locke of Portsmouth and a short account of the history of the Lockes in England*. ----: ----, ----. Facsimile reprint Bowie: Heritage Books, Inc., 1993, p. 568.]

ACKERMAN, JULIA - res: Terre Haute, then at Wade & Plum for one week before she died; d 13 Jul 1873, age 10m, cause: "inanition;"

---

[109] Tibbetts, Charles W., *The New Hampshire Genealogical Record. An illustrated quarterly magazine devoted to genealogy, history and biography. Vol. V, January 1908 - October 1908* (Dover: Charles W. Tibbetts, 1908. Facsimile reprint Bowie: Heritage Books, Inc., 1988), p. 136.
[110] Ibid., p. 138.
[111] Ibid., p. 183.
[112] Ibid., p. 187.

bur: St John. [Hughes, Lois E., *Hamilton County, Ohio, Death Records, 1870-1873, Volume II, Book A, A-K.* Bowie: Heritage Books, Inc., 1992, p. 2.]

ACKERMAN, JULIA - alive 1908; res: 70 Main [St?], Exeter NH. [Mitchell, Harry Edward, *Exeter & Hampton, New Hampshire, Census & Business Directory, 1908.* Augusta: Mitchell-Cony Company, 1908. Facsimile reprint Bowie: Heritage Books, Inc., 1979.]

AUCKERMAN, JULIANNA - b 7-9-1828 Lawrence Co OH; d/o John Auckerman & Annie Dorrathea Shaver; m 19 Dec 1846 in Lawrence Co OH to William Welch; d1887. [Correspondence dated 3 Sep. 2000 from Dorothy Pray Wilson.]

ACKERMANN, JURGEN - b1936; occ: director at "Deutsche Forschungsanstalt fur Luft - und Raumfahrt eV, Laboratory for Flight Systems Dynamics, 1971;" res: GE. [----, *Who's Who in Science in Europe: a biographical guide to science, technology, agriculture, and medicine, 9th ed., Volume 1.* London: Cartermill Publishing, 1995, p. 5.]

ACKERMANN, JURGEN EDEN - b 24 Jun 1792 Strackholt GE; m 25 Feb 1815 in Strackholt GE to Trientje Eilers b 22 Jan 1794 Strackholt GE, d 18 May 1869 Strackholt GE; ch: Gretje Jurgens b 9 Sep 1817 qv, Eilert b 14 May 1820 qv, Edo Jurgens b 5 May 1823 qv, Hilke Jurgen b 6 Feb 1825 qv, Eke Jurgens b 7 Dec 1826 Strackholt GE & d 7 Jul 1841 Strackholt GE, Antje Jurgens b 28 Oct 1828 qv, Trientje Jurgens b 28 Oct 1830 qv, Jurgen Jurgens b 12 Dec 1832 Strackholt GE & d 21 Feb 1833 Strackholt GE; d 20 May 1852 Strackholt GE. [Correspondence dated 1 Oct. 2000 from Eddie Dirks.]

ACKERMAN, MRS K - bc1838 [based on age at death]; d 25 Dec 1907 Ukiah, age 69. [Mendocino Coast Genealogical Society, *Births, Deaths and Marriages on California's Mendocino Coast: Volume One, 1889-1909.* Bowie: Heritage Books, Inc., 1995, p. 71.]

AKERMAN, KATHERINA - m 9 Jun 1555 in Westminster, St Martin in the Fields to Peerce Foxe. [Correspondence (undated) from Bob G.[?], courtesy of Robert H. Ackerman, 22 Mar. 2000.]

ACKERMAN, KIMBERLY ROSE - alive 1999. Descendant of Joseph Locklear, pioneer of Alachua FL. [----, "The Florida Pioneer Descendants Committee 1999 Certificate Awards Presentation," *The Florida Genealogist*, Volume XXII #4 (Winter 1999), p. 126.]

ACKERMAN, KOBUS - m 27 Nov 1782 Betjie Belser. [Versteeg, Dingman and Thomas E. Vermilye, Jr., *Bergen Records. Records of the Reformed Protestant Dutch Church of Bergen in New Jersey, 1666 to 1788.* Originally published in the *Year Book of the Holland Society of New York*, 1914. Reprint Baltimore:Clearfield Publishing Co., Inc., 1990, p. 80.]

ACKERMANN, KONRAD ERNST - b1710; occ: actor, manager; d1771. [Waring, J. P., *American and British Theatrical Biography: a directory.* Metuchen: The Scarecrow Press, Inc., 1979, p. 14.]

ACKERMAN, LARRY JOS - b 8 Jan 1939; mil: permanent rank of Captain received 7 Jan 1968; edu: 2 or more yrs of college. [----, *U. S. Army Register, Volume 1: regular army active list, 1 January 1974.* Washington: U. S. Government Printing Office, 1974, p. 1.]

ACKERMAN, LAURENCE - ch: J C d by 2 Oct 1870 qv; d 2 Oct 1870 NY. [Kelsey, Michael et al, *"The Southern Argus:" obituries, death notices, and implied deaths June 1869 through June 1874.* Bowie: Heritage Books, Inc., 1996, p. 71.]

ACKERMAN, LAUREN VEDDER - b 12 Mar 1905; s/o John Walter Ackerman & Bertha Vedder; m 7 May 1938 Elizabeth Fitts; ch: John, Gretchen, Jennifer, Alison; res: St Louis MO; occ: physician, educator; edu: MD University of Rochester 1932, DSc Hamtilon College 1962. [Debus, Allen G., *World Who's Who in Science: a biographical dictionary of notable scientists from antiquity to the present.* Chicago: Marquis-Who's Who, Inc., 1968, p. 8.]

ACKERMAN, LAURENS - alive 1678; rel: received into the church 2 Apr 1678. [Versteeg, Dingman and Thomas E. Vermilye, Jr., *Bergen Records. Records of the Reformed Protestant Dutch Church of Bergen in New Jersey, 1666 to 1788. Originally published in the Year Book of the Holland Society of New York*, 1915. Reprint Baltimore: Clearfield Publishing Co., Inc., 1990, p. 62.]

ACKERMAN, LAURENS - alive 1679; rel: received into the church 23 Jun 1679. [Versteeg, Dingman and Thomas E. Vermilye, Jr., *Bergen Records. Records of the Reformed Protestant Dutch Church of Bergen in New Jersey, 1666 to 1788.* Originally published in the *Year Book of the Holland Society of New York*, 1915. Reprint Baltimore: Clearfield Publishing Co., Inc., 1990, p. 63.]

ACKERMAN, LAURUS - alive 1680; m Geertje Egberts; ch: Jannetje bapt 18 Apr 1680. [Versteeg, Dingman and Thomas E. Vermilye, Jr., *Bergen Records. Records of the Reformed Protestant Dutch Church of Bergen in New Jersey, 1666 to 1788.* Originally published in the *Year Book of the Holland Society of New York*, 1913. Reprint Baltimore: Clearfield Publishing Co., Inc., 1990, p. 27.]

ACKERMAN LAWRENCE B - alive 1854. Received 550 acres on the south side of the Edisto River from D S H Ackerman. Date of instrument: 1854; date of record: 24 Sep 1870; kind of instrument: title. [For the full record, see Book D p. 338 of the Direct Index to Deeds, 1865-1974, for Colleton County SC.][113] This is probably the same Lawrence B Ackerman who received property in St Bartholomew's Parish from Benj Risher. Date of instrument: 3 Jan 1855; date of record: 24 Sep 1870; kind of instrument: conveyance. [For the full record, see Book D p. 339 of the Direct Index to Deeds, 1865-1974, for Colleton County SC.][114]

ACKERMAN, LEONA - d/o Enoch Ackerman & ----; m Patrick Adams b 7 Feb 1874 Haverhill; ch: none; res: Bristol. [Musgrove, R. W., *History of the Town of Bristol, New Hampshire*. ----: Richard W. Musgrove, 1904. Reprint with a new foreword by Charles E. Greenwood, Somersworth: New Hampshire Publishing Company, 1976, p. 3 (Volume II).]

AKERMAN, LEONARD - ch: Caroline Elizabeth bc1832 [based on age at death] & dc 26 Dec 1837 Portsmouth age 3y. [Chipman, Scott Lee, *New England Vital Records from the "Exeter News-Letter," 1831-1840*. Camden: Picton Press, 1993, p. 148.]

---

[113] McElligott, Carroll Ainsworth and Ronald J. McElligott II, *A Guide to the Pre-Civil War Land Records of Colleton County, South Carolina* (Bowie: Heritage Books, Inc., 2000), p. 3.

[114] Ibid., p. 92.

AKERMAN, LEONARD - ch: Thomas Curtis bc1832 [based on age at death] & dc 24 Jul 1838 age 6y (killed by being run over by a horse cart). [Chipman, Scott Lee, *New England Vital Records from the "Exeter News-Letter," 1831-1840*. Camden: Picton Press, 1993, p. 159.]

AKERMAN, LEONARD - alive 1822; ch: Gustavus L bc1822 qv. [Chipman, Scott Lee, *New England Vital Records from the "Exeter News-Letter," 1847-1852*. Camden: Picton Press, 1994, p. 107.]

AKERMAN, LEONARD - ch: Henrietta P mc 18 Jun 1849 qv. [Chipman, Scott Lee, *New England Vital Records from the "Exeter News-Letter," 1847-1852*. Camden: Picton Press, 1994, p. 85.]

AKERMAN, LEONARD - ch: William W P bc1832 [based on age at death] & dc 23 Jan 1854 Portsmouth at age 22. [Chipman, Scott Lee, *New England Vital Records from the "Exeter News-Letter," 1853-1858*. Camden: Picton Press, 1994, p. 45.]

AKERMAN, LEONARD - m Emeline A ---- bc1799 [based on age ate death], d 18 Mar 1853 Portsmouth, age 54. [Chipman, Scott Lee, *New England Vital Records from the "Exeter News-Letter," 1853-1858*. Camden: Picton Press, 1994, p. 11.]

AKERMAN, LEONARD - alive c1805-1814; scholar at Master Taft's school sometime between 1804 & 1814. [Brewster, Charles W., *Rambles About Portsmouth: second series*. ----: Lewis W. Brewster, 1869. Facsimile reprint Somersworth: New Hampshire Publishing Company, 1972, p. 319.]

AKERMAN, LEONARD - alive 1850; res: Portsmouth, Rockingham Co NH. [See page 43 of the original census for full record.] [Jackson, Ronald Vern and Gary Ronald Teeples, *New Hampshire 1850 Index Census*. Bountiful: Accelerated Indexing Systems, Inc., 1978, p. 3.]

AKERMAN, LEONARD - alive 1855; ch: Esther Annie mc 26 Nov 1855 qv; res: Portsmouth. [Chipman, Scott Lee, *New England Vital Records from the "Exeter News-Letter," 1853-1858*. Camden: Picton Press, 1994, p. 138.]

AKERMAN, LEONARD - m 31 Jul 1856 in Boston to Sarah B Hall; res: Portsmouth. [Chipman, Scott Lee, *New England Vital Records from the "Exeter News-Letter," 1853-1858*. Camden: Picton Press, 1994, p. 169.]

ACKERMAN, LILLIAN - alive 1995. Co-editor with Laura F Klein of *Women and Power in Native North America*, 1995. [Isenberg, Andrew C., *The Destruction of the Bison: an environmental history, 1750-1920*. Cambridge: Cambridge University Press, 2000, p. 96.]

ACKERMAN, LILO KARJAMAKI - alive 1939; d/o Sigrud Ackerman & ----; m 14 Oct 1939 in Tenino WA to Harvey E Daniels. Marriage reported in the *Advocate* 25 Oct 1939. [Mendocino Coast Genealogical Society, *Births, Deaths and Marriages on California's Mendocino Coast, Volume 4, 1930-1939*. Bowie: Heritage Books, Inc., 1998. p. 256.]

-----

The following five entries may be the same man.

AKERMAN, LINCOLN - m Jun 1941; ch: Brian b Sep 1942; mil: left for basic training at Fort Devens MA in Jul 1941.[115] "Ironically, the first draftee from Hampton was the first local man killed in the war. Newlywed Lincoln Akerman, a native of Hampton Falls, was living in Hampton with his wife when he joined the service. He was the first local man sent overseas and the first local soldier to become a father. His son, Brian, was born in September 1942, just two months before his father was killed 'somewhere in the South Pacific.' The Hampton Falls school has been named in Akerman's honor."[116] "In 1953, several bridges were named as memorials: ... Exeter Road, Hampton Falls, for Lincoln Akerman."[117]

AKERMAN, LINCOLN - alive 1941; m Patricia ---- [this may be the Patricia W Akerman who also lives on Exeter Rd]; occ: chauffeur; res: house on Exeter Rd either in Hampton or Hampton Falls.

---

[115] Randall, Peter Evans, *Hampton, a century of town and beach, 1888-1988* (Portsmouth: Peter E. Randall, Publisher, 1989), p. 663.
[116] Ibid., p. 671.
[117] Ibid., p. 500.

[Crowley & Lunt, *Exeter, Hampton, & N. H. Coast Directory.* Beverly: Crowley & Lunt, Publishers, 1941, p. 324.]

AKERMAN, LINCOLN H - b 20 Mar 1916; s/o Charles I Akerman & Mary M McConnell; m 7 May 1941 Patricia W Butler. [Hunt, James K. Jr., *Hampton Vital Records and Genealogy, 1889-1986.* Portsmouth: Peter E. Randall, Publisher, 1988, p. 2.]

AKERMAN, LINCOLN H - alive 1935; occ: laborer; res: boarded with C I Akerman in Hampton Falls NH. [Crowley & Lunt, *Exeter, Hampton, & N. H. Coast Directory.* Beverly: Crowley & Lunt, Publishers, 1935, p. 398.]

AKERMAN, LINCOLN H - alive 1941; occ: laborer; res: Hampton Falls, Hampton. [Crowley & Lunt, *Exeter, Hampton, & N. H. Coast Directory.* Beverly: Crowley & Lunt, Publishers, 1941, p. 420.]

-----

AKERMAN, LINDA - alive 1960; res: Brown Rd, Hampton NH. [----, *Exeter, Brentwood, East Kingston, Greenland, Kensington, Newfield, and Stratham Directory, 1960.* New Haven: The Price & Lee Co., 1960, p. 473.]

ACKERMAN, LISEBET - alive 1715. [Pearson, Jonathan, "Extracts from the Doop-Boek, or Baptismal Register of the Reformed Protestant Dutch Church of Schenectady, N. Y." *The New England Historical & Genealogical Register*, Volume XX (July 1866), p. 219.]

ACKERMAN, LIZZIE - m 5 Nov 1884 James M Taylor; res: Licking Co OH. [----, "1884-Marriages-1884," *The Licking Lantern*, Vol. XXIII #1 (March 1998), p. 9.]

ACKERMAN, LODEWYCK - alive 1694; witnessed bapt of Adriaen (26 Mar 1694) s/o Abraham Ackerman & Aeltje van Laer. [Versteeg, Dingman and Thomas E. Vermilye, Jr., Bergen Records. *Records of the Reformed Protestant Dutch Church of Bergen in New Jersey, 1666 to 1788.* Originally published in the *Year Book of the Holland Society of New York*, 1913. Reprint Baltimore: Clearfield Publishing Co., Inc., 1990, p. 41.]

ACKERMAN, LONI ZOE - bc1864 [based on age at death]; res: US; occ: actress; d1949, age 85. [Waring, J. P., *American and British Theatrical Biography: a directory*. Metuchen: The Scarecrow Press, Inc., 1979, p. 14.]

ACKERMAN, LOUIS - alive 1868; res: IA. He is referred to several times in the diaries of Brown Munro Sr., especially in regards to Munro's transactions at the business of Ackerman & Metzger. [Diary extracts contributed in letter dated 8 Apr. 2000 by Nancy Brown Brooker Bowers.]

ACKERMAN, LOUIS - alive 1930; m Anne Mukasie; ch: Norman Bernard b 27 Nov 1930 qv. [Debus, Allen G., *World Who's Who in Science: a biographical dictionary of notable scientists from antiquity to the present*. Chicago: Marquis-Who's Who, Inc., 1968, p. 8.]

ACKERMAN, LOUIS J - bc1841 [based on his age of 40y in 1881]; m Mary Mitinger; ch: dau b 10 Nov 1881. Louis J Ackerman was 40 in 1881 & Mary Mitinger was 26. [Brennan, Robert, "Records of Town of Wallkill, Orange County, NY" *The Orange County Genealogical Society Quarterly*, Vol. 30 #3 (August 2000), p. 23.]

AKERMAN, LOUISA - m 24 Aug 1795 in Bethnal Green, St Matthew to Robert Stokes. [Correspondence (undated) from Bob G.[?], courtesy of Robert H. Ackerman, 22 Mar. 2000.]

AKERMAN, LOUISA - m 17 Oct 1839 in St Pancras, Old Church to William Jackson. (Louisa's surname may be Bowman.) [Correspondence (undated) from Bob G.[?], courtesy of Robert H. Ackerman, 22 Mar. 2000.]

ACKERMAN, LOUISA - alive 1857; m Julius Rikelt; res: Louisville, Jefferson Co KY; color: white. [Darnell, Betty R., "Jefferson County Births, 1857," *Lines and By Lines*, Vol. XIV #4 (Winter 1999), p. 110.]

ACKERMAN, LOUISE C - res: Webster; race: white; d 3 Mar 1868, age 17d, cause: convulsions. [Hughes, Lois E., *Hamilton County, Ohio, Death Records, 1865-1869, Volume I*. Bowie: Heritage Books, Inc., 1992, p. 1.]

ACKERMANN, LOUISE VICTORINE CHOQUET - b1813; res: FR; occ: poetess; d1890. [Hyamson, Albert M., *A Dictionary of Universal Biography of All Ages and All Peoples.* London: ----, 1916. Reprint Clearfield Company, Inc., 1995, p. 4.]

ACKERMAN, LOURUS - m 3 Aug 1679 Geertje Egbers, from N Albany; res: "from Geffen, in the Meiery of 's Hertogenbosch." [Versteeg, Dingman and Thomas E. Vermilye, Jr., *Bergen Records. Records of the Reformed Protestant Dutch Church of Bergen in New Jersey, 1666 to 1788.* Originally published in the *Year Book of the Holland Society of New York,* 1914. Reprint Baltimore: Clearfield Publishing Co., Inc., 1990, p. 60.]

ACKERMAN, LOURUS - alive 1684. [Versteeg, Dingman and Thomas E. Vermilye, Jr., *Bergen Records. Records of the Reformed Protestant Dutch Church of Bergen in New Jersey, 1666 to 1788.* Originally published in the, 1913. Reprint Baltimore: Clearfield Publishing Co., Inc., 1990, p. 31.]

AKERMAN, LUCY D - mc 6 Dec 1858 in Portsmouth to John Sharper. [Chipman, Scott Lee, *New England Vital Records from the "Exeter News-Letter," 1853-1858.* Camden: Picton Press, 1994, p. 277.]

AKERMAN, LUCY H [sic?] - alive 1850; res: Portsmouth, Rockingham Co NH. [See page 1 of the original census for full record.] [Jackson, Ronald Vern and Gary Ronald Teeples, *New Hampshire 1850 Index Census.* Bountiful: Accelerated Indexing Systems, Inc., 1978, p. 3.]

ACKERMAN, LYDDIA - m 4 May 1839 Adam Gottschall. [Kieffer, Henry Martyn, *Some of the First Settlers of "The Forks of the Delaware" and Their Descendants. Being a translation from the German of the record books of the First Reformed Church of Easton, Penna. From 1760 to 1852.* Easton: ----, 1902. Facsimile reprint Bowie: Heritage Books, Inc., 1995, p. 389.]

ACKERMAN, LYMAN - alive 1812; res: Brownville, Jefferson Co NY; mil: awarded $47.00 claim as a soldier of the War of 1812. [----, *Index of Awards on Claims of the Soldiers of the War of 1812, as audited and allowed by the adjutant and inspector generals, pursuant to chapter 176, of the laws of 1859.* Albany: Weed, Parsons and Company, Printers, 1860, p. 4.]

AKKERMAN, LYSEBETH - alive 1711. [Pearson, Jonathan, "Extracts from the Doop-Boek, or Baptismal Register of the Reformed Protestant Dutch Church of Schenectady, N. Y." *The New England Historical & Genealogical Register*, Volume XIX (January 1865), p. 73.]

AKKERMAN, M - alive 1971; mil: E-6; res: 151-E 10 Patch at Fort Monroe, moved in Nov 1971 & moved out Jun 1975. [McClellan, Phyllis I., *The Artillerymen of Historic Fort Monroe, Virginia.* Bowie: Heritage Books, Inc., 1991, p. 101.]

ACKERMAN, M D THERESIA - b Cincinnati; res: 110 Bank; race: white; d 2 Apr 1874, age 28m, cause: scarlet fever; bur: St Johns.[118]

AKERMAN, M F - m Mary M ----; ch: Charlotte A bc1839 qv. [Sanborn, George Freeman Jr. & Melinde Lutz Sanborn, *Vital Records of Hampton, New Hampshire, to the end of the year 1900.* Boston: New England Historic Genealogical Society, 1992, p. 301, 329.]

ACKERMANN, M KATHARINA - d 13 Oct 1849, age 5m; bur: 13 Oct 1849, Old St Mary Roman Cath Ch, Hamilton Co OH. [Hamilton County Chapter of the Ohio Genealogical Society, *Hamilton County, Ohio, Church Death Records, 1811-1849.* Bowie: Heritage Books, Inc., 2000, p. 1.]

ACKERMAN, MABELA - m bond 19 Apr 1842 Morgan Berry. [McClure, Paul, *Early Marriages in Bath County, Kentucky: bonds 1811-1850 and returns 1811-1852.* Bowie: Heritage Books, Inc., 1994, p. 12.]

ACKERMAN, MAGE - alive 1892. Purchased a coffin & box ($17.00) for Nancey Hanes on 21 Feb 1892. [----, "Account Book of

---

[118] Hughes, Lois E., *Hamilton County, Ohio, Death Records, 1874-1877, Volume III, Book A, A-K* (Bowie: Heritage Books, Inc., 1992), p. 1. M D Theresa Ackerman - d 2 Apr 1874, age 28m. Herbert, Jeffrey G., *Index of Death and Marriage Notices appearing in the "Cincinnati Daily Gazette," 1827-1881* (Bowie: Heritage Books, Inc., 1993), p1.

Daniel C., Daniel R. & Clarence W. Adams, Undertakers of Northwest Ford HD., Sussex Co., DE, near Bloomery, Caroline Co., MD," *Delaware Genealogical Society Journal*, Vol. 10 #2 (October 1999), p. 31]

ACKERMAN, MALISSA - b 15 Jul 1850 VA; d/o Andrew Ackerman & Sarah Schades; d 6 Jul 1921 Beardstown, Cass Co IL. [Pedigree chart prepared 1984 and contributed by Teresa Durbin.]

AKERMAN, MARGARET F - mc 8 Feb 1858 in San Francisco to Wm Graham of Stockton; res: Portsmouth. [Chipman, Scott Lee, *New England Vital Records from the "Exeter News-Letter," 1853-1858*. Camden: Picton Press, 1994, p. 240.]

AKERMAN, MARGARETT - m 7 Mar 1680 in St James Dunes Pl, London to Griffith Powell. [Correspondence (undated) from Bob G.[?], courtesy of Robert H. Ackerman, 22 Mar. 2000.]

AKERMAN, MARGERITTE - m 1 Sep 1707 in Charterhouse Chappel, Finsbury to Thomas Lawrence. [Correspondence (undated) from Bob G.[?], courtesy of Robert H. Ackerman, 22 Mar. 2000.]

ACKERMAN, MARIA - d/o David Ackerman & Ann Gale; m 10 Jan 1875 George W S Brown. [Labaw, George Warne, *A Genealogy of the Warne Family in America: principally the descendants of Thomas Warne, born 1652, died 1722, one of the twenty-four proprietors of east New Jersey*. New York: Frank Allaben Genealogical Company, 1911, p. 574]

ACKERMANN, MARIA CATHARINA - bc1845 [based on age at death]; d 16 Jul 1849, age 4y; bur: 17 Jul 1849, Old St Mary Roman Cath Ch, Hamilton Co OH. [Hamilton County Chapter of the Ohio Genealogical Society, *Hamilton County, Ohio, Church Death Records, 1811-1849*. Bowie: Heritage Books, Inc., 2000, p. 1.]

ACKERMANN, MARIA E - alive 1871; res: OH Co WV. Her guardian was Frederick Nolte in 1871. [For full record, see order book 41, page 189.] [Craft, Kenneth Fischer Jr., *Ohio County (WV) Index, Volume 3: index to county court order books (part 3), 1777-1881*. Bowie: Heritage Books, Inc., 1999, p. 600.]

ACKERMAN, MARIA ELIS - b1750; m Peter Felder; res: Lingenfeld; d1794. [Ancestor table submitted by Enid Eleanor (Smith) Adams to *The American Genealogist*, Vol. 63 #2 (April 1988), p. 115.]

ACKERMANN, MARIA ELISABETH - bc1801 [based on age at death]; m Georg Miller; d age 47; bur: 28 Dec 1848, St Peter German Evangelical Ch. [Hamilton County Chapter of the Ohio Genealogical Society, *Hamilton County, Ohio, Church Death Records, 1811-1849*. Bowie: Heritage Books, Inc., 2000, p. 135.]

ACKERMAN, MARIANNE - name embroidered on an undated friendship quilt found at a Shipshewana auction. [Malak, Paula, "A Friendship Quilt," *Where the Trails Cross*, Vol. 28 #2 (Winter 1997/98), p. 57]

ACKERMAN, MARITIE - alive 1742. "A 1742 incident near Ramapo in Bergen County provided James Alexander with an opportunity to display his benevolent paternalism to the yeomen of one part of the countryside. The widow Maritie Ackerman's trials and tribulations allowed Alexander to act as an arbitrator of the social order and in so doing, he illuminated his perceptions of normal patriarchial behavior. On August 20, 1742, Alexander reported to the Board that the distraught widow had spoken to him about damage done to her family. She complained bitterly that her deceased husband's nephew had approached an unknowing Alexander, who had leased out the family's two hundred acre farm to the man, unaware that his uncle had died or that the dead man's family remained on the property. The impassioned widow told Alexander that 'her husband died suddenly when Mr. Ashfield [the Board's agent] was at Romopock, otherwise he would have come and taken a lease,' and 'represented the hardship should her land be leased to Hannis Akerman of which her husband had been eighteen years in possession, as by Edsal's [a proprietor agent's] survey.' She herself would have appeared had she not been 'lying in of the child in her arms at that time,' as well as caring for her 'eight other children.' The widow informed Alexander 'that all of the people cried out upon Hannis Akerman for his barbarity,' a claim which was no doubt true, as the younger man had violated kinship ties and social conventions to suit his own ends. Alexander knew well that the troubled county's residents would observe and measure his response to this sad tale.

(The author cites his source as George J. Miller, ed., *Minutes of the Board of Proprietors of the Eastern Division of New Jersey, Vol. 2* (Newark: ----, [c1950?]), pp. 196, 197.)

"Here was Alexander's opportunity to act the role of paternal patriarch. He 'told her he was sorry for what had passed, and thought Hannis [the nephew] much in the wrong,' but always the legalist, Alexander remarked that 'as he [Hannis] had the promise of the lease...said Alexander thought himself obliged to justify him in what he had done.' Nonetheless, Alexander immediately sent a messenger to 'forbid him to do more, and would give her the lease of the land.' (Ibid.) Alexander's action typified the way the gentry tried to use selective largesse to stabilize their status." [McConville, Brendan, *These Daring Disturbers of the Public Peace: the struggle for property and power in early New Jersey*. Ithaca: Cornell University Press, 1999, p. 196, 197]

AKERMAN, MARK - ch: Salome qv; res: Portsmouth; occ: yeoman; d by 1784. [Evans, Helen F., *Abstracts of the Probate Records of Rockingham County, New Hampshire, 1771-1799, Volume 1.* Bowie: Heritage Books, Inc., 2000, p. 8.]

AKERMAN, MARK - bc1773 [based on age at death]; dc 28 Feb 1848 Alms-house, age 75. [Chipman, Scott Lee, *New England Vital Records from the "Exeter News-Letter," 1847-1852.* Camden: Picton Press, 1994, p. 40.]

AKARMAN, MARK - alive 1797; res: Portsmouth; occ: baker. [Evans, Helen F., *Abstracts of the Probate Records of Rockingham County, New Hampshire, 1771-1799.* Bowie: Heritage Books, Inc., 2000, p. 716.]

AKERMAN, MARK - alive 1800; res: Portsmouth. Free white males under 10y = 0, 10-16y = 0, 16-26y (including heads of households) = 1, 26-45y (including heads of households) = 0, 45y & upwards (including heads of households) = 0. Free white females under 10y = 0, 10-16y = 0, 16-26y (including heads of households) = 1, 26-45y (including heads of households) = 0, 45y & upwards (including heads of households) = 0. [----, *Heads of Families at the Second Census of the United States Taken in the Year 1800: New Hampshire.* Madison: John Brooks Threlfall, 1973, p. 145.]

AKERMAN, MARK - alive 1850; res: Portsmouth, Rockingham Co NH. [See page 49 of the original census for full record.] [Jackson, Ronald Vern and Gary Ronald Teeples, *New Hampshire 1850 Index Census*. Bountiful: Accelerated Indexing Systems, Inc., 1978, p. 3.]

AKERMAN, MARK JR - bc1793 [based on age at death]; dc 2 Aug 1831 Portsmouth, age 38. "For several days previous to his decease, he had been subject to mental derangement - and on Friday week; at two o'clock in the morning, he arose from his bed, leaped from his chambers window, and fell (a distance of about fifteen feet) upon the pavement. He survived the accident only about twenty four hours." [Chipman, Scott Lee, *New England Vital Records from the "Exeter News-Letter," 1831-1840*. Camden: Picton Press, 1993, p. 10.]

ACKERMAN, MARMADUKE - alive 1776; witnessed land transaction. [Davis, John David, *Bergen County, New Jersey, Deed Records, 1689-1801*. Bowie: Heritage Books, Inc., 1995, p. 213]

ACKERMANN, MARRITJE - b 10 Mar 1722; m 22 Jan 1743 David Demarest b 12 Oct 1720, d Nov 1795. [Mayo, Mary E., *Sixteen Hundred Lines to Pilgrims. Lineage Book III.* Baltimore: Genealogical Publishing Co., Inc., 1982, p. 303.]

ACKERMAN, MARTHA - alive 1845; m Mathew Person. [Durie, Howard I., "Pascack Reformed Dutch Church Baptisms 1814-1850," *The American Genealogist*, Vol. 48 #2, p. 114.]

AKERMAN, MARTHA - alive 1850; res: Portsmouth, Rockingham Co NH. [See page 27 of the original census for full record.] [Jackson, Ronald Vern and Gary Ronald Teeples, *New Hampshire 1850 Index Census*. Bountiful: Accelerated Indexing Systems, Inc., 1978, p. 3.]

ACKERMANN, MARTHA - alive 1884; res: "Pfieffe by Eschwege;" left Hamburg or LeHavre on 22 Nov 1884 on board the *Westphalia* and arrived in NY. [Holtmann, Antonius, "Germans to America -- 50 volumes that are not to be trusted," *The Palatine Immigrant*, Vol. XXII #2 (March 1997), p. 83.] [The criticism apparently lies with the omission of her place of residence from the fifty-volume set *Germans to America: lists of passengers arriving at U.S. ports* by Ira A. Glazier and William P. Filby, published 1988-1996.]

ACKERMAN, MARTHA J - bc1857 [based on age at death]; dc 3 Jun 1881 Varick NY, age 24y. [Jackson, Mary S. and Edward F. Jackson, *Marriage and Death Notices from Seneca County, New York, Newspapers, 1817-1885.* Bowie: Heritage Books, Inc. 1997, p. 114.]

ACKERMAN, MARTHA MARIA - m 20 Apr 1879 in St Pancras to Robert William Young. [Correspondence (undated) from Bob G.[?], courtesy of Robert H. Ackerman, 22 Mar. 2000.]

AKERMAN, MARTHA S - mc 19 Oct 1863 in Portsmouth to Porter Cleaves of Boston; res: Portsmouth. [Chipman, Scott Lee, *New England Vital Records from the "Exeter News-Letter," 1859-1865.* Camden: Picton Press, 1996, p. 208.]

ACKERMAN, MARTIN - alive 1860; mil: 7 Artillery. [Wilt, Richard A., *New York Soldiers in the Civil War: a roster of military officers and soldiers who served in New York regiments in the Civil War as listed in the annual reports of the Adjutant General of the State of New York.* Bowie: Heritage Books, Inc., 1999, p. 2.]

ACREMAN, MARY - m 16 Feb 1603 in St Giles Cripplegate, London to Fraunc Wolvesley. [Correspondence (undated) from Bob G.[?], courtesy of Robert H. Ackerman, 22 Mar. 2000.]

ACREMAN, MARY - m 24 Nov 1681 in St James Dunes Pl, London to Humphry Welsh. [Correspondence (undated) from Bob G.[?], courtesy of Robert H. Ackerman, 22 Mar. 2000.]

AKERMAN, MARY - m "6th 2mo. 1686" Joseph Charley. [Quaker marriage date.] [Lee, Francis Bazley, *Genealogical and Personal Record of Mercer County, New Jersey.* New York: The Lewis Publishing Company, 1907. Facsimile reprint Bowie: Heritage Books, Inc., 1989, p. 810.]

AKERMAN, MARY - alive 1713; d/o ---- Akerman & Sarah ----; m1 Henry Tibbetts; m2 1713 ---- Samson. [Noyes, Sybil et al, *Genealogical Dictionary of Maine and New Hampshire.* Portland: ----, 1928-1939. Reprint Baltimore: Genealogical Publishing Company,

1996, p. 59.]

ACREMAN, MARY - m 9 Nov 1727 Jno Bedden. [----, "Births, Marriages, and Deaths in Portsmouth, N.H.," *The New England Historical and Genealogical Register*, Vol. XXIV (Oct. 1870), p. 359.]

AKERMAN, MARY - alive 1790; res: Portsmouth Town NH. Free white males of 16y & upwards, including heads of families = 0. Free white males under 16y = 0. Free white females, including heads of families = 2. [----, *Heads of Families at the First Census of the United States Taken in the Year 1790: New Hampshire.* Washington: Government Printing Office, 1907. Reprint Baltimore: Genealogical Publishing Company, 1966, p. 81.]

AKERMAN, MARY - alive 1800; res: Portsmouth. Free white males under 10y = 0, 10-16y = 0, 16-26y (including heads of households) = 0, 26-45y (including heads of households) = 0, 45y & upwards (including heads of households) = 0. Free white females under 10y = 3, 10-16y = 0, 16-26y (including heads of households) = 1, 26-45y (including heads of households) = 0, 45y & upwards (including heads of households) = 1. [----, *Heads of Families at the Second Census of the United States Taken in the Year 1800: New Hampshire.* Madison: John Brooks Threlfall, 1973, p. 145.]

AUCKERMAN, MARY - b 2-4-1816; d/o John Auckerman & Annie Dorrathea Shaver; m lic 15 Nov 1836 in Adams Co OH to Penrod Coneway. [Correspondence dated 3 Sep. 2000 from Dorothy Pray Wilson.]

ACKERMAN, MARY - alive 1872; res: 134 Hamilton Rd; ch: stillborn d 13 Dec 1872 & bur: Carthage Rd; race: white. [Hughes, Lois E., *Hamilton County, Ohio, Death Records, 1870-1873, Volume II, Book A, A-K.* Bowie: Heritage Books, Inc., 1992, p. 2.]

ACKERMAN, MARY - bc1872 [based on age at death] Cincinnati; res: St Michels; race: white; d 18 Jan 1874, age 2y, cause: scarlet fever; bur: St Joseph. [Hughes, Lois E., *Hamilton County, Ohio, Death Records, 1874-1877, Volume III, Book A, A-K.* Bowie: Heritage Books, Inc., 1992, p. 1.]

ACKERMAN, MARY - bc1901 [based on age at death]; d 15 Jun 1972 Nashua NH, age 71. [Nash, Gerald Q. et al, *The Vital Records of Hudson, New Hampshire, 1734-1985*. Bowie: Heritage Books, Inc., 1997, p. 492.]

AUCKERMAN, MARY CATHERINE - b 17 Noc 1812; d/o John Auckerman & Annie Dorrathea Shaver; m 29 Dec 1831 in Adams Co OH to John Robbins. [Correspondence dated 3 Sep. 2000 from Dorothy Pray Wilson.]

ACKERMAN, MARY E - bc1867 [based on age at death]; d 23 Nov 1912 Hudson NH, age 45y 9m 26d. [Nash, Gerald Q. et al, *The Vital Records of Hudson, New Hampshire, 1734-1985*. Bowie: Heritage Books, Inc., 1997, p. 492.]

AKERMAN, MARY E - mc 31 Aug 1857 in Portsmouth to Thomas Watkins of P[ortsmouth?]; res: P[ortsmouth?]. [Chipman, Scott Lee, *New England Vital Records from the "Exeter News-Letter," 1853-1858*. Camden: Picton Press, 1994, p. 218.]

AKERMAN, MARY ELEANOR - mc 30 Sep 1850 in Boston to Isaac Tower of Boston; res: Portsmouth. [Chipman, Scott Lee, *New England Vital Records from the "Exeter News-Letter," 1847-1852*. Camden: Picton Press, 1994, p. 138.]

ACKERMAN, MARY ELIZABETH - m 27 Aug 1861 in West Camp at the Lutheran parsonage to Wesley Low of Pine Bush; res: Saugerties. [Klinkenberg, Audrey M., *Marriages from "The Saugerties Telegraph," 1846-1870, and Obituaries, Death Notices and Genealogical Gleanings from "The Ulster Telegraph," 1846-1848*. Bowie: Heritage Books, Inc., 1998, p. 284.]

AKERMAN, MARY FRANCIS - mc 17 Dec 1833 in Portsmouth to Amos Chase of Saco ME. [Chipman, Scott Lee, *New England Vital Records from the "Exeter News-Letter," 1831-1840*. Camden: Picton Press, 1993, p. 82.]

ACKERMAN, MARY J - b NH; age 18 in 1850; res: Manchester, Hillsborough Co NH. Lived with Hannah Ackerman, b NH & age 20 in 1850, & many other people as family #1605 in dwelling #1448.

[*New Hampshire 1850 Census*, p. 39 at familytreemaker.com, accessed 27 August 2000.]

ACKERMAN, MARY JANE - b 30 Nov 1834 Alexandria; d/o John Ackerman & Abigail Gray; m 7 Nov 1857 James William Saunders b 17 Jan 1833 Strafford, s/o Joel Saunders & Phebe Scott; d 29 Jan 1903 Bristol, age "68-1-29." [Musgrove, R. W., *History of the Town of Bristol, New Hampshire.* ----: Richard W. Musgrove, 1904. Reprint with a new foreword by Charles E. Greenwood, Somersworth: New Hampshire Publishing Company, 1976, p. 382 (Volume II).]

ACKERMAN, MARY LOUISE - m 5 Aug 1885 in Newburyport MA ("in the home of the bride") to Frank M. Allen of Sturgis City SD. [----, "*Champaign County Herald* - Sheaves of 1885," *Champaign County Genealogical Society Quarterly*, Vol. 21 #4 (Spring 2000), p. 126.]

AKERMAN, MARY O - mc 18 Sep 1832 in Boston to Levi Liscan; res: Portsmouth, Boston. [Chipman, Scott Lee, *New England Vital Records from the "Exeter News-Letter," 1831-1840.* Camden: Picton Press, 1993, p. 54.]

ACKERMAN, MARY S - d/o Jona C Ackerman of New Brunswick NJ; m 3 Feb 1870 Ezra P Hoyt b 17 Jun 1826 NY, s/o Ezra Hoyt & Eliza ----. [Hoyt, David W., *A Genealogical History of the Hoyt, Haight, and Hight Families: with some account of the earlier Hyatt families, a list of the first settlers of Salisbury and Amesbury, Mass., etc.* ----: ----, 1871. Facsimile reprint Bowie: Heritage Books, Inc., 1992, p. 562.]

ACKERMAN, MAURICE WM - m 6 Jun 1937 in Fairlee VT to Florence J Butman. [Nash, Gerald Q. et al, *The Vital Records of Hudson, New Hampshire, 1734-1985.* Bowie: Heritage Books, Inc., 1997, p. 245.]

ACKERMAN, MERMKE - alive 1793; res: New Barbadoes Twp, Bergen Co NJ. [Davis, John David, *Bergen County, New Jersey, Deed Records, 1689-1801.* Bowie: Heritage Books, Inc., 1995, p. 303]

ACKERMAN, MEYER H - alive 1921; m Frieda Broadman; ch: Ralph Emil b 21 Aug 1921 qv. [----, *Who's Who in Frontier Science and Technology.* Chicago: Marquis Who's Who, Inc., 1984, p. 3.]

ACREMAN, MICHAEL - alive 1661; m Barbara ----; ch: Margrett chr 12 Apr 1661 at St Dunstan (Stepney). [Correspondence (undated) from Bob G.[?], courtesy of Robert H. Ackerman, 22 Mar. 2000.]

ACKERMAN, MICHAEL - alive 1860; mil: 52 Infantry, 156 Infantry. [Wilt, Richard A., *New York Soldiers in the Civil War: a roster of military officers and soldiers who served in New York regiments in the Civil War as listed in the annual reports of the Adjutant General of the State of New York.* Bowie: Heritage Books, Inc., 1999, p. 2.]

ACKERMAN, MICHAEL - ch: Joseph b1883; res: Coatsburg (Adams Co) IL in 1880, Lawrence Co MO in 1883. [----, "Southwest Missouri Ozarks Migration Project," *Ozar'kin: the people who settled the Missouri Ozarks,* Vol. XX #3 (Fall 1998), p. 125.] [The full record from Ozarks Genealogical Society, Inc. includes the following additional information: Michael arrived in IL from GE in 1853, his son Joseph was b1883 MO, & Michael lived in the Marionville area of Lawrence Co MO. Michael's wife may have been Christina Louisa Felsman; her name is connected to his without explanation. Correspondence dated 18 February 2000 from the society.]

-----

The following two entries are probably the same man.

ACKERMAN, MICHAEL - alive 1886; res: road 2 in Alexandria (Grafton Co) NH; occ: farmer with 125 acres; mil: served in 12th NH Vols Co C. [Child, Hamilton, *Business Directory of Grafton County, N. H., 1885-1886.* Syracuse: The Syracuse Journal Company, Printers and Binders, c1886, p. 3.]

AKERMAN, MICHAEL - mil: 12th Infantry Co C (NH); d1924; bur: Alexandria NH. [Longver, Phyllis O., *New Hampshire Civil War Death and Burial Locations.* Bowie: Heritage Books, Inc., 2000, unpaginated.]

-----

ACKERMAN, MICHAEL W - b 17 Dec 1946; edu: high school graduate; mil: permanent grade 1$^{st}$ Lt. [----, *U. S. Army Register, Volume II: army, NGUS, USAR, and other active lists, 1 January 1970*. Washington: U. S. Government Printing Office, 1970, p. 3.]

AKERMAN, MICHAELL - alive 1651; m Barbara ----; ch: Mary chr 9 Sep 1651 at St Dunstan (Stepney). [Correspondence (undated) from Bob G.[?], courtesy of Robert H. Ackerman, 22 Mar. 2000.]

ACREMAN, MICHAELL - alive 1661; m Barbara ----; ch: Martha chr 12 Apr 1661 at St Dunstan (Stepney). [Correspondence (undated) from Bob G.[?], courtesy of Robert H. Ackerman, 22 Mar. 2000.]

ACKERMAN, MOSES - alive 1793; res: Hackensack Twp, Bergen Co NJ. [Davis, John David, *Bergen County, New Jersey, Deed Records, 1689-1801*. Bowie: Heritage Books, Inc., 1995, p. 293.]

AKERMAN, MR - alive 1739. "Eodm Die. A message sent to his Excelly by Mr. Akerman to tell him a Quorum of the members were met." [This quote was taken from the section entitled "Journal of the House."] [Bouton, Nathaniel, *Provincial Papers. Documents and Records Relating to the Province of New-Hampshire, from 1738 to 1749: containing very valuable and interesting records and papers relating to the expedition against Louisbourg, 1745. Volume V.* Nashua: Orren C. Moore, State Printer, 1871, p. 10.]

ACKERMAN, MR - alive c1777. Robbed by ---- Cole & others c1777. [Leiby, Adrian C., *The Revolutionary War in the Hackensack Valley: the Jersey Dutch and the neutral ground, 1775-1783*. New Brunswick: Rutgers University Press, 1962, p. 194.]

AKERMAN, MR - alive 1865; owned house on State Street in Portsmouth NH which was burned. The fire was announced in the newspaper dated 25 Dec 1865. [Chipman, Scott Lee, *New England Vital Records from the "Exeter News-Letter," 1859-1865*. Camden: Picton Press, 1996, p. 301.]

ACKERMAN, MR - alive 1891; elected to serve as Assistant Chemist to Prof. Martin of Clemson College. [Rich, Peggy Burton & Marion Ard Whitehurst, *The Pickens Sentinel: favorite newspaper of Pickens*

*County. Pickens Court House, South Carolina, 1872-1893, historical and genealogical abstracts.* Bowie: Heritage Books, Inc., 1994, p. 425.]

ACKERMAN, MYRON - alive 1935; m Leona Auerbach; ch: Robert Harold b 1 Jun 1935 qv. [----, *Who's Who in Frontier Science and Technology.* Chicago: Marquis Who's Who, Inc., 1984, p. 3.]

ACKERMAN, MYRTLE - alive 1905; res: Stafford Twp, Renville Co ND. Purchased federal land on 28 Sep 1905: section 15, twp 163, range 87. [Mogren, John, "Federal Land Tract Records," *North Central North Dakota Genealogical Record,* #78 (March 1999), p. 13.]

ACKERMAN, NAHAM - alive 1786; occ: appointed post-rider for the "northern route" c1786 [it is unclear what the route was] & in 1791 he was post-rider for the following route (which was called the northern route): Concord to Boscawen, Salisbury, Andover, New Chester, Plymouth, Haverhill, Piermont, Orford, Lyme, Hanover, Lebanon, Enfield, Canaan, Grafton, Alexandria, and Salisbury, back to Concord. [Musgrove, R. W., *History of the Town of Bristol, New Hampshire.* ----: Richard W. Musgrove, 1904. Reprint with a new foreword by Charles E. Greenwood, Somersworth: New Hampshire Publishing Company, 1976, p. 138 (Volume I).]

AKERMAN, NAHUM - alive 1773; occ: boatbuilder; res: Portsmouth. Acted as surety for estate of Josiah Akerman dc 1773. [Evans, Helen F., *Abstracts of the Probate Records of Rockingham County, New Hampshire, 1771-1799, Volume 1.* Bowie: Heritage Books, Inc., 2000, p. 6, 7.]

AKERMAN, NAHUM - alive 1774; res: Portsmouth; occ: yeoman. [Evans, Helen F., *Abstracts of the Probate Records of Rockingham County, New Hampshire, 1771-1799.* Bowie: Heritage Books, Inc., 2000, p. 519.]

AKARMAN, NAHUM - alive 1776; res: Portsmouth. [Batchellor, Albert Stillman, *Miscellaneous Revolutionary Documents of New Hampshire including the association test, the pension rolls, and other important papers. Vol. 30.* Manchester: The John B. Clarke Co.,

1910, p. 118.]

AKERMAN, NAHUM - alive 1776; signed Association Test of 1776 in which he agreed to "oppose the Hostile Proceedings of the British Fleets, and Armies, against the United American Colonies." [Brewster, Charles W., *Rambles About Portsmouth: first series.* ----: Charles W. Brewster, 1859. Facsimile reprint of second edition published 1873 Somersworth: New Hampshire Publishing Company, 1971, p. 215.]

AKERMAN, NAHUM - alive 1777; occ: boatbuilder; res: Portsmouth. Surety for Daniel Callender. [Evans, Helen F., *Abstracts of the Probate Records of Rockingham County, New Hampshire, 1771-1799.* Bowie: Heritage Books, Inc., 2000, p. 130.]

AKERMAN, NAHUM - alive 1787. Chosen to be a constable at the annual town meeting on 26 Mar 1787. [The newspaper was published in Portsmouth NH so it is presumed that Portsmouth was the town having the meeting.] [Scobie, Robert, *Genealogical Abstracts from "The New Hampshire Mercury," 1784 to 1788.* Bowie: Heritage Books, Inc., 1997, p. 109.]

AKERMAN, NAHUM - alive 1790; res: Portsmouth Town NH. Free white males of 16y & upwards, including heads of families = 3. Free white males under 16y = 2. Free white females, including heads of families = 3. [----, *Heads of Families at the First Census of the United States Taken in the Year 1790: New Hampshire.* Washington: Government Printing Office, 1907. Reprint Baltimore: Genealogical Publishing Company, 1966, p. 78.]

AKERMAN, NAHUM - alive 1800; res: Portsmouth. Free white males under 10y = 1, 10-16y = 1, 16-26y (including heads of households) = 0, 26-45y (including heads of households) = 0, 45y & upwards (including heads of households) = 1. Free white females under 10y = 1, 10-16y = 2, 16-26y (including heads of households) = 0, 26-45y (including heads of households) = 1, 45y & upwards (including heads of households) = 0. [----, *Heads of Families at the Second Census of the United States Taken in the Year 1800: New Hampshire.* Madison: John Brooks Threlfall, 1973, p. 145.]

ACKERMAN, NATHAN WARD - b 22 Nov 1908 Bessarabia (RU); s/o David Ackerman & Bertha Green; m 10 Oct 1937 in Albany NY to Gwendolyn Hill, d/o Elmer Hill of Northwood NH; ch: Jeanne m Barry Curhan, Deborah; edu: *attended public schools in NY City, graduated with a BA in 1929 & MD in 1933 from Columbia University*; occ: psychiatrist; rel: Jewish; pol: Democrat; d 12 Jun 1971 Putnam Valley NY. *Arrived in US in 1912 with his mother & settled in New York City; became a US citizen in 1920.* "...from 1942 until his death he maintained a psychiatric practice in New York City, in later years devoting most of his time to family psychotherapy." In 1957 "he started the first Family Mental Health Clinic; this was under the auspices of the Jewish Family Service, New York City. ... From 1960 until the close of his life he served as director of the professional program of The Family Institute, Inc., of which he was the founder. Ackerman was considered a leading exponent of family therapy, a concept in which families rather than individual persons received psychiatric treatment. He held that the illness of one family member could aggravate the illness of another and that frequently it was family conflict that caused patients to develop symptoms of mental or emotional illness."[119]

ACKERMAN, NATHANIEL J - ch: Ethel m Bert Clarence Hutchins b 14 Sep 1875 Alexandria. [Musgrove, R. W., *History of the Town of Bristol, New Hampshire.* ----: Richard W. Musgrove, 1904. Reprint with a new foreword by Charles E. Greenwood, Somersworth: New Hampshire Publishing Company, 1976, p. 247 (Volume II).]

AUKERMAN, NEAL - owned land (section 03, township 161) in Bowbells Twp, Burke Co ND. [Mogren, John, "Bowbells Township: names of land owners," *North Central North Dakota Genealogical Record*, #83 (June 2000), p. 6.]

AUKERMAN, NEAL O - owned land (section 03, township 161) in Bowbells Twp, Burke Co ND. [Mogren, John, "Bowbells Township:

---

[119] ---- *The National Cyclopedia of American Biography*, Vol. 56. Clifton: James T. White & Company, 1975, p. 175. [See photograph on page 174b.] Mother's name is given as Bertha Greenberg, child Jeanne married Barry Curnan, he was also an educator, and he was buried in Westchester Hills Cemetery, Hastings-on-Hudson NY. ----, *Who's Who in American History - Science and Technology* (Chicago: Marquis Who's Who, Inc., 1976), p. 3. Author of nonfiction. Havlice, Patricia Pate, *Index to Literary Biography, Volume I: A-K* (Metuchen: The Scarecrow Press, Inc., 1975), p. 6.

names of land owners," *North Central North Dakota Genealogical Record*, #83 (June 2000), p. 6.]

AKERMAN, NELLIE E - alive 1908; res: Hampton NH. [Mitchell, Harry Edward, *Exeter & Hampton, New Hampshire, Census & Business Directory, 1908*. Augusta: Mitchell-Cony Company, 1908. Facsimile reprint Bowie: Heritage Books, Inc., 1979, p. 233.]

ECKERMANN, NICOLAUS/NICOLAS GOTTFRIED C - b1784; res: GE; occ: philologist; d1813. [Hyamson, Albert M., *A Dictionary of Universal Biography of All Ages and All Peoples*. London: ----, 1916. Reprint Clearfield Company, Inc., 1995, p. 190.]

ACKERMAN NORBERT JOSEPH - alive 1942; m Lusella Smith; ch: Norbert Joseph Jr b 3 Jul 1942 qv. [----, *Who's Who in Frontier Science and Technology*. Chicago: Marquis Who's Who, Inc., 1984, p. 4.]

ACKERMAN, NORBERT JOSEPH JR - b 3 Jul 1942 Chattanooga; s/o Norbert Joseph Ackerman & Lusella Smith; m ----; ch: Dori, Nancy, Andy, Jill; div; occ: energy technology co executive; edu: BS University of Tennessee 1965 & MS 1967 & PhD 1971; res: Knoxville TN. [----, *Who's Who in Frontier Science and Technology*. Chicago: Marquis Who's Who, Inc., 1984, p. 4.]

ACKERMAN, NORMAN BERNARD - b 27 Nov 1930 NY City; s/o Louis Ackerman & Anne Mukasie; m 14 Jun 1953 Anne Linda Gross; ch: Sarah Jean, Beth Leslie, Amy Susan, Jane Ellen; res: Chestnut Hill MA; occ: surgeon; edu: MD University of Pennsylvania 1956, PhD surgery University of Minnesota 1964. [Debus, Allen G., *World Who's Who in Science: a biographical dictionary of notable scientists from antiquity to the present*. Chicago: Marquis-Who's Who, Inc., 1968, p. 8.]

AKERMAN, OLIVE - alive 1850; res: Portsmouth, Rockingham Co NH. [See page 48 of the original census for full record.] [Jackson, Ronald Vern and Gary Ronald Teeples, *New Hampshire 1850 Index Census*. Bountiful: Accelerated Indexing Systems, Inc., 1978, p. 3.]

AKERMAN, OLIVER - alive 1921; edu: 8th grade student at Hampton Jr High in 1921. [Randall, Peter Evans, *Hampton, a century of town and beach, 1888-1988.* Portsmouth: Peter E. Randall, Publisher, 1989, p. 757. See photograph on p. 757.]

ACKERMAN, OLIVER H - alive 1960; occ: letter carrier; res: Lincoln Ave, Hampton NH. [----, *Exeter, Brentwood, East Kingston, Greenland, Kensington, Newfield, and Stratham Directory, 1960.* New Haven: The Price & Lee Co., 1960, p. 472.]

AKERMAN, OLIVER H - alive 1960; occ: letter carrier; res: house on Brown Rd RD 1, Hampton NH. [----, *Exeter, Brentwood, East Kingston, Greenland, Kensington, Newfield, and Stratham Directory, 1960.* New Haven: The Price & Lee Co., 1960, p. 473.]

-----

The following two entries are probably the same man.

AKERMAN, OLIVER O - alive 1935; occ: employee at Applecrest Farm; res: boarded with C I Akerman in Hampton Falls NH. [Is this Charles I Akerman, d1935?] [Crowley & Lunt, *Exeter, Hampton, & N. H. Coast Directory.* Beverly: Crowley & Lunt, Publishers, 1935, p. 398.]

AKERMAN, OLIVER O - alive 1941; m Gertrude P ----; occ: employee at Applecrest Farm; res: house on Depot Rd RFD in Hampton Falls NH. [Crowley & Lunt, *Exeter, Hampton, & N. H. Coast Directory.* Beverly: Crowley & Lunt, Publishers, 1941, p. 420.]

-----

ACKERMAN, OREN - alive 1886; res: road 9 in Alexandria (Grafton Co) NH; occ: farmer with his father. [Child, Hamilton, *Business Directory of Grafton County, N. H., 1885-1886.* Syracuse: The Syracuse Journal Company, Printers and Binders, c1886, p. 4.]

ACKERMAN, OSCAR - alive 1917; mil: register #2350 for World War I draft. [Mendocino Coast Genealogical Society, *Births, Deaths and Marriages on California's Mendocino Coast: Volume Two, 1910-1919.* Bowie: Heritage Books, Inc., 1997, p. 243.]

ACKERMAN, OSCAR - alive 1947; m Mary Olivia Johnson b 3 Aug 1891 Finland, arrived in CA in 1903, d 8 May 1947 in the Willits Hospital, bur: Rose Memorial; ch: Ellen m ---- Loo, Milda m ---- Holmes; res: Fort Bragg. Death of Mary Olivia Ackerman reported in the *Advocate* 14 May 1947. [Mendocino Coast Genealogical Society, *Births, Deaths and Marriages on California's Mendocino Coast, Volume Five, 1940-1949.* Bowie: Heritage Books, Inc., 1999. p. 57]

ACKERMAN, PATIENCE COMFORT - b1834; m Samuel E Roberts b1826 Rochester NH, d 16 Aug 1895. [Jacobsen, Thomas A., *The Robertses of Northern New England.* Bowie: Heritage Books, Inc., 1995, p. 163.]

AKERMAN, PATRICIA W - alive 1941; m [Lincoln H Akerman ?]; occ: Bradford Shoe Co; res: house on Exeter Rd, Hampton NH. [Crowley & Lunt, *Exeter, Hampton, & N. H. Coast Directory.* Beverly: Crowley & Lunt, Publishers, 1941, p. 324.]

ACKERMANN, PATRICK - occ: director at "Universite de Clermont-Ferrand II/Universite Blaise Pascal, Unit of Technology;" res: FR. [----, *Who's Who in Science in Europe: a biographical guide to science, technology, agriculture, and medicine, 9th ed., Volume 1.* London: Cartermill Publishing, 1995, p. 5.]

ACKERMAN, PAUL - alive 1810; ch: Susan b1810 qv. [Correspondence dated August 2000 from Marian Trump. She cites her source as the James C. & Katie Ann Feltz Bible.]

ACKERMAN, PAUL - m Diane ---- alive 1999 (poet & author).[120] This is probably the Diane Ackerman b1948; occ: author of nonfiction.[121] This is probably the Diane Fink b1948 who m ---- Ackerman.[122]

ACKERMANN, PAUL KURT - m1945 ----; res: Cambridge MA; edu: AB Colgate 1945, Hervey scholar at Columbia 1945 & MA 1947, Olmstead travel fellow at Harvard 1952 & PhD 1953; occ:

---

[120] Ackerman, Diane, *Deep Play* (New York: Random House, 1999), p. 117.
[121] Havlice, Patricia Pate, *Index to Literary Biography:first supplement. Volume I: A-K* (Metuchen: The Scarecrow Press, Inc., 1983), p. 5.
[122] Bailey, Martha J., *American Women in Science 1950 to the Present* (Santa Barbara: ABC-CLIO, 1998), p. 1.

assistant professor 1953- . [Cattell, Jaques, *Directory of American Scholars: a biographical directory, 3rd edition*. New York: R. R. Bowker Company, 1957, p. 2.]

AKERMAN, PETER - bc1748 [based on age at death]; dc 5 Jun 1832 Dover, age 84y. "A Revolutionary pensioner." [Chipman, Scott Lee, *New England Vital Records from the "Exeter News-Letter," 1831-1840*. Camden: Picton Press, 1993, p. 45.]

AKERMAN, PETER - bc1750 [based on his age in 1789]; mil: pension list dated Nov 1789 gives his age as 39, notes that he served in the 3rd NH & was unfit for duty due to a stiff elbow, & was apparently to receive 20 shillings. [Hammond, Isaac W., *The State of New Hampshire. Rolls and Documents Relating to Soldiers in the Revolutionary War, with an appendix, embracing some French and Indian War rolls. Volume III of the War Rolls. Volume XVI of the Series*. Manchester: John B. Clarke, Public Printer, 1887, p. 345.]

AKERMAN, PETER - alive 1775; mil: signed his mark to acknowledge receipt of $4.00 for the regimental coat promised by the colony of NH, while in Capt Elkins' co in Col Poor's regiment. [Hammond, Isaac W., *The State of New Hampshire. Rolls of the Soldiers in the Revolutionary War, 1775, to May, 1777: with an appendix, embracing diaries of Lieut. Jonathan Burton. Volume I of the War Rolls. Volume XIV of the Series*. Concord: Parsons B. Cogswell, State Printer, 1885, p. 191, 192.]

ACKERMAN, PETER - alive 1777; m ----; ch: 4; pol: Tory. "Peter Ackerman, who had disappeared into the British lines in the spring of 1777, also was with the Tappan refugees, having come out with Grey's expedition to act as pilot and guide to the troops. He was now taking advantage of the situation to bring off his wife and four children and his few belongings." [Leiby, Adrian C., *The Revolutionary War in the Hackensack Valley: the Jersey Dutch and the neutral ground, 1775-1783*. New Brunswick: Rutgers University Press, 1962, p. 179.]

AKERMAN, PETER - alive 1780; mil: enlisted 8 Jul 1780 as a corporal in Capt Daniel Jewell's co in Col Thomas Bartlet's regiment of militia raised by NH for the defense of West Point in 1780. He was to be paid at 147 pounds 8 shillings per month & was discharged

25 Oct 1780. [Hammond, Isaac W., *The State of New Hampshire. Rolls and Documents Relating to Soldiers in the Revolutionary War, with an appendix, embracing some French and Indian War rolls. Volume III of the War Rolls. Volume XVI of the Series.* Manchester: John B Clarke, Public Printer, 1887, p. 109.]

ACKERMAN, PETER - alive 1782; res: parish of Rye. His tax rate for 1782, in the parish of Rye, was 6 shillings. [Parsons, Langdon B., *History of the Town of Rye, New Hampshire, from its discovery and settlement to December 31, 1903.* ----: ----, 1905. Facsimile reprint Bowie: Heritage Books, Inc., 1992, p. 143, 145.]

AKERMAN, PETER - alive 1785; signed a petition regarding mil grievances on 9 Feb 1785; res: Rye. "The Petition of the Inhabitants of the Parish of Rye Humbly shews - That your Petitioners by Virtue of an Act passed the last Session of the General Assembly were dissolved from their Connection with the first Regt in this State and Joined with the Regt Commanded by Coll Moulton which is very inconvenient to the Town in many respects...." [Hammond, Isaac W., *Town Papers. Documents Relating to Towns in New Hampshire, New London to Wolfeborough, with an appendix, embracing some docuemnts, interesting and valuable, not heretofore published, including the census of New Hampshire of 1790 in detail. Volume XIII.* Concord: Parsons B. Cogswell, State Printer, 1884, p. 371.]

ACKERMAN, PETER - alive 1785; ch: John bapt 20 Nov 1785, Joseph bapt Aug 1782, Peter bapt Aug 1782, Phineas bapt 22 Jun 1783. [Hosier, Kathleen E., *Vital Records of Rye New Hampshire: a transcript of the births, baptisms, marriages, and deaths in this town to the year 1890.* Bowie: Heritage Books, Inc., 1992, p. 34.]

AKERMAN, PETER - alive 1788; mil: pay roll of pensioners states that he received 63.13.4 on 10 Aug 1785 & 24.0.0 on 7 Nov 1788 & 12.0.0 on 1 Jan 1789. [Hammond, Isaac W., *The State of New Hampshire. Rolls and Documents Relating to Soldiers in the Revolutionary War, with an appendix, embracing some French and Indian War rolls. Volume III of the War Rolls. Volume XVI of the Series.* Manchester: John B. Clarke, Public Printer, 1887, p. 341, 343.]

AKERMAN, PETER - alive 1787; mil: private in US Infantry; res: Strafford Co. Placed on invalid pension roll on 7 Nov 1787 with an allowance of [$?]40.00 to commence 31 Jul 1786 persuant to the law of 7 Jun 1785. [Batchellor, Albert Stillman, *Miscellaneous Revolutionary Documents of New Hampshire including the association test, the pension rolls, and other important papers. Vol. 30.* Manchester: The John B. Clarke Co., 1910, p. 218.]

ACREMAN, PETER - alive 1790; res: Epsom Town NH. Free white males of 16y & upwards, including heads of families = 1. Free white males under 16y = 4. Free white females, including heads of families = 2. [----, *Heads of Families at the First Census of the United States Taken in the Year 1790: New Hampshire.* Washington: Government Printing Office, 1907. Reprint Baltimore: Genealogical Publishing Company, 1966, p. 66.]

AKERMAN, PETER - alive 1798; res: Rochester, Strafford Co NH. Signed petition for incorporation of North-West Parish on 6 Jun 1798. The petition was granted on 28 Nov 1798 & the "west parish was set off and incorporated into a town by the name of Famington." [Hammond, Isaac W., *Town Papers. Documents Relating to Towns in New Hampshire, New London to Wolfeborough, with an appendix, embracing some docuemnts, interesting and valuable, not heretofore published, including the census of New Hampshire of 1790 in detail. Volume XIII.* Concord: Parsons B. Cogswell, State Printer, 1884, p. 348.]

ACREMAN, PETER - alive 1800; res: Portsmouth. Free white males under 10y = 1, 10-16y = 1, 16-26y (including heads of households) = 0, 26-45y (including heads of households) = 0, 45y & upwards (including heads of households) = 1. Free white females under 10y = 1, 10-16y = 1, 16-26y (including heads of households) = 0, 26-45y (including heads of households) = 1, 45y & upwards (including heads of households) = 0. [----, *Heads of Families at the Second Census of the United States Taken in the Year 1800: New Hampshire.* Madison: John Brooks Threlfall, 1973, p. 162.]

ACKERMAN, PETER - alive 1824; m Bessie Cate; ch: Hannah O b 28 May 1824 qv, Rachel C alive 1868 qv. [Musgrove, R. W., *History of the Town of Bristol, New Hampshire.* ----: Richard W. Musgrove, 1904. Reprint with a new foreword by Charles E. Greenwood,

Somersworth: New Hampshire Publishing Company, 1976, p. 400 (Volume II).]

ACKERMAN, PETER - alive 1845. Served as bondsman for James Scott & Verva Stemort in 1845. [McClure, Paul, *Early Marriages in Bath County, Kentucky: bonds 1811-1850 and returns 1811-1852.* Bowie: Heritage Books, Inc., 1994, p. 127.]

ACKERMANN, PETER - bc1834 [based on his age of 36 in the 1870 census] Prussia; s/o foreign-born parents; w Mary --- b Switzerland (age 33 in 1870); ch: Peter b IL & age 9 in 1870, Christian b IL & age 5 in 1870, Otto b IL & age 3 in 1870, Mary b Nov 1869 (age 6m in 1870); occ: farmer with real estate valued at 4350 & personal property valued at 500; res: Marine, Madison Co IL. He & his family were family #54 in dwelling #53. Other Ackermanns living with this family were Catherine b Prussia, age 42 in 1870, & William b Prussia, age 7 in 1870. Race for all residents was white. [This family appears on page 8 of the original census.] [Wasser, Elsie M., "1870 Census - United States," *The Stalker*, Vol. 20 #1 (Spring 2000), p. 16.]

ACKERMANN, PETER - alive 1882; age 39; res: GE. Immigrated through Antwerp & arrived at NY City on 7 Oct 1882. Made his declaration of intention on 11 Sep 1889 but no naturalization record is listed. [Hughes, Lois E., *Hamilton County, Ohio, Citizenship Record Abstracts, 1837-1916.* Bowie: Heritage Books, Inc., 1991, p. 1.]

ACKERMAN, PETER A - alive 1836; m Bridget Ackerman; ch: Lea b 20 Apr 1836 & bapt 19 Jun 1836, James b 10 Oct 1838 & bapt 18 Nov 1838,[123] William b 22 Mar 1842 & bapt 15 May 1842.[124]

ACHUMAN/ACKERMAN, PETER A - alive 1842; res: TX; mil: in Capt Ewing Cameron's Company A when it surrendered at Mier on 26 Dec 1842, he was liberated on 16 Sep 1844. [----, "1842 Muster Rolls," *The Genealogical Record*, Vol. XL #3 (September 1998), p. 2.]

---

[123] Durie, Howard I., "Pascack Reformed Dutch Church Baptisms 1814-1850," *The American Genealogist*, Vol. 48 #1, p. 56, 57.
[124] Durie, Howard I., "Pascack Reformed Dutch Church Baptisms 1814-1850," *The American Genealogist*, Vol. 48 #2, p. 113.

ACKERMAN PETER H - m Elizabeth Demarest; ch: Dean d 24 Feb 1980. [Hunt, James K. Jr., *Hampton Vital Records and Genealogy, 1889-1986.* Portsmouth: Peter E. Randall, Publisher, 1988, p. 426.]

AKERMAN, PHEBE - bapt 1 Sep 1717 North Church, Portsmouth NH. [Baptized as an adult?] [Tibbetts, Charles W., *The New Hampshire Genealogical Record. An illustrated quarterly magazine devoted to genealogy, history and biography. Vol. IV, January 1907 - October 1907.* Dover: Charles W. Tibbetts, 1907. Facsimile reprint Bowie: Heritage Books, Inc., 1988, p. 101.]

AKERMAN, PHEBE - alive 1850; res: Portsmouth, Rockingham Co NH. [See page 82 of the original census for full record.] [Jackson, Ronald Vern and Gary Ronald Teeples, *New Hampshire 1850 Index Census.* Bountiful: Accelerated Indexing Systems, Inc., 1978, p. 3.]

ACKERMAN, PHILLIP - d "2-17 1895." [Correspondence dated 13 Sep. 2000 from Gail R. Thomas. He cites his source as the *Kansas City Genealogist*, April 1963; the journal includes a note that this family arrived from Bavaria.]

ACKERMAN, PHINEAS W - alive 1886; m Elizabeth Bailey, d/o Daniel Bailey & Susan Chesley; ch: Charles O, Lydia O Patten; res: road 19 in Alexandria NH.[125] Occ: shoemaker & farmer with 90 acres, 10 head of cattle, 12 sheep, 300 sugar trees.[126]

ACKERMAN, PHYLLIS - m ----; res: Cornwall Bridge CT; edu: BL CA 1914 & MA 1915 & PhD (philosophy) 1917; occ: prof cultural history, Asia Institute, NY City 1940- . [Cattell, Jaques, *Directory of American Scholars: a biographical directory, 3rd edition.* New York: R. R. Bowker Company, 1957, p. 2.]

AKERMAN, PRISCILLA A - b 26 Nov 1906; d/o Charles I Akerman & Mary M McConnell; m 25 Dec 1930 Ralph W Pratt b Ipswich MA. [Hunt, James K. Jr., *Hampton Vital Records and Genealogy, 1889-1986.* Portsmouth: Peter E. Randall, Publisher, 1988, p. 2.]

---

[125] Child, Hamilton, *Gazetteer of Grafton County, N. H., 1709-1886* (Syracuse: The Syracuse Journal Company, Printers and Binders, 1886), p. 119.
[126] Child, Hamilton, *Business Directory of Grafton County, N. H., 1885-1886* (Syracuse: The Syracuse Journal Company, Printers and Binders, c1886), p. 4.

ACKERMAN, PRUDENCE J - d/o Richard Ackerman & Caroline ---; m 31 Oct 1869 in Caton NY to Eli Beeman. [Jackson, Mary S. and Edward F. Jackson, *Marriage Notices from Steuben County, New York, Newspapers, 1797-1884.* Bowie: Heritage Books, Inc., 1998, p. 393.]

ACKERMANN, R HERBERT - alive 1925; m Isabelle Trepagnier; ch: Weston Wilbur b 15 Jun 1925 qv. [Debus, Allen G., *World Who's Who in Science: a biographical dictionary of notable scientists from antiquity to the present.* Chicago: Marquis-Who's Who, Inc., 1968, p. 9.]

ACKERMAN, R T - possible s/o Valentine Ackerman & Elizabeth Spurgeon; m1 ----; m2 ----; m3 Maggie J Berkley. [Correspondence dated 13 Sep. 2000 from Gail R. Thomas. See Descendants of John Ackerman.]

AKERMAN, RACHEL - m 28 Mar 1808 in First Congregational Church, Rochester NH to Ephraim Kimball; res: Farmington. [Tibbetts, Charles W., *The New Hampshire Genealogical Record. An illustrated quarterly magazine devoted to genealogy, history and biography. Vol. V, January 1908 - October 1908.* Dover: Charles W. Tibbetts, 1908. Facsimile reprint Bowie: Heritage Books, Inc., 1988, p. 118.]

AKERMAN, RACHEL - alive 1850; res: Alexandr, Grafton Co NH. [See page 151 of the original census for full record.] [Jackson, Ronald Vern and Gary Ronald Teeples, *New Hampshire 1850 Index Census.* Bountiful: Accelerated Indexing Systems, Inc., 1978, p. 3.]

ACKERMAN, RACHEL C - alive 1868; d/o Peter Ackerman & Bessie Cate; m1 Jonathan E Sleeper b 16 Feb 1813, s/o Nathan Sleeper & ----, d 10 May 1868 age "55-2-24;" m2 Dimond G Wells, of Rumney. [Musgrove, R. W., *History of the Town of Bristol, New Hampshire.* ----: Richard W. Musgrove, 1904. Reprint with a new foreword by Charles E. Greenwood, Somersworth: New Hampshire Publishing Company, 1976, p. 400 (Volume II).]

ACKERMAN, RALPH EMIL - b 21 Aug 1921 NY City; s/o Meyer H Ackerman & Frieda Broadman; m 13 mar 1945 Eileen E Dotta; occ: psychology educator; edu: BS Ed Ohio University 1948 & M Ed

1949, PhD University of Connecticut 1960; pol: Republican; res: Edinboro PA. [----, *Who's Who in Frontier Science and Technology.* Chicago: Marquis Who's Who, Inc., 1984, p. 3.]

ACKERMAN, RAYMOND R SR - bc1898 [based on age at death]; d 28 Jan 1967 Nashua NH, age 69. [Nash, Gerald Q. et al, *The Vital Records of Hudson, New Hampshire, 1734-1985.* Bowie: Heritage Books, Inc., 1997, p. 492.]

AKERMAN, RICHARD - alive 1346. Commission of oyer and terminer "on complaint by the said William [de Shareshull] that Thomas, bishop of Ely,... Richard Akerman,... and others laid seige to him at Dikelburgh and Norwich and the suburb of that city and threatened him with mutilation of his members and incarceration of his body, so that he dared not go out to pursue his trade by which he got food for himself and his household, carried away his goods and assaulted his men and servants whereby he lost their service for a great time." Dated 18 Sep 1346, Westminster. [---, *Calendar of the Patent Rolls... Edward III. Vol. VII. A.D. 1345-1348.* ----: ----, 1903. Reprint Germany: Kraus Reprint, 1971, p. 188.]

AKERMAN, RICHARD - alive 1346. "Commission of oyer and terminer to William de Thorpe..., on complaint by Richard Spynk, citizen of Norwich, that whereas the king by letters patent lately took him, his men and servants and goods, under his special protection, Thomas, bishop of Ely,... Richard Akerman,... and others beseiged him at Norwich while so under the king's protection, threatening him with incarceration of his body...." Dated 6 Dec 1346, Tower of London. [---, *Calendar of the Patent Rolls... Edward III. Vol. VII. A.D. 1345-1348.* ----: ----, 1903. Reprint Germany: Kraus Reprint, 1971, p. 237.]

ACREMAN, RICHARD - alive 1452. "Inspeximus and confirmation of one part of certain indentures [English] made between Master Adrian Spyerinar alias Sprynker clerk, born in Theutonia, of the one part, and [two men plus] Richard Acreman of London and [one man], of the other part, dated 3 June, 30 Henry VI, wherein Adrian grants to the others at farm a part of the mine of Beerferers, to wit, all the mineral ground called 'olde shaftis' between the middle of 'Wittesham Doune' on the South and a water coming from 'Dammewell' and going down to the sea on the north, for twelve years, they paying to the king every tenth 'bolle' of ore with the 'slagges' and 'dedwarke,' which bolls should be roasted, molten and purified at their costs, and the king shall have all metal thereof; and Adrian shall have all the 'testwerk' and 'afterwash'." Dated 14 Aug 1452, Westminster. [----, *Calendar of the Patent Rolls... Henry VI. Vol. V. A.D. 1446-1452.* ----: ----, 1909. Reprint Germany: Kraus Reprint, 1971, p. 569.]

ACREMAN, RICHARD - alive 1453. "Inspeximus and confirmaiton of one part of certain indentures [English] made between Master Adrian Speryne alias Sprinker, clerk,... of the one part,and Richard Acreman and Robert Glover of the other part, dated 1 December, 31 Henry VI, wherein Adrian grants to the others at farm a part of the mine of Berefereris, to wit, 'the Sumpte Shaft' and 'the high north shaft' with all the shafts or ground between the same...; to hold for twelve years, paying to the king every tenth 'bolle' of ore with the 'slagges' and 'dedwarke,' which bolls should be roasted, molten and purified at their costs, and the king shall have all metal thereof; and Adrian shall have all the 'testwerk' and 'afterwash'." [----, *Calendar of the Patent Rolls... Henry VI. Vol. VI. A.D. 1452-1461.* ----: ----, 1910. Reprint Germany: Kraus Reprint, 1971, p. 47.]

ACKERMAN, RICHARD - alive 1869; m Caroline ----; ch: Prudence J m 31 Oct 1869 qv. [Jackson, Mary S. and Edward F. Jackson, *Marriage Notices from Steuben County, New York, Newspapers, 1797-1884.* Bowie: Heriage Books, Inc., 1998, p. 393.]

AKERMAN, ROBERT - [dc1396?]. "Pardon to Walter Taillour of Hacche for the death of Robert Akerman, killed on Monday the eve of the Purification in the seventh year." [----, *Calendar of the Patent Rolls... Richard II. Vol. V. A.D. 1391-1396.* ----: ----, 1905. Reprint Germany: Kraus Reprint, 1971, p. 701.]

AKERMAN, ROBERT - alive 1408. "To the sheriffs of London. Writ of supersedeas omnino in respect of taking a second time of William Preston chaplain any security for keeping the peace at suit of Henry Sturmer, and order by mainprise of... Robert Akerman 'wolman'... of London, to set him free, if taken." Dated 20 Oct 1408, Westminster. [It is unclear which of the five men named in the full record should be set free if taken.] [----, *Calendar of the Close Rolls... Henry IV. Vol. III. A.D. 1405-1409.* ----: ----, 1931. Reprint Germany: Kraus Reprint, 1971, p. 465.]

ACREMAN, ROBERT - alive 1410. "To the sheriffs of London. Writ of supersedeas omnino, by mainprise of...Robert Acreman 'wolman'...of London, and upon his own undertaking, in respect of taking Thomas Larke any security for keeping the peace at suit of John Sylke 'barbour'...." Dated 6 Jun 1410. [It is unclear which of the three man named in the full record did his own undertaking.] [----, *Calendar of the Close Rolls... Henry IV. Vol. IV. A.D. 1409-1413.* ----: ----, 1932. Reprint Germany: Kraus Reprint, 1971, p. 113.]

ACREMAN, ROBERT - alive 1430; due 60 shillings from John Kympton of London 10 May 1430. [----, *Calendar of the Patent Rolls...Henry VI. Vol. II. A.D. 1429-1436.* ----: ----, 1907. Reprint Germany: Kraus Reprint, 1971, p. 19.]

ACREMAN, ROBERT - res: London 1439; occ: "wooleman." [----, *Calendar of the Patent Rolls...Henry VI. Vol. III. A.D. 1436-1441.* ----: ----, 1907. Reprint Germany: Kraus Reprint, 1971, p. 284.]

ACREMAN, ROBERT - alive 1442. "...Robert Acreman of London, merchant, staying in the parish of St. Denys in Langburn ward...." Dated 8 Sep 1442, Westminster. [He was apparently one of several men responsible for helping Simon Symond pay his fine of 166 pounds 13 shillings 4 pence to the king but the king pardoned them 8 Sep 1442.] [----, *Calendar of the Patent Rolls... Henry VI. Vol. IV. A.D. 1441-1446.* ----: ----, 1908. Reprint Germany: Kraus Reprint, 1971, p. 114.]

ACKERMANN, ROBERT - alive 1700; m Alice ----; ch: Katherine chr 8 Jan 1700 at Westminster (St Martin in the Fields). [Correspondence (undated) from Bob G.[?], courtesy of Robert H. Ackerman, 22 Mar. 2000.]

AKERMAN, ROBERT - alive 1707; m Alice - ch: Margaret chr 16 Mar 1707 at St Martin in the Fields (Westminster). [Correspondence (undated) from Bob G.[?], courtesy of Robert H. Ackerman, 22 Mar. 2000.]

AKERMAN, ROBERT - alive 1747; s/o John Akerman; res: Bromham, Wilts[hire] EN; ch: John b1747 qv. [Burke, Bernard, *A Genealogical and Heraldic History of the Colonial Gentry.*

Baltimore: Genealogical Publishing Company, 1970, p. 779.]

AUKERMAN, ROBERT - mil: PFC Army; d 5 Jul 1950, killed in action. [----, "Korean Casualties List, Ohio Soldiers," *The Quest*, Vol. 16 #6 (Nov.-Dec. 1999), p. 96.]

ACKERMAN, ROBERT HAROLD - b 1 Jun 1935 NY City; s/o Myron Ackerman & Leona Auerbach; occ: neuroscientist, neurologist/neuroradiologist; edu: BA in history from Brown University 1957, MD University of Rochester 1964; res: Gloucester MA. [----, *Who's Who in Frontier Science and Technology*. Chicago: Marquis Who's Who, Inc., 1984, p. 3, 4.]

ACKERMAN, ROMULUS ALEXANDER - b 31 Jan 1821 Waughtown, Stokes Co NC; s/o Johannes Ackerman & Anna Johanna Spaugh; m1851 Serena Rebecca Sipes; d 1 Jun 1906. [Tesh, Peggy J., "Heinrich Peter Tesch and His Descendants," *The Forsyth County Genealogical Society Journal*, Vol. XVII #1 (Fall 1998), p. 51]

ACKERMAN, ROSA G - bc1883 [based on age at death]; d/o F Ackerman & L J Ackerman; d 1 Jul 1893, age 10y. "She is not dead but sleepeth." [James Ackerman also appears on the stone but without any other information.] [Weissgerber, J. G., "St. Vrain Church of the Brethren Cemetery Records: Hygiene, Boulder County, Colorado," *Orange County, California, Genealogical Society Quarterly*, Vol. 36 #1 (April 1999), p. 48.]

ACKERMAN, ROY ALAN - b 9 Sep 1951 Brooklyn; s/o Jack Ackerman & Estelle Kuchlik; m ----; ch: Shanna Avrah; occ: biochemical engineer, research corp executive; edu: PhD University of Virginia 1984. [----, *Who's Who in Frontier Science and Technology*. Chicago: Marquis Who's Who, Inc., 1984, p. 4.]

AKERMAN, RUTH - bc1798 NH [based on her age of 62y in the 1860 census]; res: Hampton Falls. According to the 1860 census, she was family #70 in dwelling #61 & had real estate valued at 300 & a personal estate valued at 50. She had living with her Eunice E b NH & age 22, Ellen [J? or F?] b NH & age 19, Isachar b NH & age 24 (a shoemaker). [1860 Census - New Hampshire - Rockingham (part), p. 80.]

AKERMAN, SALOME - alive 1784; d/o Mark Akerman & ----. In 1784, she was "a minor under 14" and Walter Akerman was assigned as her guardian. [Evans, Helen F., *Abstracts of the Probate Records of Rockingham County, New Hampshire, 1771-1799, Volume 1.* Bowie: Heritage Books, Inc., 2000, p. 8.]

AKERMAN, SAMUEL - owned a gallery pew in North Church. [Brewster, Charles W., *Rambles About Portsmouth: first series.* ----: Charles W. Brewster, 1859. Facsimile reprint of second edition published 1873 Somersworth: New Hampshire Publishing Company, 1971, p. 330.]

AKERMAN, SAMUEL - m Amy ---- bc1780 [based on age at death], dc 1 Jun 1846 Portsmouth, age 66. [Chipman, Scott Lee, *New England Vital Records from the "Exeter News-Letter," 1841-1846.* Camden: Picton Press, 1993, p. 177.]

AKERMAN, SAMUEL - bc1771 [based on age at death]; dc 11 Jan 1847 Portsmouth, age 76. [Chipman, Scott Lee, *New England Vital Records from the "Exeter News-Letter," 1847-1852.* Camden: Picton Press, 1994, p. 1.]

AKERMAN, SAMUEL - occ: printer; dc 11 May 1805 Philadelphia, cause: small pox. [Chipman, Scott Lee, *Genealogical Abstracts from Early new Hampshire Newspapers, Vol. 1.* Bowie: Heritage Books, Inc., 2000, p. 193.]

AKERMAN, SAMUEL - alive 1800; res: Portsmouth. Free white males under 10y = 0, 10-16y = 0, 16-26y (including heads of households) = 1, 26-45y (including heads of households) = 0, 45y & upwards (including heads of households) = 0. Free white females under 10y = 1, 10-16y = 0, 16-26y (including heads of households) = 1, 26-45y (including heads of households) = 0, 45y & upwards (including heads of households) = 0. [----, *Heads of Families at the Second Census of the United States Taken in the Year 1800: New Hampshire.* Madison: John Brooks Threlfall, 1973, p. 144.]

ACKERMAN, SAMUEL - bc1829 [based on age at death] MA; d 12 Aug 1900 Ukiah, age 71y 4m. [Mendocino Coast Genealogical Society, *Births, Deaths and Marriages on California's Mendocino*

*Coast: Volume One, 1889-1909.* Bowie: Heritage Books, Inc., 1995, p. 71.]

ACREMAN, SARA - alive 1695. Sister-in-law of Edward Melcher, who, in his will, gave Sara Acreman and Walter Windsor "the Liberty to dwell where they now dwell during theire Naturall Lives." [Metcalf, Henry Harrison, *Probate Records of the Province of New Hampshire, Volume 1: 1635-1717. State papers series, Volume 31.* Concord: Rumford Printing Co., 1907. Facsimile reprint Bowie: Heritage Books, Inc., 1989, p. 410.]

ACKERMAN, SARA/ZARA - alive 1737; m Hendryck Sikels/Hendrik Siggels/Hendrick Siggels/Hendrik Sikkels/Hendrik Sickkels.[127] This is probably the same Sara Ackerman - m Hendrick Sikels; bur: 25 Jun 1736.[128]

AKERMAN, SARAH - bapt 14 Jun 1719. [Baptized as an adult?] [Tibbetts, Charles W., *The New Hampshire Genealogical Record. An illustrated quarterly magazine devoted to genealogy, history and biography. Vol. IV, January 1907 - October 1907.* Dover: Charles W. Tibbetts, 1907. Facsimile reprint Bowie: Heritage Books, Inc., 1988, p. 103.]

AKERMAN, SARAH - alive 1850; res: Portsmouth, Rockingham Co NH. [See page 48 of the original census for full record.] [Jackson, Ronald Vern and Gary Ronald Teeples, *New Hampshire 1850 Index Census.* Bountiful: Accelerated Indexing Systems, Inc., 1978, p. 3.]

AKERMAN, SARAH A - mc 17 Aug 1846 William Whidden of Portsmouth; res: Portsmouth. [Chipman, Scott Lee, *New England Vital Records from the "Exeter News-Letter," 1841-1846.* Camden: Picton Press, 1993, p. 184.]

---

[127] Versteeg, Dingman and Thomas E. Vermilye, Jr., *Bergen Records. Records of the Reformed Protestant Dutch Church of Bergen in New Jersey, 1666 to 1788* (Originally published in the *Year Book of the Holland Society of New York,* 1913. Reprint Baltimore: Clearfield Publishing Co., Inc., 1990), p. 68, 69, 72, 74, 75.
[128] Versteeg, Dingman and Thomas E. Vermilye, Jr., *Bergen Records. Records of the Reformed Protestant Dutch Church of Bergen in New Jersey, 1666 to 1788* (Originally published in the *Year Book of the Holland Society of New York,* 1915. Reprint Baltimore: Clearfield Publishing Co., Inc., 1990), p. 38.

AKERMAN, SHEM - alive 1850; res: Alexandr, Grafton Co NH. [See page 156 of the original census for full record.] [Jackson, Ronald Vern and Gary Ronald Teeples, *New Hampshire 1850 Index Census*. Bountiful: Accelerated Indexing Systems, Inc., 1978, p. 3.]

AUKERMAN, SHIRLEY - alive 1905; edu: student at Logan Co High School 1905-1906. [----, "Alphabetical Roll of Students [attending] Logan County High School for the School Year 1905-06," *Oklahoma Genealogical Society Quarterly*, Vol. 45 #2 (2000), p. 68.]

ACKERMAN, SIGRUD - alive 1939 or earlier; ch: Lilo Karjamaki alive 1939 qv; res: Fort Bragg. [Mendocino Coast Genealogical Society, *Births, Deaths and Marriages on California's Mendocino Coast, Volume Four, 1930-1939*. Bowie: Heritage Books, Inc., 1998. p. 256]

AKERMAN, SIMEON - alive 1776; signed Association Test of 1776 in which he agreed to "oppose the Hostile Proceedings of the British Fleets, and Armies, against the United American Colonies." [Brewster, Charles W., *Rambles About Portsmouth: first series*. ----: Charles W. Brewster, 1859. Facsimile reprint of second edition published 1873 Somersworth: New Hampshire Publishing Company, 1971, p. 215.]

AKERMAN, SIMEON - alive 1776; res: Portsmouth. [Batchellor, Albert Stillman, *Miscellaneous Revolutionary Documents of New Hampshire including the association test, the pension rolls, and other important papers. Vol. 30*. Manchester: The John B. Clarke Co., 1910, p. 117.]

AKERMAN, SIMEON - bc1779 [based on age at death]; d 13 Apr 1850 Portsmouth, age 71. [Chipman, Scott Lee, *New England Vital Records from the "Exeter News-Letter," 1847-1852*. Camden: Picton Press, 1994, p. 119.]

AKARMAN, SIMEON - alive 1783; res: Portsmouth; occ: gentleman. [Evans, Helen F., *Abstracts of the Probate Records of Rockingham County, New Hampshire, 1771-1799*. Bowie: Heritage Books, Inc., 2000, p. 223.]

AKERMAN, SIMEON - alive 1790; res: Portsmouth Town NH. Free white males of 16y & upwards, including heads of families = 1. Free white males under 16y = 1. Free white females, including heads of families = 2. [----, *Heads of Families at the First Census of the United States Taken in the Year 1790: New Hampshire.* Washington: Government Printing Office, 1907. Reprint Baltimore: Genealogical Publishing Company, 1966, p. 78.]

AKERMAN, SIMEON - alive 1850; res: Farmington, Strafford Co NH. [See page 311 of the original census for full record.] [Jackson, Ronald Vern and Gary Ronald Teeples, *New Hampshire 1850 Index Census.* Bountiful: Accelerated Indexing Systems, Inc., 1978, p. 3.]

ACKERMAN, SOL - b1903; d 15 May 1973. [Cohen, Edward A. & Lewis Goldfarb, *Jewish Cemeteries of Hartford, Connecticut, Volume 1.* Bowie: Heritage Books, Inc., 1995, p. 1.]

ACKERMAN, SOPHIA - b 23 Jan 1837 Salem, Stokes Co NC; d/o Johannes Ackerman & Anna Johanna Spaugh; d 8 Feb 1863. [Death date may be 1817, if children are in birth order.] [Tesh, Peggy J., "Heinrich Peter Tesch and His Descendants," *The Forsyth County Genealogical Society Journal,* vol. XVII #1, Fall 1998, p. 51]

ACKERMAN, STEPH - alive 1700. As master of a coasting vessel or lumber carrier, signed a petition. [Bouton, Nathaniel, *Provincial Papers. Documents and Records Relating to the Province of New-Hampshire, from 1692 to 1722: being part II. of papers relating to that period. Containing the "Journal of the Coucil and General Assembly." Volume III.* Manchester: John B. Clarke, State Printer, 1869, p. 104.]

AKERMAN, SUPPLY JACKSON - bapt 19 Apr 1795 North Church, Portsmouth NH; s/o Joseph Akerman Jr & ----.[129] This may be the Supply J Akerman who was a scholar at Master Taft's school sometime between 1804 & 1814.[130]

---

[129] Tibbetts, Charles W., *The New Hampshire Genealogical Record. An illustrated quarterly magazine devoted to genealogy, history and biography. Vol. VII, January 1910 - April 1910.* (Dover: Charles W. Tibbetts, 1910. Facsimile reprint Bowie: Heritage Books, Inc., 1988), p. 80.

[130] Brewster, Charles W., *Rambles About Portsmouth: second series* (----: Lewis W. Brewster, 1869. Facsimile reprint Somersworth: New Hampshire Publishing Company, 1972), p. 319.

ACKERMAN, SUSAN - b1810; d/o Paul Ackerman & ----; m Robert Lusk b 2 Dec 1813, d 21 Aug 1901; d 27 Oct 1876. [Correspondence dated August 2000 from Marian Trump. She cites her source as the James C. & Katie Ann Feltz Bible.]

AKERMAN, SUSAN - mc 4 Mar 1850 in Portsmouth to Stephen A Rice. [Chipman, Scott Lee, *New England Vital Records from the "Exeter News-Letter," 1847-1852*. Camden: Picton Press, 1994, p. 115.]

ACKERMANN, THEODOR - alive 1878; m Mathilde Fritzsche; ch: Dankwart b 11 Nov 1878 qv. [Debus, Allen G., *World Who's Who in Science: a biographical dictionary of notable scientists from antiquity to the present*. Chicago: Marquis-Who's Who, Inc., 1968, p. 8.]

AKEREMAN, THOMAS - alive 1334. Commission of oyer and terminer "to William de Shareshull... on complaint by Henry bishop of Lincoln that... Thomas Akereman of Abburbury... and others, carried away his goods at Bennebury, and assaulted Walter de Woburn, his bailiff, and Thomas de Cotesmore, clerk, while lately holding the court of his yearly fair there and other men and servants of his in full court, terrifying them so that they fled from the court to the bishop's castle in the town where they beseiged them for a long time." Dated 28 Jun 1334, Barnard Castle. [----, *Calendar of the Patent Rolls... Edward III. A.D. 1330-1334*. ---: ---, 1893. Reprint Germany: Kraus Reprint, 1972, p. 580.]

ACKERMAN, THOMAS - alive 1686; occ: mariner. Richard Cole, age 21, was bound to Thomas Ackerman in 1686 for "4 years in Virginia." [Coldham, Peter Wilson, *The Complete Book of Emigrants, 1661-1699. A comprehensive listing compiled from English public records of those who took ship to the Americas for political, religious, and economic reasons; of those who were deported for vagrancy, roguery, or non-conformity; and of those who were sold to labour in the new colonies*. Baltimore: Genealogical Publishing Co., Inc., 1990, p. 564.]

ACKERMAN, THOMAS R - m 7 Apr 1947 in Nashua NH to Drinette A Dionne; ch: Pamela L b 29 Apr 1949. [Nash, Gerald Q. et al, *The Vital Records of Hudson, New Hampshire, 1734-1985.* Bowie: Heritage Books, Inc., 1997, p. 2, 245.]

ACKERMAN, THOMPSON - alive 1884; res: Marshall Co KS; notice that he is suing Julia Ackerman for divorce appears in the 31 Oct 1884 issue of *The Franklin Bee.* [Thompson, Joyce, "The Frankfort Bee, 4 Jul - 26 Dec 1884," *Topeka Genealogical Society Quarterly,* vol. 28 #1, January 1998, p. 19]

ACKERMANN, TRIENTJE JURGENS - b 28 Oct 1830 Strackholt GE; ch/o Jurgen Eden Ackermann & Trientje Eilers; m 14 Apr 1851 in Strackholt GE to Habbe Frerichs Osterbur. [Correspondence dated 1 Oct. 2000 from Eddie Dirks.]

ACKEMANN, VALENTINE - age 30; res: Bavaria.   Immigrated through Havre & arrived at NY City on 20 Nov 1850.   Declaration of intention made 7 Oct 1854 but no record of naturalization listed. [Hughes, Lois E., *Hamilton County, Ohio, Citizenship Record Abstracts, 1837-1916.*   Bowie: Heritage Books, Inc., 1991, p. 1.] [The "R" is missing from the name but is this an Ackerman?]

ACKERMAN, VALENTINE - b Prussia; m Mary ---- b OH & age 45 in 1880; ch: Catherine, Mary, Lena; res: Franklin Co OH in 1880. Valentine Ackerman was 52y in the 1880 census.  [Correspondence dated 13 Sep. 2000 from Gail R. Thomas.]

AKERMAN, VALERIE MARGARET ELIZABETH - eldest d/o W S Akerman; m 22 Apr 1908 at Burnham, co Somerset to Charles Edward Brownrigg b 3 Feb 1865, s/o Thomas Marcus Brownrigg & Meriel Anna Watt. [Crisp, Frederick Arthur, *Visitation of England and Wales, Vol. 20.* ----: ----, 1919.  Facsimile reprint Bowie: Heritage Books, Inc., 1996, p. 64.]

ACKERMAN, VICTORIA - bc1844 [based on age at death]; res: 118 Bank; race: white; d 30 Aug 1872, age 28, cause: abdominal tumor; bur: St John. [Is she the mother of Dorie Ackerman?] [Hughes, Lois E., *Hamilton County, Ohio, Death Records, 1870-1873, Volume II, Book A, A-K.* Bowie: Heritage Books, Inc., 1992, p. 2.]

ACKERMAN, W D - m Mary P Osgood; ch: son b 20 Aug 1892; res: Alexandria NH. [Nash, Gerald Q. et al, *The Vital Records of Hudson,*

*New Hampshire, 1734-1985.* Bowie: Heritage Books, Inc., 1997, p. 2.]

AKERMAN, W S - ch: Valerie Margaret Elizabeth m 22 Apr 1908 qv. [Crisp, Frederick Arthur, *Visitation of England and Wales, Vol. 20.* ----: ----, 1919. Facsimile reprint Bowie: Heritage Books, Inc., 1996, p. 64.]

AKERMAN, WALTER - ch: ---- dc 30 May 1853. [Chipman, Scott Lee, *New England Vital Records from the "Exeter News-Letter," 1853-1858.* Camden: Picton Press, 1994, p. 17.]

AKERMAN, WALTER - bc1737 [based on age at death]; occ: tanner; d1808, age 71. [Brewster, Charles W., *Rambles About Portsmouth: second series.* ----: Lewis W. Brewster, 1869. Facsimile reprint Somersworth: New Hampshire Publishing Company, 1972, p. 355.]

AKERMAN, WALTER - alive 1773; a grantee of Success Twp 12 Feb 1773. [Batchellor, Albert Stillman, *State of New Hampshire. Town Charters granted within the present limits of New Hampshire, being the continuation and conclusion of the grants of townships issued by the provincial government of New Hampshire, presented in alphabetcical arrangement, and including all subsequent to the letter E, will illustrative maps, plans, bibliographical citations and complete indexes, and an appendix containing documents relating to the most ancient towns of this State, and historical notes and monographs. Volume XXV. Town charters, Volume II.* Concord: Edward N. Pearson, Public Printer, 1895, p. 555.]

AKERMAN, WALTER - alive 1776; res: Portsmouth. [Batchellor, Albert Stillman, *Miscellaneous Revolutionary Documents of New Hampshire including the association test, the pension rolls, and other important papers. Vol. 30.* Manchester: The John B. Clarke Co., 1910, p. 113.]

AKERMAN, WALTER - alive 1776; signed Association Test of 1776 in which he agreed to "oppose the Hostile Proceedings of the British Fleets, and Armies, against the United American Colonies." [Brewster, Charles W., *Rambles About Portsmouth: first series.* ----: Charles W. Brewster, 1859. Facsimile reprint of second edition published 1873 Somersworth: New Hampshire Publishing Company,

1971, p. 215.]

AKERMAN, WALTER - alive 1784; res: Portsmouth; occ: yeoman. Guardian of Salome Akerman. [Evans, Helen F., *Abstracts of the Probate Records of Rockingham County, New Hampshire, 1771-1799, Volume 1.* Bowie: Heritage Books, Inc., 2000, p. 8.]

AKERMAN, WALTER - alive 1785. Elected to be a fence viewer at the Portsmouth town meeting on 25 Mar 1785.[131] He is probably the same Walter Akerman elected to be a fence viewer at the Portsmouth town meeting on 25 Mar 1786.[132] He is probably the same Walter Akerman elected to be a fence viewer at the Portsmouth town meeting on 25 Mar 1787.[133]

AKERMAN, WALTER - alive 1788; res: Portsmouth; occ: tanner. [Evans, Helen F., *Abstracts of the Probate Records of Rockingham County, New Hampshire, 1771-1799.* Bowie: Heritage Books, Inc., 2000, p. 140, 697.]

AKERMAN, WALTER - bc1789 [based on age at death]; dc 8 Sep 1840 Portsmouth, age 51. [Chipman, Scott Lee, *New England Vital Records from the "Exeter News-Letter," 1831-1840.* Camden: Picton Press, 1993, p. 202.] [Is this the son of Barnet Akermann, alive 1784?]

AKERMAN, WALTER - alive 1790; res: Portsmouth Town NH. Free white males of 16y & upwards, including heads of families = 2. Free white males under 16y = 0. Free white females, including heads of families = 1. [----, *Heads of Families at the First Census of the United States Taken in the Year 1790: New Hampshire.* Washington: Government Printing Office, 1907. Reprint Baltimore: Genealogical Publishing Company, 1966, p. 78.]

AKERMAN, WALTER - alive 1800; res: Portsmouth. Free white males under 10y = 0, 10-16y = 0, 16-26y (including heads of households) = 0, 26-45y (including heads of households) = 0, 45y &

---

[131] Scobie, Robert, *Genealogical Abstracts from "The New Hampshire Mercury," 1784 to 1788* (Bowie: Heritage Books, Inc., 1997), p. 11, 12.
[132] Ibid., p. 50, 51.
[133] Ibid., p. 109.

upwards (including heads of households) = 0. Free white females under 10y = 0, 10-16y = 0, 16-26y (including heads of households) = 0, 26-45y (including heads of households) = 0, 45y & upwards (including heads of households) = 1. [----, *Heads of Families at the Second Census of the United States Taken in the Year 1800: New Hampshire.* Madison: John Brooks Threlfall, 1973, p. 144.]

AKERMAN, WALTER - alive 1807. Served as selectman for Portsmouth in 1807 & 1808. [Tibbetts, Charles W., *The New Hampshire Genealogical Record. An illustrated quarterly magazine devoted to genealogy, history and biography. Vol. II, July 1904 - April 1905.* Dover: Charles W. Tibbetts, 1905. Facsimile reprint Bowie: Heritage Books, Inc., 1988, p. 161.]

ACKERMAN, WARREN - b 27 Nov 1827 New Brunswick NJ; s/o Jonathan Combs Ackerman & Maria Smith; edu: private schools in New Brunswick "where he acquired a thorough preparatory education for mercantile life;" res: New Brunswick, moved to Newark to live with his married sister Caroline E; occ: owned shares in his father's Newark Indian Rubber Company & elected to its board of directors. "Owing largely to his individual efforts, the company was very successful until about the year 1850, when, in opposition to his advice and that of others, an inferior article of rubber was purchased and manufactured into goods which proved worthless, and nearly ruined the credit and business of the company. Warren Ackerman, as soon as practicable thereafter, secured enough of the capital stock of the company to give him the entire control of its management and its manufactured goods thenceforth bore a reputation for uniform excellence. ... Mr. Ackerman subsequently bought the controlling interest in other rubber companies, and during the late civil war supplied the United States government with a large portion of its best rubber goods. ... In 1879 he sold out all his rubber interests and turned his attention to the development of the cement industry, especially that of the Lawrence Cement Company, of Ulster County, New York, some shares of which he had received from his father in the year 1853. He secured as rapidly as possible a controlling interest in the company, and was made its president. Under his management additional territory was purchased, new buildings erected, the most approved machinery was introduced, and the annual output increased from one hundred and forty thousand barrels to over one million barrels a year. Besides the Lawrence Cement Company, Mr.

Ackerman controlled the Rosendale Cement Company, of Ulster County, New York; the Cumberland Hydraulic Cement and Manufacturing Company, of Cumberland, Maryland; and he also owned, in Pennsylvania, extensive quarries from which is produced the finest quality of Portland cement.

"In 1860 Warren Ackerman purchased a farm of about fifty acres, in Scotch Plains, Union County, New Jersey. [He named it Lyde Park, in honor of his wife; it adjoined the residence property of his brother-in-law, Dr. Abraham Coles. See photographs on pages 624 and 626.] Later he bought many other farms, including the 'Deserted Village,' originally called Feltville, now the well known and popular summer resort named Glenside Park. [See photograph p. 622] Upon these he expended large sums of money. Perhaps to no one is the public in general more indebted for the present system of good roads in New Jersey than to Warren Ackerman." Married 1876 Lydia P Platt, d/o Isaac L Platt; rel: Collegiate Dutch Church, NY City. "To the efficient help rendered by Warren Ackerman and others was due the prevention of the foreclosure of the mortgages on the Central Railroad of New Jersey, in 1877." Died 30 Aug 1893, after a short illness. [Ricord, F. W., *History of Union County, New Jersey.* Newark: East Jersey History Company, 1897, p. 623, 625, 627.]

ACKERMANN, WESTON WILBUR - b 15 Jun 1925; s/o R Herbert Ackermann & Isabelle Trepagnier; occ: virologist; edu: PhD University of Texas 1947; res: Ann Arbor MI. [Debus, Allen G., *World Who's Who in Science: a biographical dictionary of notable scientists from antiquity to the present.* Chicago: Marquis-Who's Who, Inc., 1968, p. 9.]

ACKERMAN, WILLIAM - s/o Johannes Ackerman & Anna Johanna Spaugh; m1 Emily T Tesh bc1830, d/o Henrich Henry Tesh & Susanna Barbara Rothrock; m2 22 Jan 1848 Jenet Elisabeth Spach b 13 Dec 1826 in Friedberg (Davidson Co) NC & d 22 Jun 1860. [Tesh, Peggy J., "Heinrich Peter Tesch and His Descendants," *The Forsyth County Genealogical Society Journal*, Vol. XVII #1 (Fall 1998), p. 49, 51]

AKERMAN, WILLIAM - alive 1803; m Mary ----; ch: Joseph chr 18 Sep 1803 at St Mary AB Church (London). [Correspondence (undated) from Bob G.[?], courtesy of Robert H. Ackerman, 22 Mar. 2000.]

AUCKERMAN, WILLIAM - b 30 Apr 1811; s/o John Auckerman & Annie Dorrathea Shaver; m lic 13 Apr 1833 in Adams Co OH to Matilda Allis. [Correspondence dated 3 Sep. 2000 from Dorothy Pray Wilson.]

ACKERMAN, WILLIAM A - alive 1846; m Matilda Mouerson; ch: Abraham b 6 Sep 1846 & bapt 25 Oct 1846. [Durie, Howard I., "Pascack Reformed Dutch Church Baptisms 1814-1850," *The American Genealogist*, Vol. 48 #2, p. 114.]

ACKERMAN, WILLIAM/WILLIAM H - alive 1897; m Henrietta Lane. [Nash, Gerald Q. et al, *The Vital Records of Hudson, New Hampshire, 1734-1985*. Bowie: Heritage Books, Inc., 1997, p. 245.]

ACKERMANN, WILLIAM CARL - b 7 Oct 1913 Sheboygan WI; s/o William H Ackermann & Frances E Shirmer; m 6 May 1942 Margaret A [K?]epsell; ch: William Charles, Nancy Ann m W David price, Arthur John; res: Champaign IL; occ: hydrologist; edu: BS in Civil Engineering, with honors, from the University of Wisconsin 1935. [Debus, Allen G., *World Who's Who in Science: a biographical dictionary of notable scientists from antiquity to the present.* Chicago: Marquis-Who's Who, Inc., 1968, p. 9.]

ACKERMAN, WILLIAM F - alive 1862; mil: appears to have served in the Civil War; res: Meriden CT; bur: not in Meriden CT. [Davis, Charles Henry Stanley, *History of Wallingford, Conn., from its settlement in 1670 to the present time, including Meriden, which was one of its parishes until 1806, and Cheshire, which was incorporated in 1780.* Meriden: author, 1870, p. 376.]

ACKERMAN, W[ILLIA]M G - alive 1900; m Mary E Hamlet/Hamlett; ch: dau b 4 Nov 1900, Edna Blanche b 17 Jan 1902, Maurice W b 1 Jul 1905; res: Hill NH. [Nash, Gerald Q. et al, *The Vital Records of Hudson, New Hampshire, 1734-1985.* Bowie: Heritage Books, Inc., 1997, p. 1, 2.]

ACKERMAN, WILLIAM G - m 27 Aug 1914 in Nashua NH to Lanora P Tucker. [Nash, Gerald Q. et al, *The Vital Records of Hudson, New Hampshire, 1734-1985.* Bowie: Heritage Books, Inc., 1997, p. 245.]

ACKERMAN, WILLIAM G - d 5 Oct 1949 Nashua NH. [Nash, Gerald Q. et al, *The Vital Records of Hudson, New Hampshire, 1734-1985*. Bowie: Heritage Books, Inc., 1997, p. 492.]

AKERMAN, WILLIAM H [sic?] - alive 1850; res: Portsmouth, Rockingham Co NH. [See page 24 of the original census for full record.] [Jackson, Ronald Vern and Gary Ronald Teeples, *New Hampshire 1850 Index Census*. Bountiful: Accelerated Indexing Systems, Inc., 1978, p. 3.]

ACKERMANN, WILLIAM H - alive 1913; m Frances E Shirmer; ch: William Carl b 7 Oct 1913 qv. [Debus, Allen G., *World Who's Who in Science: a biographical dictionary of notable scientists from antiquity to the present*. Chicago: Marquis-Who's Who, Inc., 1968, p. 9.]

ACKERMAN, WILLIS D - m 2 May 1891 in Hudson NH to Mary P F Osgood. [Nash, Gerald Q. et al, *The Vital Records of Hudson, New Hampshire, 1734-1985*. Bowie: Heritage Books, Inc., 1997, p. 245.]

# FAMILY GROUPS

# DESCENDANTS OF A DAVID ACKERMAN

A David Ackermann - b1586, m A Ackerman
  David Abram - b1615, m Lysbet de Villiers
    David Abram - b1646, m Hillagoud Ver Planck
      Marilge - b1690, m Swaine Ogden


ACKERMAN, A DAVID - b1586 Berlicusor, Mayory of Bosch, HO; mc1614 A Ackerman bc1590 HO, d after 1620 HO; ch: David Abram b1615 qv; d after 1620 HO. [Correspondence dated 27 July 2000 from Keith Whiting.]

ACKERMAN, DAVID ABRAM - b1615 HO; s/o A David Ackerman & A Ackerman; m1641 in HO to Lysbet de Velliers/Elizabeth Bellier bc1621 HO, d after 1670 Hackensack (Essex Co) NJ; ch: David Abram b1646 qv; d1662 Hackensack (Essex Co) NJ or 26 Apr 1663 Hackensack (Essex Co) NJ. Immigrated from Holland, via Poland, to America on *The Fox*, 31 Aug 1662. [Correspondence dated 27 July 2000 from Keith Whiting. He cites his source for the 26 Apr. 1663 death date as *The Genealogical Magazine of New Jersey*, Vol. X, p. 48-49. He cites his source for the name of Elizabeth Bellier as *NEXUS*, Vol. XII #4 ([19?]95.]

ACKERMAN, DAVID ABRAM - b1646 HO; s/o David Abram Ackerman & Lysbet de Velliers/Elizabeth Bellier; m 13 Mar 1679/0 in NY to Hillagoud Ver Planck b1648 NY, chr 1 Nov 1648 NY, dc1695 NJ; ch: Marilge b1690 qv; dc1714 NJ. Immigrated from Amsterdam, HO to Hackensack NJ, Sep 1662, on *The Fox*. [Correspondence dated 27 July 2000 from Keith Whiting. He cites his source for the marriage date as the *Gen. of New Jersey Families*, p. 41. He cites his source for David Abram Ackerman's death date as *The Genealogical Magazine of New Jersey*, Vol. X, p. 48-49. He cites his source for Hillagoud Ver Planck's death date as *The Genealogical Magazine of New Jersey*, Vol. X, p. 48-49.]

ACKERMAN, MARILGE - b1690 Newark, Essex Co NJ; d/o David Abram Ackerman & Hillagoud Ver Planck; m 5 May 1711 in Hackensack (Bergen Co) NJ to Swaine Ogden b1687 Newark (Essex Co) NJ, d 20 Apr 1755 Orange (Essex Co) NJ, bur: Old Cemetery in Orange NJ; d 24 Nov 1756 Newark, Essex Co NJ. [Correspondence dated 27 July 2000 from Keith Whiting. He cites as his source for the marriage date *The Genealogical Magazine of New Jersey*, Vol. IV, p. 116 & *Ogden Family*, p. 56. He cites as his source for Marilge Ackerman's death date *The Genealogical Magazine of New Jersey*, Vol. IV, p. 116. He cites his source for Swaine Ogden's death date as *The Genealogical Magazine of New Jersey*, Vol. IV, p. 116. He cites as his source for Swain Ogden's burial place the *Ogden Family*, p. 56.]

# DESCENDANTS OF ABRAHAM JOHANNES ACKERMAN

Abraham Johannes Ackerman - b1730, m Lydia des Marest
   Johannes - b1760, m Elizabeth Dierman
      Margaret - b1799, m William John Winters


ACKERMAN, ABRAHAM JOHANNES - b 6 Oct 1730; m 29 Apr 1753 Lydia des Marest bapt 8 Nov 1730; ch: Johannes b 18 Mar 1760 qv; d Aug 1770. [Mayo, Mary E., *Sixteen Hundred Lines to Pilgrims. Lineage Book III.* Baltimore: Genealogical Publishing Co., Inc., 1982, p. 399.]

ACKERMAN, JOHANNES - b 18 Mar 1760; s/o Abraham Johannes Ackerman & Lydia des Marest; mc1781 Elizabeth Dierman b 21 May 1767, d 20 sep 1848; ch: Margaret b 20 Sep 1799 qv; d 25 Dec 1831. [Mayo, Mary E., *Sixteen Hundred Lines to Pilgrims. Lineage Book III.* Baltimore: Genealogical Publishing Co., Inc., 1982, p. 399.]

ACKERMAN, MARGARET - b 20 Sep 1799; d/o Johannes Ackerman & Elizabeth Dierman; m 23 May 1831 William John Winters b 3 May 1795, d 23 Jul 1869; d 7 Jul 1855. [Mayo, Mary E., *Sixteen Hundred Lines to Pilgrims. Lineage Book III.* Baltimore: Genealogical Publishing Co., Inc., 1982, p. 399.]

George Ackerman - m Anna ----
  George - b1747, m Margaret Sell
    Henry - b1774, m Elizabeth Bann
      ch: Susanna, Elizabeth, John
    Johannes - b1777, m Susanna Shelly
      ch: George, John, Henry, Catherine, Jacob, Susanna,
        William, Maria
  Henry - alive 1787 - see DESCENDANTS OF HENRY ACKERMAN
  John - b1749?, m Catharine Bleam
    George
    John
      ch: Jane, James, George, Anthony, John, Jacob, David,
        Abraham, Mary
    Jacob
      ch: John, Isaac, Catherine, Elizabeth, Barbara, Margaret,
        Mary, Susanna, Lena, Lydia, Jacob J
    David
      ch: Catherine, Isaac
    Henry
      ch: Joseph, John, George, Jacob, Charles H, Henry H,
        Samuel, Isaac, Elias H, Sarah, Margaret, Lydia,
        Susanna, David
    Abraham


ACKERMAN, DAVID - s/o John Ackerman & Catharine Bleam; m -
---; ch: Catherine, Isaac.[134]

ACKERMAN, GEORGE - alive 1747; m Anna ----; ch: George
b1747 qv, Henry alive 1787 qv, John b1749? qv; d1818.[135]

---

[134] Correspondence dated 3 August 2000 from Doris Daumer. Vliet, Clair
Ackerman, *The Ackerman Family Association Comprising the Descendants of
George Ackerman, Mennonite, of Lower Milford Township, Bucks County, Pa., and
some of the descendnats of Stephen Ackerman, Lutheran, of Haycock Township,
Bucks County, Pa* (----: ----, 1950), p. 10.
[135] Correspondence dated July and August 2000 from Doris Daumer. Vliet, Clair
Ackerman, *The Ackerman Family Association Comprising the Descendants of
George Ackerman, Mennonite, of Lower Milford Township, Bucks County, Pa., and
some of the descendnats of Stephen Ackerman, Lutheran, of Haycock Township,*

ACKERMAN, GEORGE - b 8 Apr 1747; s/o George Ackerman & Anna ----; m Margaret Sell b 2 Nov 1745, d/o Henry Sell & ----, d 17 Oct 1827; ch: Henry b 2 Aug 1774 qv, Johannes b 1 Mar 1777 qv; res: Lower Milford Twp (Bucks Co) PA 1772-1784; occ: Mennonite minister; d 16 Sep 1818; bur: East Swamp Burying Ground.[136]

ACKERMAN, HENRY - b 2 Aug 1774; s/o George Ackerman & Margaret Sell; m Elizabeth Bann; ch: Susanna, Elizabeth, John.[137]

ACKERMAN, HENRY - s/o John Ackerman & Catharine Bleam; m - ---; ch: Joseph, John, George, Jacob, Charles H, Henry H, Samuel, Isaac, Elias H, Sarah, Margaret, Lydia, Susanna, David.[138]

ACKERMAN, JACOB - s/o John Ackerman & Catharine Bleam; m --- --; ch: John, Isaac, Catherine, Elizabeth, Barbara, Margaret, Mary, Susanna, Lena, Lydia, Jacob J.[139]

ACKERMAN, JOHANNES - b 1 Mar 1777; s/o George Ackerman & Margaret Sell; m Susanna Shelly; ch: George, John, Henry, Catherine, Jacob, Susanna, William, Maria.[140]

ACKERMAN, JOHN - s/o John Ackerman & Catharine Bleam; m --- -; ch: Jane, James, George, Anthony, John, Jacob, David, Abraham, Mary.[141]

ACKERMAN, JOHN - b1749?; s/o George Ackerman & Anna ----; m Catharine Bleam; ch: George unm, John qv, Jacob qv, Henry qv, David qv, Abraham; d1823.[142]

---

*Bucks County, Pa.* (----: ----, 1950), p. 10. See Descendants of Henry Ackerman for continuation of this line.
[136] Ibid., correspondence and see pages 10, 11, 13.
[137] Ibid., correspondence and see pages 10, 13.
[138] Ibid., correspondence and see page 10.
[139] Ibid., correspondence and see page 10.
[140] Ibid., correspondence and see pages 10, 13.
[141] Ibid., correspondence and see page 10.
[142] Ibid., correspondence and see page 10.

# DESCENDANTS OF HANS GEORG ACKERMANN

Hans Georg Ackermann - m1697 Anna Maria Gerlach
 Johann Wendel - b1703, m Anna Maria Schick
  Johann Henrich - b1726
  Johann Georg - b1728, m Catharina Danningerin
   Ch: Johann Wendel, Johann Wendel, Johann Georg,
    Elisabet, Johannes, Catharina Elisabet, Christina,
    Georg, Johann Philip, Christina Anna,
   Georg - b1773, m Catharine Stahl
    Philip - b1806
    George W - b1807, m Mary ("Muzzie") Reese
     William - b1832
     Mary Ellen - b1826
     Edwin H - b1838
     John S - b1841
     George W - b1842
     Chauncey Forward - b1845
      George
      Mary Zella - b1886
      Lottie Dee - b1888
      Carl C - b1890, m Lydia Carlson
      Harry Staymen - b1893
      William Lloyd - b1895, m Stella Anne Saul
       Robert Lloyd - b1925, m Margaret D Ansty
      Leaota - b1900
      Dorothy - b1911
    John - b1814, m Nancy O ----
    Elizabeth
    Rebecca
   Johann Jacob - b1778
   Johann Heinrich - b1780
  Johann Leonhard - b1730
  Maria Barbara - b1732
  Georg Balthasar - b1736
  Maria Christina - b1739

ACKERMAN, CARL C - b 29 Oct 1890 Greensburg PA; s/o Chauncey Forward Ackerman & Sadie Connell Dugan; m Lydia Carlson, who lived near Tyrone PA; ch: Betty; d 10 Jun 1915 near New Alexandria PA by drowning in Keystone Reservoir. [Materials dated 6 Jan. 2000 and 12 Sep. 2000 contributed by Robert L. Ackerman. Carl C. Ackerman "had one child (Dorothy) with Anna McGlaughlin, who was adopted by Grandma Ackerman."]

ACKERMANN, CATHERINE - b1767 southeastern PA (?); d/o Christoff Ackermann & Maria Magdalena ----; d 21 Mar 1846 near Lycippus, Westmoreland Co PA. [Correspondence dated 23 Sep. 1999 from Robert L. Ackerman.]

ACKERMAN, CHAUNCEY FORWARD - b1845 Stoystown, Somerset Co PA; s/o George W Ackerman & Mary "Muzzie" Reese; m1 Martha Ann ---- div 15 Sep 1884 in Somerset PA; m2 26 Nov 1885 in Pittsburgh PA to Sadie Connell Dugan b 5 Jun 1865 Pittsburgh PA (?), d 2 Nov 1942 Greensburg PA, bur: St Clair Cem in Greensburg PA; ch: by Martha Ann ----: George; ch by Sadie Connell Dugan: Mary Zella b 9 Dec 1886 qv, Lottie Dee b 26 Feb 1888 qv, Carl C b 29 Oct 1890 qv, Harry Staymen b 3 Mar 1893 qv, William Lloyd b 26 Mar 1895 qv, Leaota b 4 May 1900 qv, Dorothy b 13 May 1911 qv; occ: taught school for 10y, farming on his father's place 1884; d Jun(?) 1913 Greensburg PA; bur: St Clair Cem, Greensburg PA.[143]

ACKERMAN, DOROTHY - b 13 May 1911 Greensburg PA; d/o Chauncey Forward Ackerman & Sadie Connell Dugan; m Harry E ("Buzz") McNerny; d 27 Dec 1977 Reading PA. [Materials dated 6 Jan. 2000 contributed by Robert L. Ackerman.]

---

[143] Materials dated 6 Jan. 2000 and 12 Sep. 2000, and contributed by Robert L. Ackerman. Occupation information cited as being from Waterman-Watkins, *Ex History of Bedford, Somerset, & Fulton Counties, PA* (----: ----, 1884). In earlier correspondence, Chauncey Forward Ackerman's military service was given; he "enlisted in the Union Army as a substitute volunteer, but only served three months before the Civil War ended." Correspondence dated 23 Sep. 1999 from Robert L. Ackerman.

ACKERMAN, EDWIN H - b 8 Mar 1838 near Stoystown PA; s/o George W Ackerman & Mary ("Muzzie") Reese; unm; 15 Dec 1869 near Stoystown PA. Military service: he is mentioned in the official records of 54th PA Reg, Co B, at Paw Paw VA. "He was one of two scouts to first report the advance on Company B of Col. John Imboden's Raiders (CA) near Little Cacapon Bridge. He spent time in Libby Prison at Richmond, Virginia." [Correspondence dated 23 Sep. 1999 and 6 Jan. 2000 from Robert L. Ackerman.]

ACKERMAN, GEORG - bc 26 Nov 1773 Lancaster Co PA; chr: Lancaster Co PA; s/o Johann Georg Ackermann & Catharina Danningerin; m 19 Apr 1803 in Trinity Lutheran Church, Lancaster PA to Catharine Stahl b Lancaster Co PA, d/o Jacob Stahl & Anna Margaretha ----, d before 1837; ch: Philip b 22 Feb 1806 qv, George W b1807 qv, John b1814 qv, Elizabeth b Lancaster Co PA, Rebecca b Lancaster Co & m ---- Fordney; occ: blacksmith; d1837 [estate records are dated 5 May 1837]. [Materials dated 23 Sep. 1999 and 6 Jan. 2000 from Robert L. Ackerman.]

ACKERMANN, GEORG BALTHASAR - b 19 May 1736 Neckar-bischofsheim Parish, Northern Kraichgau; s/o Johann Wendel Ackermann & Anna Maria Schick; m1 Christina ----; m2 18 Jun 1771 Elisabeth Albrecht (a widow of Gorg Albrecht); ch by Christina ----: Maria Barbara (?) b 30 Jul 1799 assumed Lancaster PA; naturalized Fall 1765 but "not taking an oath;" d assumed Lancaster PA. [Correspondence dated 23 Sep. 1999 and 28 Sep. 1999 from Robert L. Ackerman.]

ACKERMAN, GEORGE W - b 17 Feb 1807 Lancaster Co PA; s/o Georg Ackermann[144] & Catharine Stahl; m in Stoystown (Somerset Co) PA to Mary ("Muzzie") Reese b 10 Mar 1812 Stoystown PA (?), d 4 Oct 1897 near Stoystown PA, bur: Lambertsville Cem in Lambertsville PA; ch: William b1832 qv, Mary Ellen b1836 qv, Edwin H b 8 Mar 1838 qv, John S b 3 Apr 1841 qv, George W b 14 Jun 1842 qv, Chauncey Forward b1845 qv; res: Somerset Co 1828, Stoney Creek Twp 1884; occ: blacksmith, farmer, kept hotel in Stoystown, justice of the peace in Quemahoning; d 12 May 1897 of typhoid fever near Stoystown PA; bur: Lambertsville Cem, Lambertsville PA (near Stoystown PA). [Materials dated 23 Sep.

---

[144] The spelling of Ackermann changes at this point, going from the father's double "n" to the son's single "n."

1999 and 6 Jan. 2000 from Robert L. Ackerman. Residence and occupation data cited as being from Waterman-Watkins, *Ex History of Bedford, Somerset, & Fulton Counties, PA*, ----:----, 1884. Birth date of 1807 comes from census records; tombstone gives birth date as 17 Feb 1818. Cause of death information cited as being from notes received from Anne S. Ackerman. Catharine Stahl's name is spelled Catherine Stahl on the pedigree chart devoted to George W. Ackerman.]

ACKERMAN, GEORGE W - b 14 Jun 1842 near Stoystown PA; s/o George W Ackerman & Mary ("Muzzie") Reese; m Amanda ----; d 4 Apr 1869 near Stoystown PA. Military service: "he had the military distinction of being a sharpshooter in Company D, 142nd Pennsylvania Regiment which fought in every action of the Army of the Potomac from the creation of the Regiment to the end of the War. George is listed as actually enaged in seventeen actions including: Fredericksburg, Chancellorsville, Wilderness, Spotsylvania, and the surrender of Lee's Army at Appomattox." [Materials dated 23 Sep. 1999 and 6 Jan. 2000 contributed by Robert L. Ackerman.]

ACKERMANN, HANS GEORG - b "assume Northern Kraichgau;" m 11 May 1697 in Adersbach Parish, Northern Kraichgau to Anna Maria Gerlach b Schultheiss in Hasselbach, d/o Thomas Gerlach, d "assume No Kraichgau;" ch: Johann Wendel b 5 Jan 1703 qv; occ: smith (farrier); rel: Lutheran; res: Bischofsheim, Northern Kraichgau. [Letter dated 23 Sep. 1999 from Robert L. Ackerman.]

ACKERMAN, HARRY STAYMEN - b 3 Mar 1893 Greensburg PA; s/o Chauncey Forward Ackerman & Sadie Connell Dugan; m in Greensburg PA to Flora Norman; d 23 Nov 1962 Greensburg PA. [Materials dated 6 Jan. 2000 from Robert L. Ackerman.]

ACKERMANN, JOHANN GEORG - b 17 Sep 1728 Neckar-bischofsheim Parish, Northern Kraichgau; s/o Johann Wendel Ackermann & Anna Maria Gerlach; m 22 Jan 1758 in Tr Luth Ch, Lancaster PA to Catharina Danningerin b Duren/Duhren (nr Bretten) No K or GE, d Lancaster PA; ch: Johann Wendel b 2 Dec 1758 in Lacaster PA & dc1759, Johann Wendel b 11 Jan 1760 & dc 1814-1816 ("Perhaps this son was later called 'Georg' and became 'Georg Wackerman'?"), Johann Georg b 11 Jan 1760 (twin?), Elisabet b 31 Oct 1761 & d before Nov 1769, Johannes b 21 Apr 1763 & dc 10 Sep

1782 in Lancaster PA of a sudden chill in water, Catharina Elisabet b 12 Nov 1764 in Lancaster PA & confirmed as 'Elisabet,' Christina b 14 Jul 1766 in Lancaster PA, Georg bc 1 Dec 1767 in Lancaster PA & dc 27 May 1769 in Lancaster PA of smallpox, Johann Philip b 3 Jan 1770 in Lancaster PA, Christina Anna b 16 Dec 1771 in Lancaster PA, Georg b 26 Nov 1773 qv, Johann Jacob b 9 Jun 1778 in Lancaster PA, Johann Heinrich b 2 May 1780 in Lancaster PA & dc 23 Nov 1781 in Lancaster PA of smallpox; naturalized Fall 1765 in Philadelphia but "not taking an oath;" dc1786 assumed Lancaster PA. [Correspondence dated 23 Sep. 1999 & 28 Sep. 1999 from Robert L. Ackerman.]

ACKERMANN, JOHANN WENDEL - b 5 Jan 1703 Northern Kraichgau, Neckarbischofsheim; s/o Hans Georg Ackermann & Anna Maria Gerlach; m 4 Sep 1725 in Neckarbischofsheim Parish, North Kraichgau to Anna Maria Schick b Northern Kraichgau, d/o Johann Georg Schick & ----, d 1782 or later in Lancaster PA, bur: Trinity Lutheran Church Cem; ch: Johann Henrich b 13 Aug 1726 in Neckarbischofsheim Parish & d assumed Neckarbischofsheim Parish, Johann Georg b 17 Sep 1728 qv, Johann Leonhard b 3 Aug 1730 in Neckarbischofsheim Parish & d young in Neckarbischofsheim Parish, Maria Barbara b 1 Oct 1732 qv, Georg Balthasar b 19 May 1736 qv, Maria Christina b 18 Dec 1739 qv; occ: farrier & armorer in Europe, in Lancaster PA he "established a smithy...on the west side of Prince Street, bounded by Orange and Water Streets. This property remained in the Ackermann family until 1839;" d 31 Mar 1764 Lancaster PA (will dated 5 Mar 1764); bur: Trinity Lutheran Church Cem, Lancaster PA. "Johann Wendel with his second son Johann Georg arrived at Philadelphia, on board the ship *Osgood* out of Rotterdam via Cowes, on 29th September 1750. Anna Maria, Maria Barbara, Georg Balthasar, and Maria Christina soon followed. We know this because there is a Trinity Lutheran Church, Lancaster, Pennsylvania, record of the family attending communion service on 17th February 1751." [Correspondence dated 23 Sep. 1999, 28 Sep. 1999 and 12 Sep. 2000 from Robert L. Ackerman.]

ACKERMAN, JOHN - b1814 Lancaster Co PA; s/o Georg Ackerman & Catharine Stahl; m Nancy O ----; ch: L C (a son who was a saddler in Stoystown); res: arrived in Stoystown c1830; occ: blacksmith, farmer; d1895 near Stoystown PA. [Materials dated 6 Jan. 2000 from Robert L. Ackerman. Residence, occupation, and son's information cited as being from Waterman-Watkins, *Ex History of Bedford, Somerset, & Fulton Counties, PA*, ----: ----, 1884.]

ACKERMAN, JOHN S - b 3 Apr 1841 near Stoystown PA; s/o George W Ackerman & Mary ("Muzzie") Reese; unm; d 6 Dec 1866 near Stoystown PA. [Materials dated 6 Jan. 2000 contributed by Robert L. Ackerman.]

ACKERMAN, LEAOTA - b 4 May 1900 Greensburg PA; d/o Chauncey Forward Ackerman & Sadie Connell Dugan; m Charles ("Chad") Truxal; d 2 Mar 1985 Baltimore MD. [Materials dated 6 Jan. 2000 contributed by Robert L. Ackerman.]

ACKERMAN, LOTTIE DEE - b 26 Feb 1888 Mutual PA; d/o Chauncey Forward Ackerman & Sadie Connell Dugan; m in New York City NY to Joseph McLaughlin; d Feb 1975 FL. [Materials dated 6 Jan. 2000 and contributed by Robert L. Ackerman.]

ACKERMANN, MARIA BARBARA - b 1 Oct 1732 Neckar-bischofsheim Parish; d/o Johann Wendel Ackermann & Anna Maria Schick; m 27 Apr 1755 Joh Georg Federhaaf; d assumed Lancaster PA. [Correspondence dated 28 Sep 1999 from Robert L. Ackerman.]

ACKERMANN, MARIA CHRISTINA - b 18 Dec 1739 Neckar-bischofsheim Parish; d/o Johann Wendel Ackermann & Anna Maria Schick; m 9 Feb 1761 Abraham Myer; d assumed Lancaster PA. [Correspondence dated 28 Sep. 1999 from Robert L. Ackerman.]

ACKERMAN, MARY - b1836 near Stoystown PA; d/o George W Ackerman & Mary ("Muzzie") Reese; m Samuel Wilt. [Materials dated 6 Jan. 2000 contributed by Robert L. Ackerman.]

ACKERMAN, MARY ZELLA - b 9 Dec 1886 Mutual PA; d/o Chauncey Forward Ackerman & Sadie Connell Dugan; m Frank Hershey; d 22 Aug 1974 Carlisle PA. [Materials dated 6 Jan. 2000 contributed by Robert L. Ackerman.]

ACKERMAN, PHILIP - b 22 Feb 1806 Lancaster Co PA; s/o Georg Ackerman & Catharine Stahl; probably never married; d 5 Dec 1890 Somerset Co PA. [Materials dated 6 Jan. 2000 contributed by Robert L. Ackerman.]

ACKERMAN, ROBERT LLOYD - b 3 Sep 1925 Greensburg PA; s/o William Lloyd Ackerman & Stella Anne Saul; m 30 May 1959 in Greensburg PA to Margaret D Ansty b 19 Nov 1934 Lyndurst (Hampshire) EN; ch: Julia Anne b 4 Dec 1959, Janet Deborah b 15 Sep 1961, Robert Peter b 2 Sep 1969. [Correspondence dated 23 Sep. 1999 and 12 Sep. 2000 from Robert L. Ackerman. He cites his source for the children as Marquis' *Who's Who in the World* 16th ed., 1999.]

ACKERMAN, WILLIAM - b1832 near Stoystown PA; s/o George W Ackerman & Mary ("Muzzie") Reese; ch: Lola; d El Paso IL (?). [Materials dated 6 Jan. 2000 contributed by Robert L. Ackerman. The name of Lola is cited as coming from the notes of A. S. Ackerman.]

ACKERMAN, WILLIAM LLOYD - b 26 Mar 1895 Greensburg PA; s/o Chauncey F Ackerman & Sadie Connell Dugan; m 20 Sep 1919 in Leighton PA to Stella Anne Saul b 14 Feb 1895 near Delmont PA, d/o George Saul & Charlotte Mears, d 1 Sep 1988 near New Alexandria PA; ch: Robert Lloyd b 3 Sep 1925 qv; d 6 Nov 1960 Greensburg PA. [Materials dated 23 Sep. 1999 and 6 Jan. 2000 contributed by Robert L. Ackerman. William Lloyd Ackerman is called Lloyd W. Ackerman in correspondence dated 23 Sep. 1999 from Robert L. Ackerman.]

# DESCENDANTS OF HENRY ACKERMAN

Henry Ackerman - alive 1787, m Barbara ----
  Daughter
  Daughter
  Jacob - b1787, m Elizabeth Kochline
    Anna Elizabeth - b1813
    Catharine - b1815
    Peter - b1816
    Susanna - b1817
    Rebecca - b1818
    Jacob - b1820, m Carolyn Woodring/Watring
      Edmund - b1843, m Maria Sybilla Minner
        Ida - d age 1 1/2
        Jonas Jefferson - b1872, m Sarah Sterner Schneck
          Viola - b1893, m Wirefield Nugle
          Grace - b1895, m Wm Bierman
          Ralph Jacob - b1897
          Robert Henry - b1899, m Helen Elizabeth Kipp
            Doris May - b1923, m Edward George Daumer
            Joyce Mary - b1925, m Constantine Mourat
          Harvey Jonas - b1901
            Shirley Olivia - d1999, m 4 times
            Neil Schlegel
              Keith - m Karen Zehner
            Jan - m Harold Christman
            Rudy Schlegel - m Rose Erkalini
          Verna May - b1904, m Claude Lutz/Paul Moyer
        Henry - b1874
        Maryann - b1876
      Jacob or Henry - b1848, m Sarah Ann Krause
      Henry - b1853, m Helen Walters
    Wm Heinrich - b1821
    Maria - b1822
    Sophia Caroline - b1824
    Henrietta - b1829
    Stephen K - b1827
    Richard W - b1829
    Elizabeth - b1831
    Edward Owen - b1833

ACKERMAN, DORIS MAE - b 15 Dec 1923; d/o Robert Henry Ackerman & Helen Elizabeth Kipp; m 23 Jan 1946 Edward George Daumer b 10 Jul 1923. [Correspondence dated July 2000 from Doris Daumer.]

ACKERMAN, EDMUND - b 14 Jan 1843? Bushkill Twp; s/o Jacob Ackerman & Carolyn Woodring/Watring; m Maria Sybilla Minner b 6 Apr 1851, d/o Jonas Minner & Maria Derr, d 26 Sep 1928; ch: Ida d age 1 1/2, Jonas Jefferson b 3 Nov 1872 qv, Henry b 30 Oct 1874 & d 24 Mar 1901, Maryann b 26 Oct 1876 & d 6 Oct 1900; d 4 Jun 1927 OH. [Correspondence dated July 2000 from Doris Daumer.]

ACKERMAN, EMMA JANE - b 12 Jun 1876; d/o Henry Ackerman & Sarah Ann Krauss; m 25 Dec 1894 William Elmer Steinmetz; d 25 Jan 1958; bur: Grandview Cem. [Correspondence dated January 2001 from Elaine C. Matthews.]

ACKERMAN, GRACE MAY - b 22 May 1906; d/o William Henry Ackerman & Amy Hoffman; m Paul Hoffman. [Correspondence dated January 2001 from Elaine C. Matthews.]

ACKERMAN, HARVEY JONAS - b 21 Sep 1901; s/o Jonas Jefferson Ackerman & Sarah Sterner Schneck; m1 Frances LaTiere; m2 Alma Schlegel; ch by Alma Schlegel: Shirley Olivia d1999 qv, Neil Schlegel d by Jul 2000 qv, Jan m Harold Christman, Rudy Schlegel qv. [Correspondence dated July 2000 from Doris Daumer.]

ACKERMAN, HELEN IRENE - b 2 Nov 1910; d/o William Henry Ackerman & Amy Hoffman; m Paul Desch; d 12 Dec 1995. [Correspondence dated January 2001 from Elaine C. Matthews.]

ACKERMAN, HENRY - alive 1787; s/o George Ackerman & Anna - ---; m Barbara ----; ch: dau, dau, Jacob b 25 Feb 1787 qv.[145]

---

[145] Correspondence dated July and August 2000 from Doris Daumer. Vliet, Clair Ackerman, *The Ackerman Family Association Comprising the Descendants of George Ackerman, Mennonite, of Lower Milford Township, Bucks County, Pa., and some of the descendnats of Stephen Ackerman, Lutheran, of Haycock Township, Bucks County, Pa* (----: ----, 1950), p. 10. See Descendants of George Ackerman for the father's line.

ACKERMAN, HENRY - b 28 Dec 1848; s/o Jacob Ackerman & Caroline Woodring; m 10 Sep 1870 Sarah Ann Krauss b 5 Jul 1849, d/o Joseph Krauss & Maria Kulp, d 24 Jan 1924 Allentown PA, bur: Greenwood Cem; ch: Arthur Wilson b 13 Jul 1873 Allentown (Lehigh Co) PA & unm, Emma Jane b 12 Jun 1876 qv, Lillie Louise b 15 Apr 1879 (twin) qv, William Henry b 15 Apr 1879 (twin) qv, Minnie Elmira b 22 Jun 1883 qv; occ: worked a short while for his nephew Jonas Ackerman who was a building contractor for Schaffer & Ackerman; res: Allentown 1920; d "19-20-1922" Allentown PA; bur: Greenwood Cem, on the south side of Chew Street, in lot #2484 block R. [Correspondence dated January 2001 from Elaine C. Matthews. She notes that Jonas Ackerman was a county commissioner in the 1930s. She states that the *Genealogical Record of the Schwenkfelder Families* gives Henry Ackerman's address as 512 Gordon Street, Allentown PA in 1919.]

ACKERMAN, HENRY - b 10 Mar 1853; s/o Jacob Ackerman & Carolyn Woodring/Watring; m Helen Walters. [Correspondence dated July 2000 from Doris Daumer.]

ACKERMAN, JACOB - b 25 Feb 1787; m Elizabeth Kochline b 9 Oct 1792, d/o Peter Kochline & Elizabeth Gress; ch: Anna Elizabeth b 24 Nov 1813, Catharine b 13 Feb 1815, Peter b 8 May 1816, Susanna b 21 Aug 1817, Rebecca b 20 Nov 1818, Jacob b 9 Feb 1820 qv, Wm Henrich b 18 Jul 1821, Maria b 18 Oct 1822, Sophia Carolina b 27 Apr 1824, Henrietta b 19 Jan 1829, Stephen K b 27 Jun 1827, Richard W b 11 Sep 1829, Elizabeth b 25 Jul 1831, Edward Owen b 12 Feb 1833. [Correspondence dated July 2000 from Doris Daumer.] Jacob Ackerman d 20 Feb 1846. [Correspondence dated 3 August 2000 from Doris Daumer.]

ACKERMAN, JACOB - b 9 Feb 1820 Forkstrup; s/o Jacob Ackerman & Elizabeth Kochline; m Carolyn Woodring/Watring b 13 Apr 1813, d 18 Sep 1891; ch: Edmund b 14 Jan 1843? qv, Jacob b1848 qv, Henry b 10 Mar 1853 qv; d 27 May 1870. [Correspondence dated July 2000 from Doris Daumer.]

ACKERMAN, JACOB - b1848; s/o Jacob Ackerman & Carolyn Woodring/Watring; m Sarah Ann Krause. [Correspondence dated July 2000 from Doris Daumer.]

ACKERMAN, JONAS JEFFERSON - b 3 Nov 1872; s/o Edmund Ackerman & Maria Sybilla Minner; m Sarah Sterner Schneck b 29 Mar 1871, d/o James Schneck & Esther Sterner, d 22 May 1928; ch: Viola b 8 Jul 1893 & m Wirefield Nugle, Grace b 24 Jul 1895 & m Wm Bierman, Ralph Jacob b 24 Aug 1897 qv, Robert Henry b 8 Sep 1899 qv, Harvey Jonas b 21 Sep 1901 qv, Verva May b 6 Apr 1904 qv; d 1 Jan 1949. Jonas Jefferson Ackerman changed his middle name to Minner. [Correspondence dated July 2000 from Doris Daumer.]

ACKERMAN, JOYCE MARY - b 24 May 1925; d/o Robert Henry Ackerman & Helen Elizabeth Kipp; m Constantine Maurat d by Jul 2000. [Correspondence dated July 2000 from Doris Daumer.]

ACKERMAN, KEITH - s/o Neil Schlegel Ackerman & Elizabeth Bauer; m Karen Zehner; ch: Andora Eliese m Michael Hartman, Aaron Elijah, Mary Elizabeth, Henrich Christian, Sarah Elizabeth, Emmett Jeremiah, Andrew Jonas. [Correspondence dated July 2000 from Doris Daumer.]

ACKERMAN, LILLIE LOUISE - b 15 Apr 1879; d/o Henry Ackerman & Sarah Ann Krauss; m 20 Jun 1901 Carson A Semmel b 12 Oct 1879, s/o Willoughby Semmel & Mary A Laubach; d 24 Sep 1907. [Correspondence dated January 2001 from Elaine C. Matthews.]

ACKERMAN, MINNIE ELMIRA - b 22 Jun 1883; d/o Henry Ackerman & Sarah Ann Krauss; m 25 Dec 1903 Elwood James Anthony b 9 Apr 1879, s/o Benjamin F Anthony & Ellen J Heckman. [Correspondence dated January 2001 from Elaine C. Matthews.]

ACKERMAN, NEIL SCHLEGEL - s/o Harvey Jonas Ackerman & Alma Schlegel; m1 Elizabeth Bauer; m2 Annabell Zimmerman; ch by Elizabeth Bauer: Keith. [Correspondence dated July 2000 from Doris Daumer.]

ACKERMAN, RALPH JACOB - b 24 Aug 1897; s/o Jonas Jefferson Ackerman & Sarah Sterner Schneck; m1 Ruth Schell; m2 Elizabeth Hancock; ch: Jean m John Reifsnyder, Ralph Jr. [Correspondence dated July 2000 from Doris Daumer.]

ACKERMAN, ROBERT HENRY - b 8 Sep 1899; s/o Jonas Jefferson Ackerman & Sarah Sterner Schneck; m 4 Sep 1920 Helen Elizabeth Kipp b 11 May 1903, d/o Edward Kipp & Manie Etta Freeman/Fryman, d 22 Jan 1990; ch: Doris Mae b 15 Dec 1923 qv, Joyce Mary b 24 May 1925 qv; d 18 Mar 1976. [Correspondence dated July 2000 from Doris Daumer.]

ACKERMAN, RUDY SCHLEGEL - s/o Harvey Jonas Ackerman & Alma Schlegel; m Rose Erkolini; ch: Sally Ann, Ann m John M Lolik. [Correspondence dated July 2000 from Doris Daumer.]

ACKERMAN, SHIRLEY OLIVIA - d/o Harvey Jonas Ackerman & Alma Schlegel; m1 Forest Lentz; m2 Wm Albitz; m3 Louis Sommers; m4 John Steupeak; d1999. [Correspondence dated July 2000 from Doris Daumer.]

ACKERMAN, VERVA MAY - b 6 Apr 1904; d/o Jonas Jefferson Ackerman & Sarah Sterner Schneck; m1 Claude Lutz; m2 Paul Moyer. [Correspondence dated July 2000 from Doris Daumer.]

ACKERMAN, WILLIAM HENRY - b 15 Apr 1879; s/o Henry Ackerman & Sarah Ann Krauss; m 5 Aug 1905 Amy Hoffman b 14 Jan 1882, d/o Josiah P Hoffman & Alice J Kuntz, d 19 Mar 1965; ch: Grace May b 22 May 1906 qv, Helen Irene b 2 Nov 1910 qv; res: 1029 Kinden Street in Allentown; d 8 Nov 1964; bur: Greenwood Cem. [Correspondence dated January 2001 from Elaine C. Matthews.]

# DESCENDANTS OF JOHANNES ACKERMAN

Johannes Ackerman - of Berlicum, HO
  David Ackerman - bc1608, m Lysbet Bellier/Lysbeth De Villiers
    Abraham Ackerman - b1659
      David Abraham - m Margruitie Jurcksen
        David D - m Juanetie Van Der Beck
          David - m Jane Blauvelt
            David D - m Martha Stevens
              James A - alive 1872, m Sarah Ann Turner
                David D - b1872, m Ethel May Serviss
      Guilian/Guilean/Geleyn Ackerman - b1697
        Abraham Ackerman - b1728
          John Ackerman - b1757
            Catherine/Caterine - b1803
            John - b1805
            Abraham Ackerman - b1808
              Jacob Ackerman - b1846
                Ira Franklin Ackerman - b1881
                  William Patterson Ackerman - b1908
                    Donna Ackerman - alive 2000
            Mary Ackerman - b1810

ACKERMAN, ABRAHAM - b 3 May 1659 Nord Brabant HO; s/o David Ackerman & Lysbet Bellier; m 28 May 1683 Altze/Aeltie Van Leer b 14 May 1663 Kingston NY; ch: Guilian/Geleyn b1697 qv.[146] Abraham Ackerman - b 3 May 1659 Berlicum (near Den Bosch), Nord Brabant; bapt 15 May 1659; s/o David Ackerman & Elisbeth Bellier; m 28 May 1683 in Reformed Dutch Church of Flatbush, Long Island NY to Aeltie Van Laer b14 May 1663, bapt 26 Apr 1666 Kingston NY, d/o Adrian Van Laer & Abigail Ver Planken; res: Bedford in Long Island NY; rel: joined Bergen Reformed Church of Jersey City NJ 1 Apr 1684, dismissed to Hackensack NJ 3 Oct 1696. Abraham Ackerman owned land along the Hackensack and Saddle rivers, covers today's towns of Woodridge, Hasbrouck Heights, and

---

[146] Correspondence dated 25 Oct. 2000 from Mary V. Alexander. This is probably the same Abraham David Ackerman who married Aaltie Van Laren. ----, *The National Cyclopaedia of American Biography...Volume XXVII* (New York: James T. White Company, 1939), p. 179. Abraham Ackerman - b 3 May 1659 Nord (North) Brabant HO; s/o David Ackerman & Lysbeth De Villiers; ch: Guilean/Geleyn b1697 qv. Correspondence dated 16 Oct. 2000 contributed by Donna Kaser.

several other small towns.[147]  Abraham Davidse Ackerman - b 3 May 1659 Berlicum, Noord Brabant, HO, Netherlands; s/o David Ackerman & Elizabeth Bellier; m 28 May 1683 in Flatbush, Long Island NY to Aeltie VanLaer b 14 May 1663 Kingston (Ulster Co) NY; d Hackensack, Bergen Co NJ.[148]

ACKERMAN, ABRAHAM - b 2 May 1728; s/o Guilean/Geleyn Ackerman & ----; ch: John b 24 Nov 1757 qv. [Correspondence dated 16 Oct. 2000 contributed by Donna Kaser. The name appears as Guilian Ackerman in correspondence from Mary V. Alexander.]

ACKERMAN, ABRAHAM - b 8 Jul 1808 possibly in Bedford Co PA; s/o John Ackerman & ----; ch: Jacob b 14 Sep 1846 qv; d 26 Mar 1862 Salem NE.[149]  Abraham Ackerman b 8 Jul 1808 Bedford Co PA; s/o John Ackerman & Amy (Barton) Roberts; m1830 Isabel Green b1812, d 30 May 1886; d May 1862.[150]

ACKERMAN, ABRAHAM GELEYN - b 2 May 1728 NJ; s/o Guilian/Geleyn Ackerman & Rachel Van Voorhees; mc1756 Jannetje/Jane Romeyn b1738 Bergen Co NJ, bapt 10 Dec 1738, d/o Jan Romeyn & Catrina Outwater, d 12 Apr 1808, bur: Reformed Dutch Churchyard in New Brunswick NJ; ch: John b 24 Nov 1757 qv; d 15 Dec 1810 Reformed Dutch Churchyard, New Brunswick NJ. [Correspondence dated 25 Oct. 2000 from Mary V. Alexander.]

ACKERMAN, CATHERINE/CATERINE - b 20 Dec 1803 Bedford PA; d/o John Ackerman & Amy (Barton) Roberts; m 16 Oct 1825 in Knox Co OH to Thomas Singrey b 10 Mar 1801 Baltimore MD, s/o Jacob Singrey & Rebecca Marshall, d 20 Sep 1885 near Albion (Noble Co) IN, bur: Sweet Cem near Skinner Lake (Jeff Twp, Noble Co) IN; d 5 Dec 1881; bur: Sweet Cem, Albion, Noble Co IN. [Correspondence dated 25 Oct. 2000 from Mary V. Alexander.]

ACKERMAN, DAVID - bc1608 Berlicum HO; s/o Johannes Ackerman & ----; m1641 Lysbeth De Villiers; ch: Abraham b 3 May 1659 qv.   Arrived in America in 1662 & settled in New

---

[147] Pedigree chart prepared by Ruth Ackerman Herzberg and purchased from Yates Publishing Co.

[148] Pedigree chart prepared by Patricia J. Zumwalt and purchased from Yates Publishing Co.

[149] Correspondence dated 16 Oct. 2000 contributed by Donna Kaser.

[150] Correspondence dated 25 Oct. 2000 from Mary V. Alexander.

Amsterdam.[151]   David Ackerman - b1613 Nord Brabant HO; m 16
Sep 1641 Lysbet Bellier b1616 Dordrecht HO; ch: Abraham b 3 May
1659 qv.[152]   David Ackerman - b1613 Oss, Nord Brabant, Dutch
Republic of HO; m 16 Sep 1613 Elisbeth Bellier b 24 Jan 1616, d/o
Jean Bellier & Catharine Herque, d 29 Jan 1668; res: Berlicum in
North Brabant c1662; d between Nov 1662 & Mar 1663.[153]   David
Ackerman - b1614 Oss, Noord Brabant, HO, Netherlands; m 16 Sep
1641 Elizabeth Bellier b 24 Jan 1615/1616, d 1671 Harlem (Erie Co)
NY; d1662.[154]   David Ackerman - b1615 Berlicum HO; s/o
Jo[h]annes Ackerman & Anneken Adianse; m1641 in HO to Lysbeth
de Velliers b1615 HO, d/o Louis de velliers & Anna Schuyler, dc1679
New Harlem NY; dc1662.[155]   David Ackerman - alive 1662; m
Lysbet De Villiers. "[S]ailed for New Amsterdam from Amsterdam,
Holland, with his wife and children in 1662 but died at sea en
route."[156]

ACKERMAN, DAVID D - b 13 Dec 1872 NY City; s/o James A
Ackerman & Sarah Ann Turner; m 22 Jun 1899 in Closter NJ to Ethel
May Serviss, d/o John Henry Serviss & ----; ch: Ruth Serviss, David
D; occ: lawyer, admitted to the NY bar in 1896 & the NJ bar in 1900;
edu: AB 1894 & LLB 1896 at Columbia University; rel:
Congregationalist; d 18 Aug 1936 Closter NJ. [ ----, *The National
Cyclopaedia of American Biography... Volume XXVII*. New York:
James T. White Company, 1939, p. 179. See photograph p. 180.]

ACKERMAN, DONNA - alive 2000; d/o William Patterson
Ackerman & ----; m ---- Kaser. [Correspondence dated 16 Oct. 2000
contributed by Donna Kaser.]

---

[151] Correspondence dated 16 Oct. 2000 contributed by Donna Kaser.
[152] Correspondence dated 25 Oct. 2000 from Mary V. Alexander.
[153] Pedigree chart prepared by Ruth Ackerman Herzberg and purchased from Yates
Publishing Co.
[154] Pedigree chart prepared by Patricia J. Zumwalt and purchased from Yates
Publishing Co.
[155] Pedigree chart prepared by Lynne Moretti and purchased from Yates Publishing
Co. She states that David, Lysbeth, and son Louerence arrived in New Amsterdam
on "2-9-1662." By 1663, Lysbeth was a widow and the housekeeper for Anthony
Deicksen, an official for the West Indian Co. until 1665 when she took him to court
to pay back wages; she moved to New Harlem in 1668. Ibid.
[156] ----, *The National Cyclopaedia of American Biography... Volume XXVII* (New
York: James T. White Company, 1939), p. 179.

ACKERMAN, GUILIAN/GUILEAN/GELEYN - b1697 Hackensack NJ; s/o Abraham Ackerman & Altze/Aeltie Van Leer; mc1723 Rachel Van Voorhees bapt 4 Oct 1702; ch: Abraham Geleyn b 2 May 1728 qv.[157] Guilean/Geleyn Ackerman - b Dec 1697 Hackensack NJ; s/o Abraham Ackerman & ----; ch: Abraham b 2 May 1728 qv.[158]

ACKERMAN, IRA FRANKLIN - b 28 Dec 1881; s/o Jacob Ackerman & ----; ch: William Patterson b 23 Apr 1908 qv; d 24 Mar 1947 Whitehouse OH. [Correspondence dated 16 Oct. 2000 contributed by Donna Kaser.]

ACKERMAN, JACOB - b 14 Sep 1846 Richland Co OH; s/o Abraham Ackerman & ----; ch: Ira Franklin b 28 Dec 1881 qv; d 14 May 1901 Toledo OH. [Correspondence dated 16 Oct. 2000 contributed by Donna Kaser.]

ACKERMAN, JOHANNES - ch: David bc1608 qv; res: Berlicum HO. [Correspondence dated 16 Oct. 2000 contributed by Donna Kaser.]

ACKERMAN, JOHN - b 24 Nov 1757; s/o Abraham Ackerman & ----; ch: Abraham b 8 Jul 1808 qv; mil: Rev War soldier; d1841, age 83y. [Correspondence dated 16 Oct. 2000 contributed by Donna Kaser.] John Ackerman b 24 Nov 1757 Bergen Co NJ; s/o Abraham Geleyn Ackerman & Jannetje/Jane Romeyn; m1 Hanna(h) --- b 5 Apr 1766, d 22 Apr 1802 Bedford Co PA; m2 17 Feb 1803 Amy (Barton) Roberts b 18 Aug 1777, d/o ---- Barton & ----, d 12 Aug 1775; ch by Amy (Barton) Roberts: Catherine/Caterine b 20 Dec 1803 qv, John b 15 Nov 1805 qv, Abraham b 8 Jul 1808 qv, Mary b 5 Oct 1810 qv; d 8 Sep 1841 near Waterford, Knox Co OH; bur: North Fork Cem, Morrow Co OH.[159]

ACKERMAN, JOHN - b 15 Nov 1805 Bedford Co PA; s/o John Ackerman & Amy (Barton) Roberts; m 20 Jan 1829 Idah Cook bc1810, d 23 Dec 1862, bur: North Fork Cem in Morrow Co OH; d 3

---

[157] Correspondence dated 25 Oct. 2000 from Mary V. Alexander.

[158] Correspondence dated 16 Oct. 2000 contributed by Donna Kaser.

[159] Correspondence dated 25 Oct. 2000 from Mary V. Alexander. John Ackerman served in the Revolutionary War. Correspondence dated 16 Oct. 2000 from Donna Kaser.

Sep 1873; bur: North Fork Cem, Morrow Co OH. [Correspondence dated 25 Oct. 2000 from Mary V. Alexander.]

ACKERMAN, MARY - b 5 Oct 1810 Bedford Co PA; d/o John Ackerman & Amy (Barton) Roberts; m John Lewis b1806, d 13 Jan 1879, bur: North Fork Cem; d 21 Mar 1885; bur: North Fork Cem. [Correspondence dated 25 Oct. 2000 from Mary V. Alexander.]

ACKERMAN, WILLIAM PATTERSON - b 23 Apr 1908 Carey OH; s/o Ira Franklin Ackerman & ----; ch: Donna alive 2000 qv; d 17 Dec 1980 Toledo OH. [Correspondence dated 16 Oct. 2000 contributed by Donna Kaser.]

# DESCENDANTS OF JOHN ACKERMAN

John Ackerman
    Valentine - b1825, Jane Elizabeth Spurgeon
        Benjamin - bc1853
        John J - bc1856, m Josie
            Fred Fay - m Elizabeth Valentine Tipton
                Walter T - b1909
        Margaret Anne - b1862
        Henry Valentine - b1864, m1 Kath. Brown, m2 Belle Koup
            Henry Raymond - b1890
                James Henry - b1911, m Eva ----
                Jesse Winsford - b1913, m Nellie Gertrude Geilert
                Norman Wallace - m ----
                    Ch: John Fitzgerald, David Michael, Paul Martin
                Samuel Sherman - b1927, married three times
                    Ch: Michael William, Mark Andrew, Dorothy Ruth
            Alma Julia - b1892
            Effie Elizabeth - b1894
            Virgil
            Viola
        George - bc1867, m Gertrude Ramsey
            Ch: Ralph, Myrtle, Alta/Alma Mae
        Anna Elizabeth - b1874
    Phillip - bc1829
    George W - m Rita J Sigafoos
    Melissa


AKERMAN, ALMA JULIA - b 3 Jan 1892 Waverly KS; d/o Henry Valentine Ackerman & Katherine Brown; m 5 Nov 1913 in Waverly KS to John Walter Thomas b 19 Oct 1888 California (Moniteau Co) MO, d 12 Feb 1969 Garnett KS; d 6 Jun 1975 Tulsa OK; bur: Garnett KS.[160] Alma Julia Akerman "was always known by her middle name, Julia, which was sometimes shown as Juel. ... While she was not certain, she always believed that her grandfather, Valentine Akerman, came to Columbus, Ohio, with her great-grandfather, possibly named

---

[160] The spelling of the Ackerman surname differs between father and daughter in the addendum. Thomas, Gail Robert, *Daniel Thomas of Prince George's County, Maryland* (----: ----, 1996), addendum 1/15/2000.

John, in about 1833."[161]    "Julia was a beautiful young lady, with brown hair and brown eyes, of medium build and being about five feet two inches tall. Her education included only elementary school which was the custom in the rural areas of Kansas at that time."[162] After marrying, she and her husband "set up housekeeping on a farm five miles north of Wesphalia. ... In 1918 they sold the first farm and bought a second one in the same area (in section 1-21S-17E) which they later sold at a good profit and bought a well improved 320 acre farm in an area known as 'French Ridge' 3.5 miles west of the Anerson-Coffee County lines in Coffee County, KS. This farm was in secion 7-17S-17E...."[163]    She and her husband "moved from their farm eleven miles northeast of Burlington to a house in Burlington. ... They also purchased a small 26 acre farm at the southwest edge of Burlington.... In 1959, several years after her husband retired, they sold their place at Burlington and bought a small two bedroom home at 715 East 4$^{th}$, Garett, Kansas."[164]    In 1974, Alma Julia Akerman moved to the Skyline Nursing Home in Tulsa OK, where she lived until her death."[165]

AKERMAN, ANNA ELIZABETH - b 20 Sep 1874 Council Bluffs IA; d/o Valentine Ackerman & Jane Elizabeth Spurgeon; m1 23 Jul 1892 Harry Putnam Newcomb d 7 Dec 1928; m2 before 21 Jan 1932 Albert S Mortimer b 14 Oct 1864, d 29 Apr 1949, bur: Glendale Cem in Pottawatomie Twp KS; d 21 Jan 1932. [Thomas, Gail Robert, *Daniel Thomas of Prince George's County, Maryland.* ----: ----, 1996, addendum 1/15/2000.]

ACKERMAN, EFFIE ELIZABETH - b 9 Jun 1894 Waverly, Coffey Co KS; d/o Henry Valentine Ackerman & Katherine Brown; m Apr 1909 in Kansas City Wyandotte Co KS to Arthur Henry Van Wye; d 7 Dec 1917 Sunnyside WA; bur: Terrace Heights Mem Park.[166]    Effie Elizabeth Ackerman "insisted the name was spelled with a 'C'."[167]

[161] Thomas, Gail Robert, *Daniel Thomas of Prince George's County, Maryland* (---- : ----, 1996), p. 171.
[162] Ibid., p. 174.
[163] Ibid., p. 169.
[164] Ibid., p. 175.
[165] Ibid., p. 176.
[166] Thomas, Gail Robert, *Daniel Thomas of Prince George's County, Maryland* (---- : ----, 1996), addendum 1/15/2000.
[167] Thomas, Gail Robert, *Daniel Thomas of Prince George's County, Maryland* (---- : ----, 1996), p. 172.

AKERMAN, FRED FAY - s/o John J Akerman & Josie ----; m Elizabeth Valentine Tipton; ch: Walter T b 14 Dec 1909. [Thomas, Gail Robert, *Daniel Thomas of Prince George's County, Maryland.* ----: ----, 1996, addendum 1/15/2000.]

ACKERMAN, GEORGE - bc1867 OR; s/o Valentine Ackerman & Jane Elizabeth Spurgeon; m Gertrude Ramsey; ch: Ralph, Myrtle m ---- Harris, Alta/Alma Mae; d Baldwin, Douglas Co KS. [Thomas, Gail Robert, *Daniel Thomas of Prince George's County, Maryland.* ----: ----, 1996, addendum 1/15/2000.]

ACKERMAN, HAZEL MAE - b 24 Feb 1918; d/o Henry Raymond Ackerman & Margaret Ethel Christina Hulse; m Truman Mansell b 18 Oct 1918; d 5 Jan 2000 Kansas City MO. [Thomas, Gail Robert, *Daniel Thomas of Prince George's County, Maryland.* ----: ----, 1996, addendum 1/15/2000.]

ACKERMAN, HENRY RAYMOND - b 13 Feb 1890 Coffey Co KS; s/o Henry Valentine Ackerman & Katherine Brown; m1 before 1911 Margaret Ethel Christina Hulse b 30 Sep 1893, d 19 Oct 1963; m2 after 1952 Edith Roberts; ch by Margaret Ethel Christina Hulse: James Henry b 8 Jan 1911 qv, Jesse Winsford b 28 May 1913 qv, Hazel Mae b 24 Feb 1918 qv, Gertrude Juanita b 10 Sep 1920, Theresa Maria b 18 Jul 1922 & m ---- Riffle, Robert Wesley b 8 Mar 1924 & m Mary McMillon, Samuel Sherman b 16 May 1927 qv, Dorothy Ruth b 22 Apr 1931 & m James Ulrey; d 21 Sep 1960 Kansas City KS.[168] Gertrude Juanita Ackerman "Died young - by letter 9 Sept. 1974, Nellie Ackerman wrote that Gertrude was poisoned by her mother."[169]

ACKERMAN, HENRY VALENTINE - b 24 Feb 1864 Portland OR; s/o Valentine Ackerman & Jane Elizabeth Spurgeon; m1 3 Jun 1889 in Ft Scott KS to Katherine Brown b 8 Oct 1865 Cincinnati (Hamilton Co) OH, d 7 Feb 1902 Bronaugh (Vernon Co) MO; m2 c 3 Nov 1902 Belle Koup; ch of Katherine Brown: Henry Raymond b 13 Feb 1890 qv, Alma Julia b 3 Jan 1892 qv, Effie Elizabeth b 9 Jun 1894 qv; ch of

---

[168] Thomas, Gail Robert, *Daniel Thomas of Prince George's County, Maryland* (----: ----, 1996), addendum 1/15/2000.
[169] Thomas, Gail Robert, *Daniel Thomas of Prince George's County, Maryland* (----: ----, 1996), p. 172.

Belle Koup: Virgil qv, Viola qv; d Sep 1930 Kansas City; bur: Mt Hope Cem, Kansas City KS.[170] Henry Valentine Akerman m2 after c1902 Belle Madison Koup, his housekeeper.[171]

ACKERMAN, JAMES HENRY - b 8 Jan 1911; s/o Henry Raymond Ackerman & Margaret Ethel Christina Hulse; m Eva ----; d 6 Apr 1968. [Thomas, Gail Robert, *Daniel Thomas of Prince George's County, Maryland*. ----: ----, 1996, addendum 1/15/2000.]

ACKERMAN, JESSE WINSFORD - b 28 May 1913; s/o Henry Raymond Ackerman & Margaret Ethel Christina Hulse; m Nellie Gertrude Geilert d 6 Mar 1985 Mansfield OH; ch: Norman Wallace alive 1996 qv; dc Oct 1994.[172] Jesse Winsford Ackerman m Nellie Gertrude Geilert, d/o Paul Geilert, d 6 Mar 1985 Mansfield MO; ch: Norman Wallace qv.[173]

ACKERMAN, JOHN - unproven father of Valentine, Phillip, George W, & Melissa; the compiler's mother was uncertain whether or not "John" was the correct name. The children were known siblings of each other, however. [Correspondence dated 3 August 2000 from Gail R. Thomas.]

AKERMAN, JOHN J - bc1856 IL; s/o Valentine Ackerman & Jane Elizabeth Spurgeon; m Josie ---- d1925, bur: Mt Hope Cem; ch: Fred Fay qv.[174] John J Akerman bc1858.[175]

AKERMAN, MARGARET ANNE - b 13 Jan 1862 IA; d/o Valentine Ackerman & Jane Elizabeth Spurgeon; m John Frank Mortimer; d 5

---

[170] Thomas, Gail Robert, *Daniel Thomas of Prince George's County, Maryland* (----: ----, 1996), addendum 1/15/2000.

[171] Surname spelling differs between book and addendum. Thomas, Gail Robert, *Daniel Thomas of Prince George's County, Maryland* (----: ----, 1996), p. 171.

[172] Thomas, Gail Robert, *Daniel Thomas of Prince George's County, Maryland* (----: ----, 1996), addendum 1/15/2000.

[173] Thomas, Gail Robert, *Daniel Thomas of Prince George's County, Maryland* (----: ----, 1996), p. 171.

[174] The spelling of the Ackerman surname is different between father and son in the addendum. Thomas, Gail Robert, *Daniel Thomas of Prince George's County, Maryland* (----: ----, 1996), addendum 1/15/2000.

[175] Thomas, Gail Robert, *Daniel Thomas of Prince George's County, Maryland* (----: ----, 1996), p. 171.

Dec 1900 Waverly, Coffey Co KS; bur: Glendale Cem, Pott Twp.[176]
Margaret Akerman bc1862 IA; m Bert Mortimer.[177]

ACKERMAN, MICHAEL WILLIAM - b 31 Oct 1953 Camp
Pendleton, Oceanside CA; s/o Samuel Sherman Ackerman & Barbara
Jean Cady; m1979 Georgina Sims.[178] Michael William Ackerman res:
San Clemente CA.[179]

ACKERMAN, NORMAN WALLACE - alive 1996; s/o Jesse
Winsford Ackerman & Nellie Gertrude Geilert; m ----; ch: John
Fitzgerald, David Michael, Paul Martin; res: Arlington TX.[180]
Norman Wallace Ackerman res: Arlington TX; edu: engr degree from
KS State. John is "Petr Engr, Tex A&M, David is pilot with UPS in
Lewisville TX, and Paul resides in Dallas TX.[181]

AKERMAN, PHILLIP - bc 20 Jan 1829 Bavaria or GE; possible s/o
John Ackerman & ----; m after 1848 in OH to Joanna Frederica
Goehring; d 27 Feb 1895 Fremont IA; bur: Cedar Cem, Mahaska Co
IA. [Pedigree chart contributed by Gail R. Thomas.]

ACKERMAN, SAMUEL SHERMAN - b 16 May 1927 LaHarpe KS;
s/o Henry Raymond Ackerman & Margaret Ethel Christina Hulse; m1
1 Oct 1951 in Kansas City MO to Barbara Jean Cady; m2 12 Jan 1961
Phylis (Klein) (Ustis) Lipton, d/o Philip Klein; m3 14 Mar 1980 in
San Antonio TX to Helen Louise Conde Brown d 29 Jun 1994; ch of
Barbara Jean Cady: Michael William  b 31 Oct 1953 qv, Mark
Andrew b 24 Dec 1955 Camp Pendleton (Oceanside) CA & res
Mission Viejo CA; ch of Helen Louise Conde Brown: Dorothy Ruth b

---

[176] The spelling of Akerman differs between father and daughter in the addendum.
Thomas, Gail Robert, *Daniel Thomas of Prince George's County, Maryland* (----: ----, 1996), addendum 1/15/2000.
[177] Thomas, Gail Robert, *Daniel Thomas of Prince George's County, Maryland* (----: ----, 1996), p. 171.
[178] Thomas, Gail Robert, *Daniel Thomas of Prince George's County, Maryland* (----: ----, 1996), addendum 1/15/2000.
[179] Thomas, Gail Robert, *Daniel Thomas of Prince George's County, Maryland* (----: ----, 1996), p. 172.
[180] Thomas, Gail Robert, *Daniel Thomas of Prince George's County, Maryland* (----: ----, 1996), addendum 1/15/2000.
[181] Thomas, Gail Robert, *Daniel Thomas of Prince George's County, Maryland* (----: ----, 19960, p. 171.

22 Apr 1931 & m James Ulrey.[182] Samuel Sherman Ackerman & Barbara Jean Cady divorced. He m2 Phylis (Klein) (Ustis) Lipton, d/o Philip Klein; she died. He m3 Helen Louise (Conde) Brown, d/o William Abram Conde & Beatrice Brumett.[183]

ACKERMAN, VALENTINE - b1825 GE or Bavaria; possible s/o John Ackerman & ----; m 3 Oct 1830 in Butler Co OH to Jane Elizabeth Spurgeon b1832 ST, d Jul 1902, bur: Mt Ida Cem in Anderson Co KS; ch: Benjamin bc1853 OH, John J bc1856 qv, Margaret Anne b 13 Jan 1862 qv, Henry Valentine b 24 Feb 1864 qv, George bc1867 qv, Anna Elizabeth b20 Sep 1874 qv; d May 1894; bur: Mt Hope Cem, Kansas City KS.[184] Valentine Akerman was a soldier in the Union army during the Civil War.[185]

ACKERMAN, VIOLA - d/o Henry Valentine Akerman & Belle Koup; m Harold Main of "Harrisonville MO?"; res: Kansas City; d by 1996. [Thomas, Gail Robert, *Daniel Thomas of Prince George's County, Maryland.* ----: ----, 1996, p. 174.]

ACKERMAN, VIRGIL - s/o Henry Valentine Akerman & Belle Koup; occ: worked in a salvage yard in Kansas City MO; m several times; res: Kansas City MO. [Spelling of surname differs between father and son in book.] [Thomas, Gail Robert, *Daniel Thomas of Prince George's County, Maryland.* ----: ----, 1996, p. 174.]

---

[182] Thomas, Gail Robert, *Daniel Thomas of Prince George's County, Maryland* (----: ----, 1996), addendum 1/15/2000. Correspondence dated 3 August 2000 from Gail R. Thomas includes Phylis Klein's father's name.

[183] Thomas, Gail Robert, *Daniel Thomas of Prince George's County, Maryland* (----: ----, 1996), p. 172.

[184] Thomas, Gail Robert, *Daniel Thomas of Prince George's County, Maryland* (----: ----, 1996), addendum 1/15/2000. A Valentine Ackerman m 3 Oct. 1850 in Butler OH to Elizabeth Jane Spurgin according to the International Genealogical Record at familysearch.com, accessed 26 August 2000. A Valentinus Ackerman was christened 31 Aug. 1827 at Roemisch-Katholische, Neuerburg Bitburg, Rheinland, Preussen, the son of Joannis Ackerman and Elisabethae Berlooss according to the International Genealogical Record at familysearch.com, accessed 26 August 2000. In a letter dated 13 Sep. 2000, Gail R. Thomas mentions an 1880 census record for Neosho County, Kansas, showing Val Akerman b GE, age 55 in 1880, with wife Jane b OH?, age 40 in 1880, and children: Benjamin b OH, John b IL, Margaret b IA, Henry, George b OR, and Anna b IA.

[185] Surname spelling differs between book and addendum. Thomas, Gail Robert, *Daniel Thomas of Prince George's County, Maryland* (----: ----, 1996), p. 171.

# DESCENDANTS OF STEPHEN AKERMAN

Stephen Akerman - bc1634, m Sarah Morse
  Benjamin - 1686
    Mary - bapt 1711
    Sarah - bapt 1711
    Elizabeth - bapt 1711
    Benjamin - m Elizabeth Mead
      Joseph - m Elizabeth Jackson
        Benjamin - alive 1821, m Olive Meloon
          Amos Tappan - 1821, m Martha Rebecca Galloway
            Joseph - 1872, m Effie Ellen Reid
              Joseph Reid
              Benjamin
              Joseph Reid
              Elizabeth
  Simeon
  Nahum
  Josiah
  Hannah

AKERMAN, AMOS TAPPAN - b 23 Feb 1821 Portsmouth NH; s/o Benjamin Akerman & Olive Meloon;[186] m Martha Rebecca Galloway,[187] d/o Samuel Galloway & Rebecca E Scudder;[188] ch:

---

[186] ----, *The National Cyclopaedia of American Biography: being the history of the United States as illustrated in the lives of the founders, builders, and defenders of the republic, and of the men and women who are doing the work and moulding the thought of the present time.* Vol. IX. (New York: James T. White & Company, 1907), p. 209. Illustration appears on p. 209. Amos Tappan Akerman b 6 Jan 1823 Keene NH. ----, *The Twentieth Century Biographical Dictionary of Notable Americans, Vol. 1* appearing at ancestry.com, accessed 6 Aug. 2000. Amos Tappan Akerman b1819. Wilson, James Grant and John Fiske, *Appleton's Cyclopaedia of American Biography* (New York: D. Appleton & Co., 1888. Reprint Detroit: Gale Research, 1968), appearing at ancestry.com, accessed 6 Aug. 2000.

[187] ----, *The National Cyclopaedia of American Biography: being the history of the United States as illustrated in the lives of the founders, builders, and defenders of the republic, and of the men and women who are doing the work and moulding the thought of the present time.* Vol. XXXIII. (New York: James T. White & Company, 1947), p. 434. According to the International Genealogical Record, Amos Tappan Akerman m1847 in GA to Martha Rebecca Galloway or Amos T Akerman m 28 May 1864 in Clark GA to Martha R Galloway. familysearch.com, accessed 6 Aug. 2000.

Joseph b 10 Aug 1872 qv;[189] occ: admitted to the bar in 1844, taught at several schools over the next six years, entered professional practice in Elberton GA in 1850, US attorney for the district of GA 1866-1870, appointed US attorney general by President Grant in 1870 (resigned 1872); edu: common schools of NH, Dartmouth College (graduated 1842); pol: conservative party, joined the Republican party after the Civil War; d 21 Dec 1880 Cartersville GA. Opposed secession, although finally went with the state (GA) and entered the service of the Confederate government in the quartermaster's department. After the Civil War, supported the reconstruction policy of the government.[190] Promised one or more pictures for the collection at Phillips Exeter Academy in Exeter NH but had not yet contributed them by Oct 1874.[191] Authored the 13-page booklet "Sketch of the Military Career of Enoch Poor, Brig. General in the Revolutionary War."[192]

[188] Cooley, Eli F., *Genealogy of the Early Settlers in Trenton and Ewing, "Old Hunterdon County," New Jersey* (----: ----, 1883. Facsimile reprint Bowie: Heritage Books, Inc., 1993), p. 252, 323.

[189] ----, *The National Cyclopaedia of American Biography: being the history of the United States as illustrated in the lives of the founders, builders, and defenders of the republic, and of the men and women who are doing the work and moulding the thought of the present time.* Vol. XXXIII. (New York: James T. White & Company, 1947), p. 434.

[190] ----, *The National Cyclopaedia of American Biography...* Vol. IX, p. 209. Died 22 Nov 1880 according to Rich, Peggy Burton & Marion Ard Whitehurst, *The Pickens Sentinel: favorite newspaper of Pickens County. Pickens Court House, South Carolina, 1872-1893, historical and genealogical abstracts* (Bowie: Heritage Books, Inc., 1994), p. 80. Also served as the principal of Male School and was considered a "distinguished lawyer" who "practiced his profession" in GA. Winborne, Benjamin B., *The Colonial and State Political History of Hertford County, North Carolina* (----: ----, 1906. Reprinted as *The Colonial and State History of Hertford County, North Carolina* with new material added by Baltimore: Genealogical Publishing Co., Inc., 1976), p. 87. "[A]dmitted to the bar in 1844, and practised in New Hampshire until 1850, when he removed to Georgia. Here he continued the practice of law...." Amos Tappan Akerman was the quartermaster and served through the war. He resigned as U. S. attorney general on 14 Dec. 1871 and returned to Georgia. Unsuccessful candidate for the U. S. senate in 1873. ----, *The Twentieth Century Biographical Dictionary of Notable Americans, Vol. 1* appearing at ancestry.com, accessed 6 Aug. 2000.

[191] ----, "Portraits of New-Hampshire Governors...," *The New England Historical and Genealogical Register*, Vol. XXVIII (Oct. 1874), p. 447.

[192] ----, "Recent Publications," *The New England Historical and Genealogical Register*, Vol. XXXII (July 1878), p. 370.

AKERMAN, BENJAMIN - s/o Benjamin Akerman & Mary Hodge; m Elizabeth Mead; ch: Joseph m Elizabeth Jackson qv.[193]

AKERMAN, BENAJMIN - b1686 Newbury, Essex Co MA;[194] m1 1708 Elizabeth Hodge;[195] m2 c1729 Mary Broughton[196] or Mary Bradden, d/o John Bradden & Prudence Mitchell;[197] ch [possibly not in birth order]: Mary bapt 26 Aug 1711 at North Church in Portsmouth NH, Sarah bapt 26 Aug 1711 at North Church in Portsmouth NH, Elizabeth bapt 26 Aug 1711 at North Church in Portsmouth NH,[198] Benjamin bapt 4 Jul 1714 at North Church in Portsmouth NH,[199] Simeon, Nahum, Josiah, Hannah;[200] occ: butcher,

[193] ----, *The National Cyclopaedia of American Biography: being the history of the United States as illustrated in the lives of the founders* (New York: James T. White & Company, 1947), p. 434. According to Elizabeth Graham Eckland, Benjamin Akerman b1714; chr: 4 Jan 1714 North Church, Portsmouth NH; m 29 Jul 1745 in Portsmouth NH to Elizabeth Mead; d 24 Aug 1783 Portsmouth, Rockingham Co NH. Contribution by Elizabeth Graham Eckland to familysearch.org, accessed 6 Aug. 2000.
[194] Contributed by Elizabeth Graham Eckland to familysearch.org, accessed 6 Aug. 2000.
[195] Noyes, Sybil et al, *Genealogical Dictionary of Maine and New Hampshire* (Portland: ----, 1928-1939. Reprint Baltimore: Genealogical Publishing Company, 1996), p. 59. Tibbetts identifies Benjamin's wife only as Eliz. Tibbetts, Charles W., *The New Hampshire Genealogical Record. An illustrated quarterly magazine devoted to genealogy, history and biography. Vol. IV, January 1907 - October 1907* (Dover: Charles W. Tibbetts, 1907. Facsimile reprint Bowie: Heritage Books, Inc., 1988), p. 56. Hammond identifies Benjamin's wife only as Mary. Hammond, Otis G., *Probate Records of the Province of New Hampshire, Vol. 6, 1757-1760. State Papers Series Vol. 36* (----: The State of New Hampshire, 1938. Facsimile reprint Bowie: Heritage Books, Inc., 1989), p. 208, 209.
[196] Contributed by Elizabeth Graham Eckland to familysearch.org, accessed 6 Aug. 2000.
[197] Noyes, Sybil et al, *Genealogical Dictionary of Maine and New Hampshire* (Portland: ----, 1928-1939. Reprint Baltimore: Genealogical Publishing Company, 1996), p. 59.
[198] Tibbetts, Charles W., *The New Hampshire Genealogical Record. An illustrated quarterly magazine devoted to genealogy, history and biography. Vol. IV, January 1907 - October 1907* (Dover: Charles W. Tibbetts, 1907. Facsimile reprint Bowie: Heritage Books, Inc., 1988), p. 56.
[199] Ibid., p. 98. Noyes identifies only Benjamin by name and notes that there are seven other children. Noyes, Sybil et al, *Genealogical Dictionary of Maine and New Hampshire* (Portland: ----, 1928-1939. Reprint Baltimore: Genealogical Publishing Company, 1996), p. 59.
[200] Hammond, Otis G., *Probate Records of the Province of New Hampshire, Vol. 6, 1757-1760. State Papers Series Vol. 36.* ----: The State of New Hampshire, 1938. Facsimile reprint Bowie: Heritage Books, Inc., 1989, p. 208, 209.

doorkeeper to the court;[201] res: Portsmouth;[202] d Jan 1758 Portsmouth, Rockingham Co NH.[203] Benjamin Akerman m Mary Hodge [Is this a combining of Elizabeth Hodge and Mary Broughton/Bradden?]; res: EN, Portsmouth NH. Benjamin came from EN prior to 1716 & settled in Portsmouth NH.[204] [Did he go from EN to MA to NH?] In his will dated 31 Dec 1757 - 25 Jan 1758, Benjamin Akerman left his son Benjamin "the Tanyard at Islington that was Kirke's"[205] and signed his name Benja Akarman.[206] The following information pertains to Benjamin Akerman's service as doorkeeper to the court. It is assumed that all records refer to the same man. He would have been about 30 years old when he started the work and he appears to have continued until his death, when he was about 72 years old. The name appears variously as Benj., Benja., Benjamin, Akerman, and Acreman. Benjamin Akerman took the oath as doorkeeper on 12 Jan 1716.[207] It was recorded in the journal of the General Assembly for 17 Aug 1722 that he was to receive 7 pounds for his service as door keeper in 1721.[208] He served as doorkeeper & carrier of expresses,

[201] Noyes, Sybil et al, *Genealogical Dictionary of Maine and New Hampshire* (Portland: ----, 1928-1939. Reprint Baltimore: Genealogical Publishing Company, 1996), p. 59.

[202] Ibid., p. 59. See also Hammond, Otis G., *Probate Records of the Province of New Hampshire, Vol. 6, 1757-1760. State Papers Series Vol. 36.* (----: The State of New Hampshire, 1938. Facsimile reprint Bowie: Heritage Books, Inc., 1989), p. 208, 209.

[203] Contributed by Elizabeth Graham Eckland to familysearch.org, accessed 6 Aug. 2000.

[204] ----, *The National Cyclopaedia of American Biography: being the history of the United States as illustrated in the lives of the founders, builders, and defenders of the republic, and of the men and women who are doing the work and moulding the thought of the present time.* Vol. XXXIII. (New York: James T. White & Company, 1947), p. 434.

[205] Noyes, Sybil et al, *Genealogical Dictionary of Maine and New Hampshire* (Portland: ----, 1928-1939. Reprint Baltimore: Genealogical Publishing Company, 1996), p. 59.

[206] Hammond, Otis G., *Probate Records of the Province of New Hampshire, Vol. 6, 1757-1760. State Papers Series Vol. 36.* (----: The State of New Hampshire, 1938. Facsimile reprint Bowie: Heritage Books, Inc., 1989), p. 208, 209.

[207] Bouton, Nathaniel, *Provincial Papers. Documents and Records Relating to the Province of New-Hampshire, from 1692 to 1722: being part II. of papers relating to that period. Containing the "Journal of the Coucil and General Assembly." Volume III.* (Manchester: John B. Clarke, State Printer, 1869), p. 661.

[208] Bouton, Nathaniel, *Provincial Papers. Documents and Records Relating to the Province of New-Hampshire, from 1722 to 1737: containing important records and papers, pertaining to the settlement of the boundary lines between New-Hampshire*

etc, & was allowed 7 pounds 10 shillings for his service, as recorded in the journal of the General Assembly on 12 Jun 1724.[209]   He was paid 7 pounds for his service in 1724, as recorded in the journal of the General Assembly on 21 May 1725.[210]   He was voted, on 8 Jan 1725, to "be allowed & paid out of the publick Treasury the Sum of three pounds more than formerly allowed him for this Present year not to be paid till ye year is up, and that for ye future he be allowed and paid out of ye Publick Treasury (after ye Present year) the Sum of ten pounds pr annum for his attenda on the Govr Counl and assembly."[211] According to the journal of the House dated 29 Apr 1729, he was to receive 10 pounds for his service as "Dore Keeper" for 1728.[212]   He was recorded in the journal of the Council and Assembly on 13 May 1729 as receiving 10 pounds for service as doorkeeper.[213]   He received 10 pounds for his service as doorkeeper in 1729, as recorded in the journal of the General Assembly dated 1 Sep 1730.[214] According to the journal of the House dated 4 May 1731, he was paid 10 pounds for service as "Dore Keeper" in 1730.[215]   He was paid 10 pounds for his service as doorkeeper in 1731, as recorded in the journal of the House dated 16 Jan 1733.[216]   He was paid paid 10 pounds for service as doorkeeper as recorded in the journal of the House for 12 May 1732.[217]   He was to be paid 40 pounds for 4 years as doorkeeper to 15 Apr 1735, as recorded in the journal of the House dated 16 May 1735.[218]   He was to receive 60 pounds for 6 years of service as doorkeeper to 15 Apr 1737, as recorded in the journal of the House dated 23 Mar 1736.[219] According to the "Journal of the House," he was to receive 7 pounds 10 shillings "Proclamation money" for his service as a "doorkeeper for the yeare 1742 Ending

---

*and Massachusetts. Volume IV.* (Manchester: John B. Clarke, State Printer, 1870), p. 52.

[209] Ibid., p. 142.

[210] Ibid., p. 174.

[211] Ibid., p. 203. The journal of the House records the above item being voted on on 8 Jan 1725 and approved for Benjamin Akerman. Ibid., p. 416.

[212] Ibid., p. 507.

[213] Ibid., p. 545.

[214] Ibid., p. 760.

[215] Ibid., p. 593.

[216] Ibid., p. 658.

[217] Ibid., p. 619.

[218] Ibid., p. 693.

[219] Ibid., p. 723.

April next."[220]   A further record appeared in the "Journal of the House" records for 2 Jul 1743 pertaining to 1742: "Whereas in the last Supply Bill in the Estimate of the charge for the year 1742, there was put therein for Benja Akerman as doorkeeper the sum of three pounds fifteen shillings; And since that act passed, viz. on the first day of December 1742, there was a vote passed in the House of Represents that there be paid Benja Akerman for his service as Dorekeeper for the yeare 1742, ending at April 1743, the sum of seven pounds ten shillings Proclamation money: And whereas the said Benja Akerman has recd the sum of three pounds fifteen shillings Proclamation money as allowed in the estimate aforesaid-- Voted that there be paid out of the Publick Treasury the sum of three pounds fifteen shillings Proclamation money, in full for his service as Dore keeper for the yeare 1742, Ending April last, out of the Contingencies."[221]   The "Journal of the House" records: "Eodm Die. Voted that Benjamin Akerman be paid out of the Publick Treasury (out of the money laid in for contingencies &c) the sum of forty pounds old Tenor for his service as dore keeper...for the year 1743 from the 15th of April 1743 to the 15th April 1744 in full."[222]   As doorkeeper, he was instructed on 3 Jan 1745 to inform people of a meeting time.[223]   The House voted that Benjamin Akerman be paid ten pounds "out of ye money in the Publick Treasury for defraying the charge of the Government in full for his service of one year to the fifteenth of Apl 1745."[224] "Journal of the House" records dated 20 May 1746 noted that he was to be paid 11 pounds for his service "as doorkeeper to ye 25th of March last past."[225]   According to the "Journal of the House" records dated 27 May 1748, he was to be paid 13 pounds for his service "as Door Keeper for ye year 1747 to ye 25th of March last past to be paid out of ye money in ye publick Treasury."[226]   This is probably the Mr. Akerman who was to be paid a "door-keeper allowance, from 5th Mar. 1753 to 5th Mar. 1755" of 50 pounds.[227]   Benjamin Akerman

[220] Bouton, Nathaniel, *Provincial Papers. Documents and Records Relating to the Province of New-Hampshire, from 1738 to 1749: containing very valuable and interesting records and papers relating to the expedition against Louisbourg, 1745. Volume V.* (Nashua: Orren C. Moore, State Printer, 1871), p. 178.
[221] Ibid., p. 208, 679.
[222] Ibid., p. 251, 721.
[223] Ibid., p. 399.
[224] Ibid., p. 358.
[225] Ibid., p. 420, 445, 822.
[226] Ibid., p. 584, 883.
[227] Bouton, Nathaniel, *Provincial Papers. Documents and Records Relating to the Province of New-Hampshire, from 1749 to 1763: containing very valuable and*

was to be paid 30 pounds for his service as door keeper, 1755-1756.[228] "Votes of allowance were concurred as follows[:] Door-keeper Acreman's acct, for the year, 1756 [-] 30 [pounds]."[229] Benjamin Akerman was dead by 31 Mar 1758 because his door-keeper allowance of 18 pounds 15 shillings was paid "to his legal Representative."[230]

AKERMAN, BENJAMIN - alive 1821; s/o Joseph Akerman & Elizabeth Jackson; m Olive Meloon; ch: Amos Tappan b 23 Feb 1821 qv.[231]

AKERMAN, JOSEPH - s/o Benjamin Akerman & Elizabeth Mead; m Elizabeth Jackson; ch: Benjamin alive 1821qv. [----, *The National Cyclopaedia of American Biography: being the history of the United States as illustrated in the lives of the founders, builders, and defenders of the republic, and of the men and women who are doing the work and moulding the thought of the present time.* Vol. XXXIII. New York: James T. White & Company, 1947, p. 434.]

AKERMAN, JOSEPH - b 10 Aug 1872; s/o Amos Tappan Akerman & Martha Rebecca Galloway; m 7 Jun 1906 in Charlotte NC to Effie Ellen Reid, d/o Jonathan Reid; ch: Joseph Reid d in infancy, Benjamin, Joseph Reid, Laura, Elizabeth m John David Withrow Jr; occ: obstetrician, professor of obstetrics at Univ of GA School of Medicine from 1922 until his death; edu: AB 1894 from Univ of GA, MD 1900 from Johns Hopkins; rel: Reid Memorial (Presbyterian) Church, he was an elder; pol: independent; d 9 Dec 1943 Augusta GA. [----, *The National Cyclopaedia of American Biography: being the history of the United States as illustrated in the lives of the founders, builders, and defenders of the republic, and of the men and*

---

*interesting records and papers relating to the Crown Point expedition, and the "Seven Years French and Indian Wars," 1755-1762. Volume VI.* (Manchester: James M. Campbell, State Printer, 1872), p. 384.

[228] Ibid., p. 525.

[229] Ibid., p. 589.

[230] Ibid., p. 666.

[231] ----, *The National Cyclopaedia of American Biography: being the history of the United States as illustrated in the lives of the founders, builders, and defenders of the republic, and of the men and women who are doing the work and moulding the thought of the present time.* Vol. XXXIII. (New York: James T. White & Company, 1947), p. 434. According to the International Genealogical Index, Benjamin Akerman mc1820 in Portsmouth NH to Olive Meloon. Familysearch.org, accessed 6 Aug. 2000.

*women who are doing the work and moulding the thought of the present time.* Vol. XXXIII. New York: James T. White & Company, 1947, p. 434. See photograph on page 434.]

ACREMAN/ACKERMAN, STEPHEN - bc1634 Newbury, Essex Co MA;[232] m 17 Dec 1684 in Newbury [Essex Co] MA to Sarah Morse d 7 Dec 1711 Newbury;[233] ch: Benjamin b1686 qv; d after 1695 Portsmouth NH.[234] Stephen Ackerman/Acreman m1 17 Dec 1684? in Newbury to Sarah (Morse) Stickney d1711.[235]

---

[232] Contributed by Elizabeth Graham Eckland to familysearch.org, accessed 6 Aug. 2000.

[233] Roth, Jean A., "The Luke Woodbury Saunders Family Part II: the maternal ancestry of Mary Ann (Montgomery) Saunders," *Seattle Genealogical Society Bulletin*, Vol. 49 #2 (Winter 2000), p. 64.

[234] Contributed by Elizabeth Graham Eckland to familysearch.org, accessed 6 Aug. 2000.

[235] Torrey, Clarence Almon, *New England marriages Prior to 1700* (Baltimore: Genealogical Publishing Co., Inc., 1985), p. 2, 710. Stephen Ackerman first colonial record, his marriage in 1684 at Newbury, Mass. Holmes, Frank R., *Directory of the Ancestral Heads of new England Families, 1620-1700* (New York: ----, 1923. Reprint Baltimore: Genealogical Publishing Co., Inc., 1989), p. i.

# BIBLIOGRAPHY

Correspondence
    Robert H. Ackerman
    Robert L. Ackerman
    Mary V. Alexander
    Nancy Brown Brooker Bowers
    Christy Baize Cave
    Marian A.Coberly
    Doris Daumer
    Eddie Dirks
    Teresa Durbin
    Marjorie Jackson
    Donna Kaser
    Elaine C. Matthews
    Gail R. Thomas
    Marian Trump
    Carl W. Weil
    Keith Whiting
    Dorothy Pray Wilson

Primary Sources
    Rockingham County, New Hampshire, 1860 Census
    Rockingham County, New Hampshire, 1880 Census
    Rockingham County, New Hampshire, 1900 Census

Secondary Sources

----. "Account Book of Daniel C., Daniel R. & Clarence W. Adams, Undertakers of Northwest Ford HD., Sussex Co., Delaware, near Blommery, Caroline Co., Maryland." *Delaware Genealogical Society Journal*, Vol. 10 #2 (October 1999).

----. *An Illustrated Historical Atlas of Lucas and Part of Wood Counties, Ohio.* Chicago: Andreas & Baskin, 1875. Facsimile reprint Bowie: Heritage Books, Inc., 1999.

----. "Alphabetical Roll of Students [attending] Logan County High School for the School Year 1905-06." *Oklahoma Genealogical Society Quarterly*, Vol. 45 #2 (2000).

----. "Births, Marriages, and Deaths in Portsmouth, N.H." *The New England Historical and Genealogical Register*, Vol. XXIV (Oct. 1870).

----. "Births, Marriages, and Deaths in Portsmouth, N. H." *The New England Historical and Genealogical Register*, Vol. XXV (April 1871).

----. "Births, Marriages, and Deaths in Portsmouth, N.H.," *The New England Historical and Genealogical Register*, Vol. XXVI (Oct. 1872).

----. "Brooklyn Church Records." *The German Connection*, Vol. 23 #3 (Third Quarter 1999).

----. *Calendar of the Close Rolls...Henry IV. Vol. III. A.D. 1405-1409.* ----: ----, 1931. Reprint Germany: Kraus Reprint, 1971.

----. *Calendar of the Close Rolls...Henry IV. Vol. IV. A.D. 1409-1413.* ----: ----, 1932. Reprint Germany: Kraus Reprint, 1971.

----. *Calendar of the Patent Rolls...Edward III. A.D. 1330-1334.* ----: ----, 1893. Reprint Germany: Kraus Reprint, 1972.

----. *Calendar of the Patent Rolls...Edward III. A.D. 1338-1340.* ----: ----, 1895. Reprint Germany: Kraus Reprint, 1972.

----. *Calendar of the Patent Rolls...Edward III. Vol. VII. A.D. 1345-1348.* ----: ----, 1903. Reprint Germany: Kraus Reprint, 1971.

----. *Calendar of the Patent Rolls...Edward III. Vol. IX. A.D. 1350-1354.* ----: ----, 1907. Reprint Germany: Kraus Reprint, 1971.

----. *Calendar of the Patent Rolls...Edward IV. A.D. 1327-1330.* ----: ----, 1893. Reprint Germany: Kraus Reprint, 1972.

----. *Calendar of the Patent Rolls...Elizabeth I. Vol. V. 1569-1572.* London: Her Majesty's Stationery Office, 1966.

----. *Calendar of the Patent Rolls...Elizabeth. Vol. II. 1560-1563.* London: Her Majesty's Stationery Office, 1948. Reprint Germany: Kraus Reprint, 1976.

----. *Calendar of the Patent Rolls...Henry IV. Vol. III. A.D. 1405-1408.* ----: ----, 1907. Reprint Germany: Kraus Reprint, 1971.

----. *Calendar of the Patent Rolls...Henry VI. Vol. II. A.D. 1429-1436.* ----: ----, 1908. Reprint Germany: Kraus Reprint, 1971.

----. *Calendar of the Patent Rolls...Henry VI. Vol. IV. A.D. 1429-1436.* ----: ----, 1908. Reprint Germany: Kraus Reprint, 1971.

----. *Calendar of the Patent Rolls...Henry VI. Vol. III. A.D. 1436-1441.* ----: ----, 1908. Reprint Germany: Kraus Reprint, 1971.

----. *Calendar of the Patent Rolls...Henry VI. Vol. IV. A.D. 1441-1446.* ----: ----, 1908. Reprint Germany: Kraus Reprint, 1971.

----. *Calendar of the Patent Rolls...Henry VI. Vol. V. A.D. 1446-1452.* ----: ----, 1909. Reprint Germany: Kraus Reprint, 1971.

----. *Calendar of the Patent Rolls...Henry VI. Vol. VI. A.D. 1452-1461.* ----: ----, 1910. Reprint Germany: Kraus Reprint, 1971.

----. *Calendar of the Patent Rolls...Richard II. A.D. 1381-1385.* ----: ----, 1897. Reprint Germany: Kraus Reprint, 1971.

----. *Calendar of the Patent Rolls...Richard II. Vol. V. A.D. 1391-1396.* ----: ----, 1905. Reprint Germany: Kraus Reprint, 1971.

----. "*Champaign County Herald* - Sheaves of 1885." *Champaign County Genealogical Society Quarterly*, Vol. 21 #4 (Spring 2000).

----. "Chicago Catholic Cemetery." *Chicago Genealogist*, Vol. 32 #3 (Spring 2000).

----. "City Guard - A California Militia Unit." *Root Cellar Preserves*, Vol. 21 #3 (Jun-Jul-Aug-Sep 1999).

----, *The Compact Edition of the Oxford English Dictionary.* Oxford: Oxford University Press, 1985.

----. "Deaths Extracted from R. L. Polk & Co.'s Toledo [Ohio] Directory 1885-1886. Mortuary List. Extending from April 1, 1885 to April 1, 1886. Compiled from official records." *Fort Industry Reflections*, Vol. 18 #4.

----. "Deaths Extracted from R. L. Polk & Co.'s Toledo [Ohio] Directory 1886-1887. Mortuary List. Extending from April 1, 1886 to April 1, 1887." *Fort Industry Reflections*, Vol. XX #1 (January-February-March 2000).

----. "Douglas County Stray Records, 1885-1906." *Ozar'kin*, Vol. XX #1 (Spring 1998).

----. "1842 Muster Rolls." *The Genealogical Record*, Vol. XL #3 (September 1998).

----. "1860 U. S. Census Mortality Schedules." *The Genealogical Magazine of New Jersey*, Vol. 74 #1 (January 1999).

----. "1880 Great Register of San Bernardino County." *Valley Quarterly*, Vol. XXXVI #3 (September 1999).

----. "1884-Marriages-1884." *The Licking Lantern*, Vol. XXIII #1 (March 1998).

----. "Empire, Colorado, Empire Cemetery." *The Foothills Inquirer*, Vol. 19 #3 (Fall 1999).

----. *Everton's Genealogical Helper*, Vol. 52 #6 (1998).

----. *Exeter, Brentwood, East Kingston, Greenland, Kensington, Newfield, and Stratham Directory, 1960*. New Haven: The Price & Lee Co., 1960.

----. "The Florida Pioneer Descendants Committee 1999 Certificate Awards Presentation." *The Florida Genealogist*, Volume XXII #4 (Winter 1999).

----. "Flushing [New York] Directory, 1868, Part 1." *Queens Genealogy Workshop*, Vol. 1 #1 (Spring 2000).

----. "General Index to Estates - Palm Beach County." *Ancestry: quarterly bulletin of the Palm Beach County Genealogical Society*, Vol. XXXV #1 (January 2000).

[----, "Hamilton/Hamleton Files," *The Connector*, Vol. 21 #12 (December 1999), p. 223.]

----. *Heads of Families at the First Census of the United States Taken in the Year 1790: New Hampshire*. Washington: Government Printing Office, 1907. Reprint Baltimore: Genealogical Publishing Company, 1966.

----. *Heads of Families at the Second Census of the United States Taken in the Year 1800: New Hampshire*. Madison: John Brooks Threlfall, 1973.

----. *Heads of Families at the First Census of the United States Taken in the Year 1790: Pennsylvania*. Baltimore: Genealogical Publishing Company, 1966.

----. "Honor List of State's WWII Casualties." *Pioneer Pathfinder*, Vol. 25 #2 (April 1999).

----. "Humboldt County, World War II." *Redwood Researcher*, Vol. XXXII #2 (November 1999).

----. "Immigrant Ancestor Register." *The Palatine Immigrant*, Vol. XXIV #1 (1998).

----. "Immigrant Ancestor Register." *The Palatine Immigrant*, Vol. XXIV #2 (March 1999).

----. "Indian War Casualities from the Florida War, 1835-1842." *The Southern Genealogists Exchange Quarterly*. Vol. 39 #166 (June 1998).

----. *Index of Awards on Claims of the Soldiers of the War of 1812, as audited and allowed by the adjutant and inspector generals, pursuant to chapter 176, of the laws of 1859*. Albany: Weed, Parsons and Company, Printers, 1860.

----. "Korean Casualties List, Ohio Soldiers." *The Quest*, Vol. 16 #6 (Nov.-Dec. 1999).

----. "Lafayette County, Missouri, Naturalizations, 1870-1879." *The Kansas City Genealogist*, Vol. 39 #3 (Winter 1999).

----. "List of the Real Estate Owners, Beaver Township, Mahoning County." *Mahoning Meanderings*, Vol. 22 (September 1998).

----. "Marriages of Madison County, North Carolina." *A Lot of Bunkum*, Vol. 21 #3 (August 2000).

----. *The National Cyclopaedia of American Biography: being the history of the United States as illustrated in the lives of the founders, builders, and defenders of the republic, and of the men and women who are doing the work and moulding the thought of the present time.* Vol. IX. New York: James T. White & Company, 1907.

----. *The National Cyclopaedia of American Biography: being the history of the United States as illustrated in the lives of the founders, builders, and defenders of the republic, and of the men and women who are doing the work and moulding the thought of the present time.* Volume XXVII. New York: James T. White Company, 1939.

----. *The National Cyclopaedia of American Biography: being the history of the United States as illustrated in the lives of the founders, builders, and defenders of the republic, and of the men and women who are doing the work and moulding the thought of the present time.* Vol. XXXIII. New York: James T. White & Company, 1947.

----. *The National Cyclopaedia of American Biography: being the history of the United States as illustrated in the lives of the founders, builders, and defenders of the republic, and of the men and women who are doing the work and moulding the thought of the present time.* Vol. XLIV. New York: James T. White & Company, 1962.

---- *The National Cyclopedia of American Biography: being the history of the United States as illustrated in the lives of the founders, builders, and defenders of the republic, and of the men and women who are doing the work and moulding the thought of the present time.* Vol. 56. Clifton: James T. White & Company, 1975, p. 175.

----. "New Jersey Tidbits." *The German Connection*, Vol. 22 #4.

----. *Official Army Register January 1, 1922.* Washington: U. S. Government Printing Office, 1922.

----. *Official Army Register January 1, 1925.* Washington: U. S. Government Printing Office, 1925.

----. *Official Army Register January 1, 1945.* Washington: U. S. Government Printing Office, 1945.

----. "Orange County Cemetery Records." *Orange County, California, Genealogical Society Journal*, Vol. 34 #2 (October 1997).

----. "Orange County Wills." *The Orange County [New York] Genealogical Society Quarterly*, Vol. 29 #1 (May 1999).

----. "Oregon's Roll of Honor." *Trees From the Grove*, Vol. XI #2 (April-May-June 1998.

----. "Original Land Owners - Frankfort Township." *Where the Trails Cross*, Vol. 29 #2 (Winter 1998/1999).

----. "Original land Owners: Shiawassee Co., Michigan." *Shiawassee Steppin' Stones*, Vol. 27 #2 (February 1998).

----. "Our Fire Department: a historical look at the Cincinnati fire department." *The Tracer*, Vol. 20 #4 (December 1999).

----. *Patent Rolls of the Reign of Henry III...A.D. 1225-1232.* ----: ----, 1903. Reprint Germany: Kraus Reprint, 1971.

----, *Personal and Family Names.* Glasgow: H. Nisbet and Co., ----. Facsimile reprint Bowie: Heritage Books, Inc. and Rutland: Charles E. Tuttle, Co., Inc., 1988.

----. "Portraits of New-Hampshire Governors...." *The New England Historical and Genealogical Register*, Vol. XXVIII (Oct. 1874).

----. "Recent Publications." *The New England Historical and Genealogical Register*, Vol. XXXII (July 1878).

----. "1793 Tax, Unity and Burnt House Woods Hundred." *Western Maryland Genealogy*, Vol. 13 #2.

----. "Southwest Missouri Ozarks Migration Project." *Ozar'kin: the people who settled the Missouri Ozarks*, Vol. XX #3 (Fall 1998).

----. *U. S. Army Register, Volume 1: regular army active list, 1 January 1970.* Washington: U. S. Government Printing Office, 1970.

----. *U. S. Army Register, Volume 1: regular army active list, 1 January 1974.* Washington: U. S. Government Printing Office, 1974.

----. *U. S. Army Register, Volume II: army, NGUS, USAR, and other active lists, 1 January 1970.* Washington: U. S. Government Printing Office, 1970.

----. *Who's Who in American History - Science and Technology.* Chicago: Marquis Who's Who, Inc., 1976.

----. *Who's Who in Frontier Science and Technology*. Chicago: Marquis Who's Who, Inc., 1984.

----. *Who's Who in Science in Europe: a biographical guide to science, technology, agriculture, and medicine, 9th ed., Volume 1*. London: Cartermill Publishing, 1995.

----. *Who's Who in Show Business*. New York: Who's Who in Show Business, Inc., 1968.

----. *Who's Who in Show Business*. New York: Who's Who in Show Business, Inc., 1971.

----. "World War I Veterans of Somerset County [Pennsylvania]." *Laurel Messenger*, Vol. XLI #1 (February 2000).

----. "WPA Obituary Index." *Nemaha County Genealogical Society Newsletter*, Vol. 6 #1 (Nov. 1998).

----. *Year Book of the Society of Sons of the Revolution in the State of New York*. New York: Francis E. Fitch, 1899.

Abate, Frank R. *American Places Dictionary, Volume Two: South*. Detroit: Omnigraphics, Inc., 1994.

Abate, Frank R. *Omni Gazetteer of the United States of America. Volume 10 - National Index*. Detroit: Omnigraphics, Inc.

Ackerman, Bruce. *We The People, Volume 2: transformations*. Cambridge: The Belknap Press, 1998.

Ackerman, Diane. *Deep Play*. New York: Random House, 1999.

Ackerman, Forest J. *Ackermanthology*. Los Angeles: General Publishing Group, Inc., 1997.

Ackerman, John and David Gerboth, "Historical Review of Ackermans Cave," *Minnesota Speleology Monthly*, Vol. 25 #2.

Ackermann, Nicholas John George, *Journal of...*, Vol. 9.

Adams, Sampson, & Co. *The Salem Directory, containing the names of the citizens, city officers, a business directory, general events of the years 1856 and 1857, and an almanac for 1859. Also, a business directory of South Danvers*. Salem: Henry Whipple & Son, 1859.

Allen, Roger MacBride. *Allies and Aliens*. New York: Baen Publishing Enterprises, 1995.

Alson, Rebecca R. "Forsyth County Court of Pleas and Quarter Session, March Term 1860." *The Forsyth County [North Carolina] Genealogical Society Journal*, Vol. XVI #3 (Spring 1998).

Alson, Rebecca R. "Forsyth County Court of Pleas and Quarter Session, June Term 1860." *The Forsyth County [North Carolina] Genealogical Society Journal*, Vol. XVII #1 (Fall 1998).

Alson, Rebecca R. "Forsyth County Court of Pleas and Quarter Session, September Term 1860." *The Forsyth County [North Carolina] Genealogical Society Journal*, Vol. XVII #3 (Spring 1999).

Alson, Rebecca R. "Forsyth County Court of Pleas and Quarter Session, June Term 1860." *The Forsyth County [North Carolina] Genealogical Society Journal*, Vol. XVII #4 (Summer 1999).

Alson, Rebecca R. "Forsyth County Court of Pleas and Quarter Session, March Term 1861." *The Forsyth County [North Carolina] Genealogical Society Journal*, Vol. XVIII #1 (Fall 1999).

Alson, Rebecca R. "Forsyth County Court of Pleas and Quarter Session, June Term 1861." *The Forsyth County [North Carolina] Genealogical Society Journal*, Vol. XVIII #1 (Fall 1999).

Alson, Rebecca R. "Forsyth County [NC] Court of Pleas and Quarter Session, September Term 1861." *The Forsyth County Genealogical Society Journal*, Vol. XVIII #3 (Spring 2000).

Ancestor table submitted by Enid Eleanor (Smith) Adams to *The American Genealogist*, Vol. 63 #2 (April 1988).

Anderson, Marti. "Boulder County Divorces, 1867-1919, Part I A's - G's." *Boulder [Colorado] Genealogical Society Quarterly*, Vol. 31 #3 (August 2000).

Anderson, William, *Genealogy and Surnames: with some heraldic and biographical notices*. Edinburgh: William Ritchie, MDCCCLXV.

Baer, Mabel Van Dyke. "Abstract of Pension Record of John Ackerman." *Chips From Many Trees and Growing Roots*, Vol. 2 (Summer 1998).

Bailey, Martha J. *American Women in Science: a biographical dictionary*. Denver: ABC-CLIO, 1994.

Barnes, Donald S. "Behrens' Funeral Home: index to H. J. Behrens' mortuary records, book 4, 1930-1939." *Black Hills Nuggets*, Vol. XXXII #4 (November 1999.

Bartholomew, John. *The Oxford Advanced Atlas*. London: Oxford University Press, 1936.

Batchellor, Albert Stillman. *Miscellaneous Revolutionary Documents of New Hampshire including the association test, the pension rolls, and other important papers. Vol. 30.* Manchester: The John B. Clarke Co., 1910.

Batchellor, Albert Stillman. *The New Hampshire Grants being transcripts of the charters of townships and minor grants of lands made by the provincial government of New Hampshire, within the present boundaries of the State of Vermont, from 1749 to 1764. With an appendix containing petitions to King George the Third, in 1766, by the proprietors and settlers under the New Hampshire Grants, and lists of the subscribers; also historical and bibliographical notes relative to the towns in Vermont, by Hiram A. Huse, State Historian. Volume XXVI. Town charters, Volume III.* Concord: Edward N. Pearson, Public Printer, 1895.

Batchellor, Albert Stillman. *Provincial Papers of New Hampshire including the records of the president and council, January 1, 1679, to December 22, 1680.... Vol. XIX.* Manchester: John B. Clarke, Public Printer, 1891.

Batchellor, Albert Stillman. *State of New Hampshire. Town Charters granted within the present limits of New Hampshire, being the continuation and conclusion of the grants of townships issued by the provincial government of New Hampshire, presented in alphabetcical arrangement, and including all subsequent to the letter E, will illustrative maps, plans, bibliographical citations and complete indexes, and an appendix containg documents relating to the most ancient towns of this State, and historical notes and monographs. Volume XXV. Town charters, Volume II.* Concord: Edward N. Pearson, Public Printer, 1895.

Batchellor, Albert Stillman. *State of New Hampshire. Town Charters including grants of territory within the present limits of New Hampshire, made by the government of Massachusetts, and a portion of the grants and charters issued by the government of New Hampshire, with an appendix, consisting of papers relating to the granting of the various lines and bodies of towns, with acts in regard to town bounds in general, and many documents produced by disputes between towns concerning their boundary lines, with illustrative maps and plans and complete indexes. Volume XXIV. Town charters, Volume I.* Concord: Edward N. Pearson, Public Printer, 1894.

Batchellor, Albert Stillman. *State of New Hampshire. Township Grants of Lands in New Hampshire included in the Masonian Patent issued subsequent to 1746 by the Masonian Proprietary. Volume XXVII. Town Charters, Volume IV. Masonian Papers, Volume 1.* Concord: Edward N. Pearson, Public Printer, 1896.

Biehl, Robert. "Military Census, 1862, St. Clair County, Illinois: West Belleville and North Belleville." *St. Clair County Genealogical Society Quarterly*, Vol. 21 #2 (1998).

Boddie, William Willis. *History of Williamsburg. Something about the people of Williamsburg County, South Carolina, from the first settlement by Europeans about 1705 until 1923.* Columbia: ----, 1923. Facsimile reprint Baltimore: Clearfield Company, Inc., 1995.

Bogner, Tom. "The Old Catholic Cemetery." *The Prospector*, Vol. 19 #2 (Februrary 1999).

Bouton, Nathaniel. *Provincial and State Papers. Miscellaneous Documents and Records Relating to New Hampshire at Different Periods.... Volume X.* Concord: Edward A. Jenks, State Printer, 1877.

Bouton, Nathaniel. *Provincial Papers. Documents and Records Relating to the Province of New-Hampshire, from 1692 to 1722: being part II. of papers relating to that period. Containing the "Journal of the Coucil and General Assembly." Volume III.* Manchester: John B. Clarke, State Printer, 1869.

Bouton, Nathaniel. *Provincial Papers. Documents and Records Relating to the Province of New-Hampshire, from 1722 to 1737: containing important records and papers, pertaining to the settlement of the boundary lines between New-Hampshire and Massachusetts. Volume IV.* Manchester: John B. Clarke, State Printer, 1870.

Bouton, Nathaniel. *Provincial Papers. Documents and Records Relating to the Province of New-Hampshire, from 1738 to 1749: containing very valuable and interesting records and papers relating to the expedition against Louisbourg, 1745. Volume V.* Nashua: Orren C. Moore, State Printer, 1871.

Bouton, Nathaniel. *Provincial Papers. Documents and Records Relating to the Province of New-Hampshire, from 1749 to 1763: containing very valuable and interesting records and papers relating to the Crown Point expedition, and the "Seven Years French and Indian Wars," 1755-1762. Volume VI.* Manchester: James M. Campbell, State Printer, 1872.

Bouton, Nathaniel. *Provincial Papers. Documents and Records Relating to the Province of New-Hampshire, from 1764 to 1776; including the whole administration of Gov. John Wentworth; the events immediately preceding the Revolutionary War; the losses at the Battle of Bunker Hill, and the record of all proceedings till the end of our provincial history. Volume VII.* Nashua: Orren C. Moore, State Printer, 1873.

Bouton, Nathaniel. *Town Papers. Documents and Records Relating to Towns in New Hampshire; with an appendix embracing the constitutional conventions of 1778-1779; and of 1781-1783; and the State Constitution of 1784. Volume IX.* Concord: Charles C. Pearson, State Printer, 1875.

Brennan, Robert. "Records of Town of Wallkill, Orange County, New York." *The Orange County Genealogical Society Quarterly*, Vol. 30 #3 (August 2000).

Brewer, J. S. *Letters and Papers, Foreign and Domestic, of the Reign of Henry VIII. ... Vol. IV. - Part III. 1529-1530. With a general index.* London: Her Majesty's Stationary Office, 1876. Reprint Vaduz: Kraus Reprint Ltd., 1965.

Brewster, Charles W. *Rambles About Portsmouth: first series.* ----: Charles W. Brewster, 1859. Facsimile reprint of second edition published 1873 Somersworth: New Hampshire Publishing Company, 1971.

Brewster, Charles W. *Rambles About Portsmouth: second series.* ----: Lewis W. Brewster, 1869. Facsimile reprint Somersworth: New Hampshire Publishing Company, 1972.

Brown, Warren. *History of Hampton Falls, N. H., Volume II: containing the church history and many other things not previously recorded.* Concord: The Rumford Press, 1918.

Burke, Bernard. *A Genealogical and Heraldic History of the Colonial Gentry.* Baltimore: Genealogical Publishing Company, 1970.

Burke, W. J. and Will D. Howe. *American Authors and Books, 1640-1940.* New York: Gramercy Publishing Co., 1943.

Burnsad, Cathy. "Veteran's Graves Registration Project." *The Florida Genealogist*, Vol. XXII #3 (Fall 1999).

Cahill, Melinda Morgenstern & Diane Renner Walsh. "Naturalization Record Index of the County Court, St. Clair Co., Illinois, 1864-1906, A-J." *St. Clair County Genealogical Society Quarterly*, Vol. 21 #1 (1998).

Calaway, Louise Meredith. "The 1884 Great Register." *The Searcher*, Vol. 37 #4 (July/August 2000).

Carr, Mary. "Marriages - 1870, Volume 4, Delaware County, Ohio." *The Delaware Genealogist*, Vol. 15 #4 (Winter 1999/2000).

Cattell, Jaques. *Directory of American Scholars.* Lancaster: The Science Press, 1942.

Cattell, Jaques. *Directory of American Scholars: a biographical directory, 3rd edition.* New York: R. R. Bowker Company, 1957.

Child, Hamilton. *Gazetteer of Grafton County, N. H., 1709-1886.* Syracuse: The Syracuse Journal Company, Printers and Binders, 1886.

Child, Hamilton, *Business Directory of Grafton County, N. H., 1885-1886.* Syracuse: The Syracuse Journal Company, Printers and Binders, c1886.

Chipman, Scott Lee. *Genealogical Abstracts from Early New Hampshire Newspapers, Vol. 1.* Bowie: Heritage Books, Inc., 2000.

Chipman, Scott Lee. *New England Vital Records from the "Exeter News-Letter," 1831-1840.* Camden: Picton Press, 1993.

Chipman, Scott Lee. *New England Vital Records from the "Exeter News-Letter," 1841-1846.* Camden: Picton Press, 1993.

Chipman, Scott Lee. *New England Vital Records from the "Exeter News-Letter," 1847-1852*. Camden: Picton Press, 1994.

Chipman, Scott Lee. *New England Vital Records from the "Exeter News-Letter," 1853-1858*. Camden: Picton Press, 1994.

Chipman, Scott Lee. *New England Vital Records from the "Exeter News-Letter," 1859-1865*. Camden: Picton Press, 1996.

Cohen, Edward A. & Lewis Goldfarb. *Jewish Cemeteries of Five Counties of Connecticut, Volume 2*. Bowie: Heritage Books, Inc., 1998.

Cohen, Edward A. & Lewis Goldfarb. *Jewish Cemeteries of Hartford, Connecticut, Volume 1*. Bowie: Heritage Books, Inc., 1995.

Coldham, Peter Wilson. *The Complete Book of Emigrants, 1607-1660. A comprehensive listing compiled from English public records of those who took ship to the Americas for political, religious, and economic reasons; of those who were deported for vagrancy, roguery, or non-conformity; and of those who were sold to labour in the new colonies*. Baltimore: Genealogical Publishing Co., Inc., 1988.

Coldham, Peter Wilson. *The Complete Book of Emigrants, 1661-1699. A comprehensive listing compiled from English public records of those who took ship to the Americas for political, religious, and economic reasons; of those who were deported for vagrancy, roguery, or non-conformity; and of those who were sold to labour in the new colonies*. Baltimore: Genealogical Publishing Co., Inc., 1990.

Cooley, Eli F. *Genealogy of the Early Settlers in Trenton and Ewing, "Old Hunterdon County," New Jersey*. ----: ----, 1883. Facsimile reprint Bowie: Heritage Books, Inc., 1993.

Craft, Kenneth Fischer Jr. *Ohio County (WV) Index, Volume 3: index to county court order books (part 3), 1777-1881*. Bowie: Heritage Books, Inc., 1999.

Crisp, Frederick Arthur. *Visitation of England and Wales, Vol. 20*. ----: ----, 1919. Facsimile reprint Bowie: Heritage Books, Inc., 1996.

Crowley & Lunt. *Exeter & N. H. Coast Directory*. Beverly: Crowley & Lunt, Publishers, 1915.

Crowley & Lunt. *Exeter, Hampton, & N. H. Coast Directory*. Beverly: Crowley & Lunt, Publishers, 1935.

Crowley & Lunt. *Exeter, Hampton, & N. H. Coast Directory*. Beverly: Crowley & Lunt, Publishers, 1941.

Crowley & Lunt. *Exeter, Newmarket, & N. H. Coast Directory*. Beverly: Crowley & Lunt, Publishers, 1924.

Currier, John J. *History of Newburyport, Massachusetts, 1764-1905*. Newburyport: author, 1906. Rperint Somersworth: New Hampshire Publishing Company, 1977.

Dalum, Gerald. "Pomeranians and Others to Texas." *Die Pommerschen Leute*, Band 21 (Winter 1998).

Darnell, Betty R. "Jefferson County Births, 1857." *Lines and By Lines*, Vol. XIV #4 (Winter 1999).

Davis, Charles Henry Stanley. *History of Wallingford, Conn., from its settlement in 1670 to the present time, including Meriden, which was one of its parishes until 1806, and Cheshire, which was incorporated in 1780*. Meriden: author, 1870.

Davis, John David. *Bergen County, New Jersey, Deed Records, 1689-1801*. Bowie: Heritage Books, Inc., 1995.

Davis, William T. *Professional and Industrial History of Suffolk County, Massachusetts, Volume 1: history of the bench and bar*. ----: The Boston History Company, 1894.

Debus, Allen G. *World Who's Who in Science: a biographical dictionary of notable scientists from antiquity to the present*. Chicago: Marquis-Who's Who, Inc., 1968.

Dougherty, Marilyn. "The Spanish-American War, The Phillipine Campaign, Montana Edition." *Treasure State Lines*, Vol. 24 #1 (1999).

Durie, Howard I. "Pascack Reformed Dutch Church Baptisms, 1814-1850." *The American Genealogist*, Vol. 47 #3 (July 1971).

Durie, Howard I. "Pascack Reformed Dutch Church Baptisms, 1814-1850." *The American Genealogist*, Vol. 47 #4.

Durie, Howard I. "Pascack Reformed Dutch Church Baptisms, 1814-1850." *The American Genealogist*, Vol. 48 #1.

Durie, Howard I. "Pascack Reformed Dutch Church Baptisms, 1814-1850." *The American Genealogist*, Vol. 48 #2.

Eddlemon, Sherida K. *A Genealogical Collection of Kentucky Birth & Death Records, Volume 1*. Bowie: Heritage Books, Inc.

Egle, William Henry. *Pennsylvania Archives: 3$^{rd}$ Series, Vol. VI*. Harrisburg: Clarence M. Busch, Printer, 1896.

Evans, Helen F. *Abstracts of the Probate Records of Rockingham County, New Hampshire, 1771-1799*. Bowie: Heritage Books, Inc., 2000.

Federal Writers' Project, *New Jersey: a guide to its present and past*. New York: The Viking Press, 1939.

Fernow, B. *Documents Relating to the History of the Dutch and Swedish Settlements on the Delaware River.... Vol. XII.* Albany: The Argus Company, Printers, 1877.

Fry, Georgene. White's Common School Register, [Beaver Township, Mahoning County, Ohio]." *Mahoning Meanderings*, Vol. 21 (October 1997).

Fry, Georgene. White's Common School Register, [Beaver Township, Mahoning County, Ohio]." *Mahoning Meanderings*, Vol. 21 (November 1997).

Fry, Georgene. White's Common School Register, [Beaver Township, Mahoning County, Ohio]." *Mahoning Meanderings*, Vol. 22 (January 1998).

Gannett, Henry, *The Origin of Certain Place Names in the United States.* Washington: Government Printing Office, 1902. Facsimile reprint Bowie: Heritage Books, Inc., 1996.

Garrison, Linda Norman. *"The Waurika News." The Tree Tracers*, Vol. XXIII #2 (Dec. 1998-Feb. 1999).

Gascoigne, Robert Mortimer. *A Historical Catalogue of Scientists and Scientific Books from the earliest times to the close of the nineteenth century.* New York: Garland Publishing, Inc., 1984.

Germann, Jane. "Clark County [Washington] and the Civil War." *Trail Breakers*, Vol. 26 #1 (Fall 1999).

Gilman, Gerry. "Old City Cemetery." *Trail Breakers*, Vol. 25 #1.

Gnagey, Ruth Failing. "Morton County, Kansas, Marriages, Book A, 18 March 1887 to 23 March 1925." *The Treesearcher*, Vol. 40 #1 (1998).

Goode, J. Paul, *Goode's School Atlas: physical, political, and economic for American schools and colleges, revised and enlarged.* New York: Rand McNally & Company, 1946.

Gwathmey, John H. *Historical Register of Virginians in the Revolution: soldiers - sailors - marines, 1775-1783.* Richmond: The Dietz Press, Publishers, 1938.

Halpin, Cathryn. "149th Illinois Infantry Regiment, Company B." *St. Clair County [Illinois] Genealogical Society Quarterly*, Vol. 22 #4 (1999).

Hamilton County Chapter of the Ohio Genealogical Society. *Hamilton County, Ohio, Church Death Records, 1811-1849.* Bowie: Heritage Books, Inc., 2000.

Hammond, Isaac W. *The State of New Hampshire. Miscellaneous Provincial and State Papers 1725-1800. Vol. XVIII.* Manchester: John B. Clarke, Public Printer, 1890.

Hammond, Isaac W. *The State of New Hampshire. Rolls and Documents Relating to Soldiers in the Revolutionary War, with an appendix, embracing some French and Indian War rolls. Volume III of the War Rolls. Volume XVI of the Series.* Manchester: John B. Clarke, Public Printer, 1887.

Hammond, Isaac W. *The State of New Hampshire. Rolls of the Soldiers in the Revolutionary War, 1775, to May, 1777: with an appendix, embracing diaries of Lieut. Jonathan Burton. Volume I of the War Rolls. Volume XIV of the Series.* Concord: Parsons B. Cogswell, State Printer, 1885.

Hammond, Isaac W. *The State of New Hampshire. Rolls of the Soldiers in the Revolutionary War, May, 1777 to 1780: with an appendix, embracing names of New Hampshire men in Massachusetts regiments. Volume II of the War Rolls. Volume XV of the Series.* Concord: Parsons B. Cogswell, State Printer, 1886.

Hammond, Isaac W. *Town Papers. Documents Relating to Towns in New Hampshire, New London to Wolfeborough, with an appendix, embracing some docuemnts, interesting and valuable, not heretofore published, including the census of New Hampshire of 1790 in detail. Volume XIII.* Concord: Parsons B. Cogswell, State Printer, 1884.

Hammond, Otis G. *Probate Records of the Province of New Hampshire, Vol. 4, 1750-1753. State Papers Series Vol. 34.* ----: The State of New Hampshire, 1933. Facsimile reprint Bowie: Heritage Books, Inc., 1989.

Hammond, Otis G. *Probate Records of the Province of New Hampshire, Vol. 5, 1754-1756. State Papers Series Vol. 35.* ----: The State of New Hampshire, 1936. Facsimile reprint Bowie: Heritage Books, Inc., 1989.

Hammond, Otis G. *Probate Records of the Province of New Hampshire, Vol. 6, 1757-1760. State Papers Series Vol. 36.* ----: The State of New Hampshire, 1938. Facsimile reprint Bowie: Heritage Books, Inc., 1989.

Hammond, Otis G. *Probate Records of the Province of New Hampshire, Vol. 7, 1760-1763. State Papers Series Vol. 37.* ----: The State of New Hampshire, 1939. Facsimile reprint Bowie: Heritage Books, Inc., 1990.

Hammond, Otis G. *Probate Records of the Province of New Hampshire, Vol. 9, 1767-1771. State Papers Series Vol. 39.* ----: The State of New Hampshire, 1941. Facsimile reprint Bowie: Heritage Books, Inc., 1990.

Havlice, Patricia Pate. *Index to Literary Biography, Volume I: A-K.* Metuchen: The Scarecrow Press, Inc., 1975.

Havlice, Patricia Pate. *Index to Literary Biography: first supplement. Volume I: A-K.* Metuchen: The Scarecrow Press, Inc., 1983.

Heilman, Robert A. *The Heilman Family Genealogy comprising three Heilman lines in one volume: John Peter, John Adam, and William B. Heilman.* Bowie: Heritage Books, Inc.

Herbert, Jeffrey G. *Index of Death and Marriage Notices Appearing in the "Cincinnati Daily Gazette," 1827-1881.* Bowie: Heritage Books, Inc., 1993.

Hosier, Kathleen E. *Vital Records of Rye, New Hampshire: a transcript of the births, baptisms, marriages, and deaths in this town to the year 1890.* Bowie: Heritage Books, Inc., 1992.

Holmes, Frank R., *Directory of the Ancestral Heads of New England Families, 1620-1700.* New York: ----, 1923. Reprint Baltimore: Genealogical Publishing Co., Inc., 1989.

Holtmann, Antonius. "Germans to America -- 50 volumes that are not to be trusted." *The Palatine Immigrant*, Vol. XXII #2 (March 1997).

Hooff, Ronald L. and Barbara M. Hooff. *Descendants of Lorenz and Anna M. Hoff/Hooff.* Bowie: Heritage Books, Inc., 2000.

Hopper, Maria Jean Pratt. "Who Was Cornelia Hopper's Mother?" *The Genealogical Magazine of New Jersey*, Vol. 73 #3 (September 1998).

Hoyt, David W. *A Genealogical History of the Hoyt, Haight, and Hight Families: with some account of the earlier Hyatt families, a list of the first settlers of Salisbury and Amesbury, Mass., etc.* ----: ----, 1871. Facsimile reprint Bowie: Heritage Books, Inc., 1992.

Hubbard, C. Horace and Justus Dartt, *History of the Town of Springfield, Vermont, with a genealogical record, 1752-1895.* Boston: Geo. H. Walker & Co., 1895. Facsimile reprint Bowie: Heritage Books, Inc., 1998.

Hughes, Lois E. *Hamilton County, Ohio, Birth Records, 1874-1875, Volume I, Book A, A-K.* Bowie: Heritage Books, Inc., 1994.

Hughes, Lois E. *Hamilton County, Ohio, Citizenship Record Abstracts, 1837-1916.* Bowie: Heritage Books, Inc., 1991.

Hughes, Lois E. *Hamilton County, Ohio, Death Records, 1865-1869, Volume I.* Bowie: Heritage Books, Inc., 1992.

Hughes, Lois E. *Hamilton County, Ohio, Death Records, 1870-1873, Volume II, Book A, A-K.* Bowie: Heritage Books, Inc., 1992.

Hughes, Lois E. *Hamilton County, Ohio, Death Records, 1874-1877, Volume III, Book A, A-K.* Bowie: Heritage Books, Inc., 1992.

Hughes, Lois E. *Hamilton County, Ohio, Marriage Index, 1817-1845, Volume I.* Bowie: Heritage Books, Inc., 1994.

Hughes, Lois E. *Wills Filed in Probate Court, Hamilton County, Ohio, 1791-1901: Volume 1, A-K.* Bowie: Heritage Books, Inc., 1991.

Hunt, James K. Jr. *Hampton Vital Records and Genealogy, 1889-1986*. Portsmouth: Peter E. Randall, Publisher, 1988.

Hyamson, Albert M. *A Dictionary of Universal Biography of All Ages and All Peoples*. London: ----, 1916. Reprint Baltimore: Clearfield Company, Inc., 1995.

Internet
> ancestry.com
> biosci.ohio-state.edu/%7Emicrobio/aab.html
> e-bay.com
> education.canberra.edu.au/staff/pace/ackermann/ackermann.html
> familytreemaker.com
> memory.loc.gov
> music.indiana.edu/som/emi/ackerman/html
> placesnamed.com/a/c/ackerman.asp
> thewall-usa.com

Isenberg, Andrew C. *The Destruction of the Bison: an environmental history, 1750-1920*. Cambridge: Cambridge University Press, 2000.

Jackson, Mary S. and Edward F. Jackson. *Marriage and Death Notices from Seneca County, New York, Newspapers, 1817-1885*. Bowie: Heritage Books, Inc. 1997.

Jackson, Mary S. and Edward F. Jackson. *Death Notices from Steuben County, New York, Newspapers, 1797-1884*. Bowie: Heritage Books, Inc., 1998.

Jackson, Mary S. and Edward F. Jackson. *Marriage Notices from Steuben County, New York, Newspapers, 1797-1884*. Bowie: Heritage Books, Inc., 1998.

Jackson, Mary S. and Edward F. Jackson. *Marriage Notices from Washington County, New York, newspapers, 1799-1880*. Bowie: Heritage Books, Inc., 1995.

Jackson, Ronald Vern and Gary Ronald Teeples. *New Hampshire 1850 Index Census*. Bountiful: Accelerated Indexing Systems, Inc., 1978.

Jacobsen, Thomas A. *The Robertses of Northern New England*. Bowie: Heritage Books, Inc., 1995.

Jewett, Frederic Clarke. *History and Genealogy of the Jewetts of America...Vol. II*. Rowley: The Jewett Family of America. Facsimile reprint Bowie: Heritage Books, Inc., 1992.

Jones, William Haslet. *Vital Statistics of Seabrook, New Hampshire, 1768-1903*. Bowie: Heritage Books, Inc., 1998.

Jones, William Haslet. *The Yeaton Family of New England, 1650-1900*. Bowie: Heritage Books, Inc., 1997.

Kellogg, Louise Phelps. *The British Regime in Wisconsin and the Northwest*. Madison: State Historical society of Wisconsin, 1935.

Kelsey, Michael, et al. *Miscellaneous Texas Newspaper Abstracts - Deaths, Volume 2*. Bowie: Heritage Books, Inc., 1997.

Kelsey, Michael, et al. *"The Southern Argus:" obituaries, death notices, and implied deaths June 1869 through June 1874*. Bowie: Heritage Books, Inc., 1996.

Kelsey, Michael, et al. *Texas Masonic Deaths with Selected Biographical Sketches*. Bowie: Heritage Books, Inc., 1998.

Kennedy Center. *Stagebill*. December, 1999.

Kieffer, Henry Martyn. *Some of the First Settlers of "The Forks of the Delaware" and Their Descendants. Being a translation from the German of the record books of the First Reformed Church of Easton, Penna. From 1760 to 1852*. Easton: ----, 1902. Facsimile reprint Bowie: Heritage Books, Inc., 1995.

Kilner, Arthur R. *Green County, Ohio - Past and Present*. Bowie: Heritage Books, Inc., 1997.

Klinkenberg, Audrey M. *Marriages from "The Saugerties Telegraph," 1846-1870, and Obituaries, Death Notices and Genealogical Gleanings from "The Ulster Telegraph," 1846-1848*. Bowie: Heritage Books, Inc., 1998.

Klinkenberg, Audrey M. *Obituaries, Death Notices and Genealogical Gleanings from "The Saugerties Telegraph," Volume 1: 1848-1852*. Bowie: Heritage Books, Inc., 1989.

Klinkenberg, Audrey M. *Obituaries, Death Notices and Genealogical Gleanings from "The Saugerties Telegraph," Volume 3: 1861-1870*. Bowie: Heritage Books, Inc., 1989.

Knox, Grace Louise and Barbara B. Ferris. *Connecticut Divorces: superior court records for the counties of New London, Tolland, & Windham, 1719-1910*. Bowie: Heritage Books, Inc., 1987.

Labaw, George Warne. *A Genealogy of the Warne Family in America: principally the descendants of Thomas Warne, born 1652, died 1722, one of the twenty-four proprietors of east New Jersey*. New York: Frank Allaben Genealogical Company, 1911.

Ladd, Kevin. *Gone to Texas: genealogical abstracts from "The Telegraph & Texas Register," 1835-1841*. Bowie: Heritage Books, Inc., 1994.

Lawson, Rowena. *Bath County, Kentucky, 1820-1840 Censuses*. Bowie: Heritage Books, Inc., 1985.

Lawson, Rowena. *Nelson County, Kentucky, 1850 Census.* Bowie: Heritage Books, Inc., 1985.

Lee, Francis Bazley. *Genealogical and Personal Record of Mercer County, New Jersey.* New York: The Lewis Publishing Company, 1907. Facsimile reprint Bowie: Heritage Books, Inc., 1989.

Leiby, Adrian C. *The Revolutionary War in the Hackensack Valley: the Jersey Dutch and the neutral ground, 1775-1783.* New Brunswick: Rutgers University Press, 1962.

Lentz, Harris M. III. *Science Fiction, Horror & Fantasy Film and Television Credits: Volume 1.* Jefferson: McFand & Company, Inc., Publishers, 1983.

Lentz, Harris M. III. *Science Fiction, Horror & Fantasy Film and Television Credits Supplement: through 1987.* Jefferson: McFand & Company, Inc., Publishers, 1983.

Locke, Arthur H. *A History and Genealogy of Captain John Locke (1627-1696) of Portsmouth and Rye, N. H., and His Descendants. Also of Nathaniel Locke of Portsmouth and a short account of the history of the Lockes in England.* ----: ----, no date. Facsimile reprint Bowie: Heritage Books, Inc., 1993.

Longver, Phyllis O. *New Hampshire Civil War Death and Burial Locations.* Bowie: Heritage Books, Inc., 2000.

Lowell, Delmar R. *The Historic Genealogy of the Lowells of America from 1639 to 1899.* Rutland: Delmar R. Lowell, 1899. Reprint Bowie; Heritage Books, Inc., 2000.

Lower, Mark Antony. *A Dictionary of the Family Names of the United Kingdom.* ----: ----, c1860. Facsimile reprint Bowie: Heritage Books, Inc., 1996.

MacDonald, William Colt. *Trouble Shooter.* ----: Berkley Medallion, 1965.

Malak, Paula. "A Friendship Quilt." *Where The Trails Cross*, Vol. 28 #2 (Winter 1997/1998).

Maltin, Leonard. *1999 Movie & Video Guide.* New York: Signet, 1998.

Marine, William M., *The British Invasion of Maryland, 1812-1815.* ----: ----, c1899. Facsimile reprint Bowie: Heritage Books, Inc., 1998.

Martin, David Kendall. "Uncovering the Elphick Ancestry of Harriet J. Allen of Susquehanna Co., Penn." *The American Genealogist*, Vol. 64 #1 (January 1989).

Mayo, Mary E. *Sixteen Hundred Lines to Pilgrims. Lineage Book III.* Baltimore: Genealogical Publishing Co., Inc., 1982.

McClellan, Phyllis I. *The Artillerymen of Historic Fort Monroe, Virginia.* Bowie: Heritage Books, Inc., 1991.

McClure, Paul. *Early Marriages in Bath County, Kentucky: bonds 1811-1850 and returns 1811-1852.* Bowie: Heritage Books, Inc., 1994.

McConville, Brendan. *These Daring Disturbers of the public Peace: the struggle for property and power in early New Jersey.* Ithaca: Cornell University Press, 1999.

McElligott, Carroll Ainsworth and Ronald J. McElligott II. *A Guide to the Pre-Civil War Land Records of Colleton County, South Carolina.* Bowie: Heritage Books, Inc., 2000.

McElroy, Dorothy E. and Charles A. Earp. *The History and Roster of the First Christian Church (Disciples of Christ) of Baltimore, Maryland, 1810-1996.* Bowie: Heritage Books, Inc., 1996.

Mendocino Coast Genealogical Society. *Births, Deaths and Marriages on California's Mendocino Coast: Volume One, 1889-1909.* Bowie: Heritage Books, Inc., 1995.

Mendocino Coast Genealogical Society. *Births, Deaths and Marriages on California's Mendocino Coast: Volume Two, 1910-1919.* Bowie: Heritage Books, Inc., 1997.

Mendocino Coast Genealogical Society. *Births, Deaths and Marriages on California's Mendocino Coast: Volume Three, 1920-1929.* Bowie: Heritage Books, Inc., 1997.

Mendocino Coast Genealogical Society. *Births, Deaths and Marriages on California's Mendocino Coast: Volume Four, 1930-1939.* Bowie: Heritage Books, Inc., 1998.

Mendocino Coast Genealogical Society. *Births, Deaths and Marriages on California's Mendocino Coast: Volume Five, 1940-1949.* Bowie: Heritage Books, Inc., 1999.

Metcalf, Henry Harrison. *Probate Records of the Province of New Hampshire, Volume 1: 1635-1717. State papers series, Volume 31.* Concord: Rumford Printing Co., 1907. Facsimile reprint Bowie: Heritage Books, Inc., 1989.

Metcalf, Henry Harrison. *Probate Records of the Province of New Hampshire, Volume 2: 1718-1740. State papers series, Volume 32.* Bristol: R. W. Musgrove, Printer, 1914. Facsimile reprint Bowie: Heritage Books, Inc., 1989.

Metcalf, Henry Harrison. *Probate Records of the Province of New Hampshire, Volume 3: 1741-1749. State papers series, Volume 33.* Concord: The Rumford Press, 1915. Facsimile reprint Bowie: Heritage Books, Inc., 1989.

Mitchell, Harry Edward. *Exeter & Hampton, New Hampshire, Census & Business Directory, 1908*. Augusta: Mitchell-Cony Company, 1908. Facsimile reprint Bowie: Heritage Books, Inc., 1979.

Mogren, John. "Bowbells Township: names of land owners." *North Central North Dakota Genealogical Record*, #83 (June 2000).

Mogren, John. "Federal Land Tract Records." *North Central North Dakota Genealogical Record*, #78 (March 1999).

Morris Area Genealogy Society Indexing Group. "Index to Records of Greenwood Cemetery, Boonton, 1872-1899." *Morris Area Genealogy Society Newsletter*, Vol. 12 #2 (June 1999).

Movies
 *The Rookie*

Musgrove, R. W. *History of the Town of Bristol, New Hampshire*. ----: Richard W. Musgrove, 1904. Reprint with a new foreword by Charles E. Greenwood, Somersworth: New Hampshire Publishing Company, 1976. (Two volumes.)

Nash, Gerald Q., et al. *The Vital Records of Hudson, New Hampshire, 1734-1985*. Bowie: Heritage Books, Inc., 1997.

Nichipor, Ruth L. *Vital Statistics from the Town Records of Hampton Falls, New Hampshire, Through 1899*. ----: ----, 1976.

North, S. N. D. *Heads of Families at the First Census of the UnitedSstates Taken in the Year 1790: North Carolina*. Washington: Government Printing Office, 1908. Reprint Spartanburg: The Reprint Company, 1961.

Noyes, Sybil et al. *Genealogical Dictionary of Maine and New Hampshire*. Portland: ----, 1928-1939. Reprint Baltimore: Genealogical Publishing Company, 1996.

Ohles, Frederik, et al. *Biographical Dictionary of Modern American Educators*. Westport: Greenwood Press, 1997.

Palmer, Barbara. *The Civil War Veterans of San Diego*. Unpublished ms, c1998.

Parsons, Langdon B. *History of the Town of Rye, New Hampshire, from its discovery and settlement to December 31, 1903*. ----: ----, 1905. Facsimile reprint Bowie: Heritage Books, Inc., 1992.

Pearson, Jonathan. "Extracts from the Doop-Boek, or Baptismal Register of the Reformed Protestant Dutch Church of Schenectady, N. Y." *The New England Historical & Genealogical Register*, Volume XIX (January 1865).

Pearson, Jonathan. "Extracts from the Doop-Boek, or Baptismal Register of the Reformed Protestant Dutch Church of Schenectady, N. Y." *The New England Historical & Genealogical Register*, Volume XX (July 1866).

Pearson, Jonathan. "Extracts from the Doop-Boek, or Baptismal Register of the Reformed Protestant Dutch Church of Schenectady, N. Y." *The New England Historical & Genealogical Register*, Volume XXI (April 1867).

Pierce, Frederick Clifton. *Batchelder, Batcheller Genealogy. Descendants of Rev. Stephen Bachiler, of England, a leading non-conformist who settled the town of New Hampton, N. H. and Joseph, Henry, Joshua, and John Batcheller of Essex Co., Massachusetts.* Chicago: author, 1898. Facsimile reprint Bowie: Heritage Books, Inc., 1992.

Pletcher, Pamela. "Mahoning County Commutation Book for 1865 Entitled *Duplicate List of persons Liable to Military Duty.*" *Mahoning Meanderings*, Vol. 23 (February 1999).

Prather, Geraldine. "Brownstone Newspaper Obituary Index, 1910-1923." *Genealogy Jottings*, Vol. 17 #3 (September 1998).

Prevenier, Walter and Wim Blockmans. *The Burgundian Netherlands*. Cambridge: Cambridge University Press, 1986.

Query submitted by Roger D. Joslyn to *The American Genealogist*, Vol. 64 #1 (January 1989).

Radzinsky, Edvard. *The Last Tzar: the life and death of Nicholas II*. Translated from the Russian by Marian Schwartz. New York: Anchor Books, 1992.

Randall, Peter Evans. *Hampton, a century of town and beach, 1888-1988*. Portsmouth: Peter E. Randall, Publisher, 1989.

Reaney, P. H. *A Dictionary of British Surnames*. London: Routledge and Kegan Paul, 1958.

Reddy, Anne Waller and Andrew Lewis Riffle. *Richmond City, Virginia, Marriage Bonds, 1797-1853*. Baltimore: Genealogical Publishing Co., Inc., 1976.

Rich, Peggy Burton and Marion Ard Whitehurst. *The Pickens Sentinel: favorite newspaper of Pickens County. Pickens Court House, South Carolina, 1872-1893, historical and genealogical abstracts*. Bowie: Heritage Books, Inc., 1994.

Ricord, F. W. *History of Union County, New Jersey*. Newark: East Jersey History Company, 1897.

Rigdon, Walter. *The Biographical Encyclopaedia & Who's Who of the American Theatre*. New York: James H. Heineman, Inc., 1966.

Roberts, Richard P. *Alton, New Hampshire, Vital Records, 1890-1998.* Bowie: Heritage Books, Inc., 1999.

Robichaux, Albert J. Jr. *German Coast Families: European origins and settlement in colonial Louisiana.* Rayne: Hebert Publications, 1997. Book review appearing in *The American Genealogist*, Vol. 74 #3 (July 1999).

Rodabaugh, James H. *The Ohio State Archaeological and Historical Quarterly,* Vol. 58 #1 (January 1949).

Rohrbach, Lewis Bunker. *Men of Bern: the 1798 burgerverzeichnisse of Canton Bern, Switzerland.* Rockport: Picton Press, 1999. Advertisement appearing in *Everton's Genealogical Helper*, Vol. 53 #4 (July-August 1999).

Rollins, Alden M. *The Rollins Family in the New Hampshire Provincial Deeds, 1655-1771.* Bowie: Heritage Books, Inc., 1997.

Roseboom, Eugene Holloway and Francis Phelps Weisenburger. *A History of Ohio.* New York: Prentice-Hall, Inc., 1934.

Roth, Jean A. "The Luke Woodbury Saunders Family Part II: the maternal ancestry of Mary Ann (Montgomery) Saunders." *Seattle Genealogical Society Bulletin*, Vol. 49 #2 (Winter 2000).

Ruppert, Gary B. "Martin Luther Lutheran Church Records." *Maryland Genealogical Society Bulletin*, Vol. 40 #3 (Summer 1999).

Saltonstall, William G. *Ports of Piscataqua.* ----: Harvard University Press, c. 1941. Reprint Bowie: Heritage Books, Inc., 1987.

Sanborn, George Freeman Jr. & Melinde Lutz Sanborn. *Vital Records of Hampton, New Hampshire, to the end of the year 1900.* Boston: New England Historic Genealogical Society, 1992.

Sanders, Ruth Bennett. "Farmers Loan & Trust, Tax Register, 1886-1889." *Kansas Review*, Vol. 24 #2.

Sanderson, Ruth Bennett. "Kansas Casualties in the World War - 1917-1919." *Kansas Review*, Vol. 25 #2 (1999).

Sanderson, Ruth Bennett. "Johnson County, Kansas, Will Books." *The Johnson County, Kansas, Genealogist*, Vol. 28 #1 (March 2000).

Scobie, Robert. *Genealogical Abstracts from "The New Hampshire Mercury," 1784 to 1788.* Bowie: Heritage Books, Inc., 1997.

Scholl, Allen W. *Descendants of Moses and Isabell (Clark) Crawford of Bucks County, Pennsylvania.* Bowie: Heritage Books, Inc.

Sharp, Harold S. and Marjorie Z. Sharp. *Index to Characters in the Performing Arts, Part I - Non-Musical Plays: Volume 1.* Metchuen: The Scarecrow Press, Inc., 1969.

Sharp, Harold S. and Marjorie Z. Sharp. *Index to Characters in the Performing Arts, Part II - Operas and Musical Productions: A-L.* Metchuen: The Scarecrow Press, Inc., 1969.

Sharp, Harold S. and Marjorie Z. Sharp. *Index to Characters in the Performing Arts, Part II - Operas and Musical Productions: M-Z and Symbols.* Metchuen: The Scarecrow Press, Inc., 1969.

Sheppard, F. H. W. *Survey of London, Volume XXVI: the parish of St. Mary Lambeth, part two, southern area.* London: The Athlone Press, 1956.

Sherman, Renee Britt. *Brooke County, Virginia/West Virginia, Licenses and Marriages, 1797-1874.* Bowie: Heritage Books, Inc., 1991.

South King County Genealogical Society. *King County, Washington, Deaths, 1891-1907.* Bowie: Heritage Books, Inc., 1996.

Stickney, Matthew Adams. *The Fowler Family: a genealogical memoir, ten generations: 1590-1882.* ----: ---, 1883. Reprint Charleston: Garnier & Company, 1969.

Tesh, Peggy J. "Heinrich Peter Tesch and His Descendants." *The Forsyth County [North Carolina] Genealogical Society Journal,* Vol. XVII #1 (Fall 1998).

Thomas, Gail Robert. *Daniel Thomas of Prince George's County, Maryland.* ----: ----, 1996. Also, addendum dated 1/15/2000.

Thompson, Joyce. *"The Frankfort Bee, 4 Jul - 26 Dec 1884."* *Topeka [Kansas] Genealogical Society Quarterly,* Vol. 28 #1 (January 1998).

Tibbetts, Charles W. *The New Hampshire Genealogical Record. An illustrated quarterly magazine devoted to genealogy, history and biography. Vol. II, July 1904 - April 1905.* Dover: Charles W. Tibbetts, 1905. Facsimile reprint Bowie: Heritage Books, Inc., 1988.

Tibbetts, Charles W. *The New Hampshire Genealogical Record. An illustrated quarterly magazine devoted to genealogy, history and biography. Vol. IV, January 1907 - October 1907.* Dover: Charles W. Tibbetts, 1908. Facsimile reprint Bowie: Heritage Books, Inc., 1988.

Tibbetts, Charles W. *The New Hampshire Genealogical Record. An illustrated quarterly magazine devoted to genealogy, history and biography. Vol. V, January 1908 - October 1908.* Dover: Charles W. Tibbetts, 1908. Facsimile reprint Bowie: Heritage Books, Inc., 1988.

Tibbetts, Charles W. *The New Hampshire Genealogical Record. An illustrated quarterly magazine devoted to genealogy, history and biography. Vol. VI, January 1909 - October 1909.* Dover: Charles W. Tibbetts, 1909. Facsimile reprint Bowie: Heritage Books, Inc., 1988.

Tibbetts, Charles W. *The New Hampshire Genealogical Record. An illustrated quarterly magazine devoted to genealogy, history and biography. Vol. VII, January 1910 - April 1910.* Dover: Charles W. Tibbetts, 1910. . Facsimile reprint Bowie: Heritage Books, Inc., 1988.

Tiberi, Dee. "Account Book, 1853-1857." *The Delaware Genealogist*, Vol. 15 #3 (Fall 1999).

Tilton, Allyson Monroe. "1880 Federal Census - Lebanon City." *St. Clair County [Illinois] Genealogical Society Quarterly*, Vol. 22 #2 (1999).

Timman, Henry R. "Obituaries." *The Firelands Pioneer*, 3rd series, Vol. XIII.

Torrey, Clarence Almon. *New England Marriages Prior to 1700.* Baltimore: Genealogical Publishing Co., Inc., 1985.

Versteeg, Dingman, *Records of the Reformed Dutch Church of New Paltz, New York: containing an account of the organization of the church and the registers of consistories, members, marriages, and baptisms.* Volume III of the *Collections of The Holland Society of New York*. ----: ----, 1896. Reprint Baltimore: Genealogical Publishing Co., Inc., 1977. p. 58

Versteeg, Dingman and Thomas E. Vermilye, Jr. *Bergen Records. Records of the Reformed Protestant Dutch Church of Bergen in New Jersey, 1666 to 1788.* Originally published in the *Year Book of the Holland Society of New York*, 1913. Reprint Baltimore: Clearfield Publishing Co., Inc., 1990.

Versteeg, Dingman and Thomas E. Vermilye, Jr. *Bergen Records. Records of the Reformed Protestant Dutch Church of Bergen in New Jersey, 1666 to 1788.* Originally published in the *Year Book of the Holland Society of New York*, 1914. Reprint Baltimore: Clearfield Publishing Co., Inc., 1990.

Versteeg, Dingman and Thomas E. Vermilye, Jr., *Bergen Records. Records of the Reformed Protestant Dutch Church of Bergen in New Jersey, 1666 to 1788.* Originally published in the *Year Book of the Holland Society of New York*, 1915. Reprint Baltimore: Clearfield Publishing Co., Inc., 1990.

Vliet, Clair Ackerman. *The Ackerman Family Association Comprising the Descendants of George Ackerman, Mennonite, of Lower Milford Township, Bucks County, Pa., and some of the descendnats of Stephen Ackerman, Lutheran, of Haycock Township, Bucks County, Pa.* ----: ----, 1950.

Volk, Adam. "Markers in Grandview Memorial Gardens." *Champaign County [Illinois] Genealogical Society Quarterly*, Vol. 20 #2 (Fall 1998).

Waring, J. P. *American and British Theatrical Biography: a directory*. Metuchen: The Scarecrow Press, Inc., 1979.

Wasser, Elsie M. "1870 Census - United States," *The Stalker*, Vol. 20 #1 (Spring 2000).

Waters, Thomas Franklin. *Ipswich in the Massachusetts Bay Colony, Volume II. A history of the town from 1700 to 1917*. Ipswich: The Ipswich Historical Society, 1917. Reprint Newburyport: Parker River Researchers, 1988.

Weissgerber, J. G. "St. Vrain Church of the Brethren Cemetery Records." *Orange County, California, Genealogical Society Journal*, Vol. 36 #1 (April 1999).

Weller, Ralph H. "Orange County, New York, Early Marriages." *The Orange County Genealogical Society Quarterly*, Vol. 30 #3 (August 2000).

Wells, Ann. "Perfect Attendence, Union School - Crystal Lake." *McHenry County, Illinois, Connection Quarterly*, Vol. XVI #1 (Jan.-Mar. 1998).

Wells, Carol. *Edgefield County, South Carolina: deed books 32 and 33*. Bowie: Heritage Books, Inc., 2000.

Williams, Walter. *A History of Northeast Missouri, Volume 1*. Chicago: The lewis Publishing Company, 1913.

Wilt, Richard A. *New York Soldiers in the Civil War: a roster of military officers and soldiers who served in New York Regiments in the Civil War as listed in the annual reports of the Adjutant General of the State of New York*. Bowie: Heritage Books, Inc., 1999.

Winborne, Benjamin B. *The Colonial and State Political History of Hertford County, North Carolina*. ----: ----, 1906. Reprinted as *The Colonial and State History of Hertford County, North Carolina* with new material added by Baltimore: Genealogical Publishing Co., Inc., 1976.